ANCHORED

Stories of Fishes & Stitches,
Tales of Raising Seven Tails

Connie Frostman Marcy

City Heights Press
2008

City Heights Press - Ashland, Wisconsin
www.booktraveler.com
E-mail: cityheightspress@excite.com

First printing

ISBN: 1-889924-12-1

This book is dedicated to the memory of

James Henry Frostman
and
Karen Joy Frostman O'Neil

Prologue

The muscular, weatherworn commercial fisherman, the strict disciplinarian and the man who thought he was in charge of his house knelt gently down with me beside my bed and together we prayed:

"Now I lay me down to sleep,
I pray the Lord my soul to keep.
If I should die before I wake,
I pray the Lord my soul to take."

Then it was my turn to go solo, and here it got complicated. I took a deep breath and continued:

"God bless Mommy and Daddy,
Carolyn, Janis, Jimmy,
Billy, Karen, Eric,
Gramma and Grampa Frostman,
Gramma and Grampa Cousineau,
And all the people of the world.
Amen"

I gasped for air, smiled, looked up to find the familiar grin shining down on me, and jumped into bed.

That prayer took place 40-plus years ago. Sometimes I can still feel Dad's presence kneeling next to me. The words of the prayer echo in my ears, just as they did after crawling under the covers that night so long ago.

I can remember the second story roof slanting closely over my bed, and feel the wind rattling the glass in the dormer. Drawing the covers up and over my shoulders, I remember listening as the floorboards creaked under Dad's steps as he retreated down the hallway. He would grab the top of the banister with his calloused hand and turn to go down the stairs, sliding his hands on the woodwork he himself held onto as he was led up the same staircase to his bed some 30 years earlier.

My brain is cluttered with this and many other stories of my childhood, memories that bring back feelings of fondness and comfort, memories of learning right from wrong and memories so embarrassing I wish I could forget. Good, bad, impressive or embarrassing, it is who I am. And, growing up, I listened to the stories my parents told of their experiences and the stories my brothers and sisters told of their escapades. These stories lent life and history to local landmarks, and gave me a feeling of connection to the area and people from my hometown.

Time after time Mom would tell one of these stories and always lament, "I should have written a book."

She was right.

Too often we listen intently to the stories our families tell, but then later regret that we can't remember the details. The history of our daily lives is so rich, but these details are not something chronicled in the newspapers, or in the records of property deeds, births, marriages or deaths at the county court house, or in the medical records at the hospital. What makes us liked, loved, respected or memorable is our actions in our daily lives, and all too often the only documentation of this is an oral history, passed down through conversations.

Life is full of good intentions. I had always thought of writing down the special things I remembered about my childhood and giving it to my parents in the form of a letter. It would be a gift, I thought, to let them know that I loved them and appreciated all the years they devoted to raising me.

Regretfully, I dragged my feet on this endeavor, and at age 46, with my dad bedridden and dying from cancer, I finally wrote a letter to him. It wasn't exactly what I wanted to say, and at that time he was not capable of reading it. I read it to him over the phone, suppressing my sobs as my sister held the phone to his ear, half a country away from me. He was no longer capable of telling all his stories. I knew I would no longer hear his viewpoints on the economy, local politics, his choice of stocks (he favored real estate, which made his broker cringe) or the fishing industry. He couldn't comment on the birds in the birdfeeder or tell us tidbits about what the town was like when he was growing up. All the everyday unique things that he did were locked in his mind and only God could hear them.

I shuddered from my deep, raw pain, powerless to help him as he went through his misery. Soon I wouldn't be able to take comfort in knowing he would always be there, miles away, but still within reach through the touch of a phone. I would no longer hear him yell "Marce!" and annoy my mom. I would no longer hear him say, "Oh Geez..." when something annoyed him. I would not be able to watch that impish grin come across his face, not even one more time.

Cancer had been terribly cruel, bringing pain to him and everyone who loved him. I came to the realization that I had options on how to deal with this pain. I could lament and cry over the loss of my dad, or I could lament, cry, kick myself and then rejoice as friends and family selflessly shared their memories with me so I could preserve their stories. What follows I have gleaned from my mom, my brothers, sisters, cousins, and family friends and everyone else that I could annoy. To all of you, I am ever so grateful.

Glaciers to Scandinavians

You don't just stumble upon Bayfield, Wisconsin. You don't go for a Sunday drive and happen to drive through it unless you are out for a good long ride, or maybe you happen to get lost. There are no interstate highways nearby. There are no traffic lights once you get there. There are no fast food chains. No outlet malls. Some years it has even been tough to find ice cream after 9:00 p.m.

I always try to describe it as being about as far north in Wisconsin as you can go. By *car* that is; go any farther and you end up in the lake. It is 90 miles east of Duluth, Minnesota, about the same distance from the Upper Peninsula of Michigan, and right on Lake Superior. When I left home for college in central Wisconsin, I found a few fellow students who didn't know we existed. They thought the northern end of the state was somewhere around Wausau or Eau Claire. I had to convince them that there were still 214 miles of state above that, filled with towns, people, and stories.

In the 1970's Bayfield boasted a population of 874. Downtown had three grocery stores (Hillside, Andy's and Johnson's), at least four restaurants, a library, a hardware store, a lumber company, a lumber mill, drug store, theater, post office, two gas stations, about five bars, docks, fisheries, the Department of Natural Resources and more, all within a couple of blocks.

Downtown was six blocks of flatness. Everything north and west of the docks, the business district and the railroad tracks shot up at an abrupt (and annoying) angle, especially if it was winter and you didn't have chains on your tires. To the north was Catholic Hill, where the Catholic Church and its elementary school stood proudly dressed in sandstone. Clapboard siding protected the Lutheran

Church at the top of Cooper Hill and the Baptists watched over the top of Main Street (officially named Rittenhouse Avenue, but we never called it that).

The Presbyterians had the corner across from Uncle John and Aunt Eleanor's house, and the Episcopalians were in a quaint little structure on the way up the hill to the public school.

The public school spread itself across the top of Third and Fourth streets. It held about 500 children in grades K-12, all under one expansive roof. It was the scene of much of the town activity, basketball games being a big deal in the winter in Bayfield.

But I digress already. This is not a story about Bayfield during my youth, but more my parents' journey through their lives together, which played out mostly in Bayfield. So with that, lets back up to an earlier time.

The Wisconsin Glaciation period gradually receded into history 10,000 to 12,000 years ago, scouring out the Great Lakes region. Not that understanding my parents requires going back to the caveman era, but a feel for the region would be a good thing. The glaciers scraped and gouged out many geologic features throughout Wisconsin, such as end moraines, terminal moraines, and kettle moraines, drumlins, and esters. It is amazing that Rib Mountain survived the onslaught, remaining to tower majestically over the city of Wausau, way down south (I repeat, *way* down south).

The weight of ice a mile thick pressed down on the land, and as the climate warmed and the ice receded, five huge holes between the future St. Lawrence Seaway and the Port of Duluth were left exposed. The resulting melt water filled the void and created the Great Lakes. Lake Superior, farthest to the west, would become the largest fresh water lake in the world. It would be deep and cold, the lowest depth being 1,333 feet deep. Its temperature would vary from slightly numbing in the summer to frozen solid in the winter.

The glaciers also exposed Precambrian sandstone bedrock. As the waters rose in the lake, erosion began to sculpt away at the bare rock. Isostatic rebound, the rising of the land as the weight of the glaciers was removed, was also at work. The result of this geologic activity included the formation of an archipelago of 22 islands jutting out from the northeast end of the Bayfield Peninsula on the southern shore of the lake.

Long Island, the southern most, a long narrow strip of trees and sand, would guard the entrance to Chequamegon Bay. Devils Island would claim the northern most point of Wisconsin with huge sea caves howling devilish sounds. Eagle Island would keep watch to the west and Outer Island, aptly named, claimed the northeastern most point, its view extending out to encompass water and sky for as far as the eye could see. The islands provided shelter from the storms that could rage on the open lake and provided a location for folklore to thrive.

The waters around the islands were cold, clear and pristine. The sandy bottoms and rocky shoals inside the islands, and the deep waters on the outside would provide prime habitat for a select group of hardy fish species.

The sturgeon (Acipenser fulvescens) appeared to be a relic from the age of the dinosaurs. It had triangle-shaped plates sticking upright from the ridge along its back, leading to a shark-like tail. It had a flat snout with slender barbels dangling underneath. These resembled whiskers and allowed the fish to taste and smell. This boney, plated monster inhabited the shallow waters around the islands and many rivers and inland lakes in Wisconsin. It would feed off the bottom, sucking up larvae, crustaceans, leeches and snails off the bottom, along with silt, gravel, small rocks and any-thing else in the way. The indigestible material would be filtered out through the gills and the good stuff would be digested.

Slow to mature, the female sturgeon would not breed until it was almost five feet long and around 25 years of age. Then she would only spawn every 4 to 6 years. The male also waited until he reached the same length, but would spawn every other year. This rit-ual would take place up the Bad River in May or early June when waters reached around 50 degrees.

The average life span of the sturgeon was 50 years, but would be recorded to live up to 100 years old, weigh up to 310 pounds and be 90 inches long. These fish were known to leap out of the water until they appeared to be standing on their tails, then splash back in

Ashland. Ethel was born in 1911. She and her family lived in the country for nine more years before moving to town. This move was a life-changing experience for the family and especially young Ethel. The family now had to learn and use English, and for the first time Ethel would to go to school.

Bert (or 'Albert' when Ethel was upset) was the French Canadian. He had dark hair and a very dark complexion. He had a broken nose that was a little bit twisted and carried the nickname Kitty (accent on the 'Kit'). He worked for the DuPont plant between Washburn and Ashland. His job included work as a security guard during World War II, and otherwise he drove big busses from the plant to pick up workers in Washburn. He also drove snow plows. Sometimes, if there was a big storm, DuPont would bring plows to town to clear the roads as a community service. Mom remembers struggling to walk through the snow to get to school, and watching as her dad passed her by in the company bus or plow. Company policy would not allow him to give his daughters a ride.

Bert's parents were Michael and Marceline (Corrier) Cousineau. They were French Canadians that had immigrated to Washburn before Albert was born. Michael earned his living as a logger. Marceline, a tiny woman, had been a school teacher near Montreal in Canada. Mom remembers Gramma Marceline claiming to have taken a canoe to school. That was all Gramma Marceline said, leaving us wondering what she did once the ice set in.

Both grandparents spoke fluent French and Gramma Marceline would only speak French to her granddaughter when she visited. Gramma would say things over and over until Marcie understood it. And when she didn't want Marcie to understand, she would talk real fast. So as a young girl, Marcie was fairly fluent in both English and French. She can still roll "Ferme la porte!" off her tongue ("Shut the door!").

Bert spoke the language also, but after Gramma Marceline died, he didn't try to keep speaking French at home. He didn't let the ability go to waste however. Bert would use his French to frustrate his Swedish bride. After all his daughters had married, he and his

1947 - Marcie at Big Rock, perched on Jim's first brand new truck

second daughter's father-in-law, who was also French-Canadian, would annoy Gramma when they went out to dinner together. Bert and Percey would sit at the table and talk French, and then they'd look at somebody across the room and giggle. Gramma Ethel would get so mad because she didn't know what or who they were gossiping about.

Marcie was the oldest of three daughters. (There was a brother, but he died of meningitis at 11 months of age.) Marcie was christened Marcelline Joy Cousineau. Two ll's, unlike her grandmother Marceline with only one 'l'. This did lead to some confusion. Gramma Ethel had to order a copy of Marcie's birth certificate to ensure her baptism certificate was spelled correctly.

I always mused about how awful it would have been if a teacher had made her write her name on the board 100 times. The Cousineau family had a naming pattern going on. Her sisters were named Jacqueline and Kathleen. Long elegant names. Jacqueline was tall, slender and had naturally curly hair. Like the name, she always looked elegant and carried herself with poise. Kathleen on the other hand, took after Gramma Cousineau and never cleared 5 feet in height. She was perky and always had this big smile on her face. Her voice even smiled. If I ever needed a conversation, she was the one to call. In any case, the elegant, long names somehow never stuck. Their nicknames were all we ever knew them as: Mom was *Marcie,* Jacqueline was *Aunt Dolly,* and Kathleen was *Aunt Snookie.*

Just down the street was a beach and when Marcie was a kid, she and her friends used to go down to the lake and play at the beach. There was a small boat there, and one day they decided to go for a cruise. Being kids and the boat being a little row boat, one thing lead to another and they tipped it over. When Marcie finally surfaced, she was underneath the overturned boat.

As she put it, "It scared the devil out of me."

Being scared was thankfully the worst part of that day, as all the kids made it back to shore safely.

The incident did have a lasting effect as Marcie would never again voluntarily swim underwater. She will, however, swear that she was and is not afraid of the water. I quote: "I'm not afraid of the water. I want to breathe. I will swim in water over my head. As long as I know the distance I can swim. But I cannot go under the water. I just don't go under the water. Even lifeguards have tried to get me to swim under water but I can't do it."

Her aversion to submersion would stay a small but nagging stress that she would nevertheless carry through a lifetime soon to be led next to - and on top of - Lake Superior.

When Jim Met Marcie

It didn't take long for Jim and Marcie to become a couple, spending time with friends and having fun. Small black and white photographs attached to brittle album pages allow me to join them on some of these dates. They did a lot of fishing together, but not exactly sitting on a dock next to a quiet little lake with casting rods, a picnic basket and a can of worms.

Jim took Marcie and friends on the *Ione,* a commercial fish tug built for his dad, the one on which he was crew. They trolled the waters of Lake Superior, fishing for trout big enough to eat any one of my cats. The photo albums contain proof of the catch, some shots showing Mom standing on the roof, elbows straining against her waist and trout gills hooked in each hand. The tails stretched so

1940s - *Marcie standing on top of the* **Ione,** *holding lake trout caught in nets.*

far down that they swept the deck.

Photos also record these teenagers cruising with the *Ione* near Balancing Rock on the northeast coast of Stockton Island, miles from Bayfield. Balancing Rock is either a rock or a miniature island, depending on your perspective. The land eroded around it, leaving it as a sandstone monolith in a cove surrounded by steep cliffs. The cove is wide enough and deep enough for a boat to circle the rock, a boat as big as the *Ione* or even a more modern United States Coast Guard vessel.

1940s - *Balancing on 'Balancing Rock'*

One particular trip included Jim, Marcie and two other young couples. Jim convinced the "girls" that it would be great to take a picture of them standing on the rock. Being trusting souls, they agreed. Jim slowly nosed the *Ione* up to the rock and the girls scrambled off onto a ledge. He smiled from the cockpit, and put the *Ione* into reverse. The tug slowly drifted away from the rock, and then, as Jim played with the throttle and the gears, the boat came to a dead stop a short distance away. Marcie admitted feeling a bit apprehensive as she watched the boat back away. She was now on a narrow ledge, 15-20 miles out into Lake Superior, 20 feet above the lake, with maybe 30 feet of cold water below her and dependant on her new boyfriend not to abandon her.

1940s - This ice-covered vessel is likely the **Dawn,** *owned by Les Cornell. Les hired young Jim to fish with him. After Les retired, Jim hired Les to captain his trolling boat.*

She watched as the boat settled in its spot, water rippling away from the hull and gently bouncing against her rock. Then she saw the pilot house hatch pop open and Jim, smiling with camera in hand, stuck his head out of the pilot house and yelled, "Smile!"

The three girls, in their plaid wool jackets, headscarves and rolled up dungarees, laughed (albeit nervously), posed, and Jim snapped away, commemorating the event with photographs. He then disappeared into the pilot house again, the engine sputtered to life and the girls with private relief watched as the *Ione* crept back to retrieve them.

The guys then traded places with the girls and more pictures were taken. One last picture in the album was of Jim, alone on the rock. The perspective of the picture put the *Ione* a short distance away. After the picture was taken Jim did not wait for the boat to nose up so he could step back on board. Instead he let out a whoop and dove off the rock. His body splashed into the icy water and disappeared for a short eternity, then his head burst up and out of the water and he could be heard gasping, not only for breath but to recover from the shock of the cold water immersion. He swam back to the boat and the guys grabbed his arms and hauled his wet carcass back inside.

It made a lasting impression on his date.

Marcie made many other trips on the *Ione* with Jim. Now may be a good time to introduce readers to this vessel, because the Great Lakes fish tug is quite different from Georgia's shrimp boats and Alaska's trawlers, and distinction between them is important.

Named for Dad's sister, the *Ione* was a 42-foot long wooden fish tug built for Grampa Ole in 1936. Short on elegance but long on practicality, it sported a fully enclosed cabin running from bow to stern.

The Great Lakes fish tug design evolved to provide protection from the harsh elements found in boreal waters. It was in full operation from the time the ice broke in the spring until the ice locked everyone out in late fall. The weather on Lake Superior could vary from a brilliant blue sky and a 75 degree blanket of air resting on an absolutely mirror flat surface of water, to howling winds, 20-foot rolling black seas, a driving sleet and bone-chilling temperatures biting through wool underwear in a matter of hours. The enclosed cabin protected the fishermen not only from freezing winds, icy spray and rolling seas that would break over the bow, but also summer sunburns. Inside was a coal stove that could provide heat as the men set and lifted nets in the quite frigid early spring and late fall.

The boat was a fantail design, which meant instead of the stern being squared off at the waterline, the curve of the stern's hull rose up out of the water to allow water to be displaced as it cut through the waves.

The *Ione* was set up for gill net fishing. The gill nets were shaped like a volley ball net, with corks tied to the upper end and lead weights crimped to the lower to keep the mesh spread wide underwater. Numerous nets would be set strung together in "gangs," with buoys and anchors attached to each end of the gang. The mesh was of varying widths, depending on what species was being

The Ione was a 42-foot long wooden fish tug.

caught. As the fish swam through the mess and found their belly too large to fit through the mesh, they would attempt to back out and get caught in their gills - thus the "gill" net.

There were gangways (doors) at the stern and on both sides that allowed fresh air in, but more importantly allowed for the setting and lifting of the gill net. The gang was set out the stern gangway as the boat motored forward, "set" meaning the large buoy with an anchor attached, which was dragged to the stern gangway and heaved out into the water. Attached to the buoy were lead lines. The lead line was as long as the depth of the water from surface to net. Attached to the lead was a bridle, which in turn grasped the top and bottom of the end of one net. Each net was approximately 300 to 400 feet long. A long string of nets would be attached end-to-end, accumulating into hundreds if not thousands of feet of mesh spreading under the water. This made up a "gang." The anchor line was also attached to the bridle, and established the distance from the net to the lake bottom.

So out the door would go the first buoy and anchor. The drag from the anchor and the forward motion of the boat pulled the nets out of their boxes, and they would slide seemingly by themselves over the gunnels before disappearing into the deep. At the end of the nets was attached another buoy and accompanying anchor. It would be heaved overboard to mark the end of the gang.

The net would be "lifted" after a set number of nights in the water. The fisherman would return, maneuvering the boat so that the buoy was alongside the lifter adjacent to the starboard gangway. Once within reach, the buoy would be hauled into the boat through this gangway, and the lead line wrapped around the teeth of the lifter. The teeth were on a cylinder that would continuously grab the line on the outside of the boat and pull it to the inside of the boat, bringing up the nets attached to the other end of the terminal line.

Long flat tables ran the length of the boat's interior. The nets would come off the lifter and be spread the length of these tables. The fish were untangled and removed from the nets and tossed into boxes lining the deck. When a stretch of net was clear, the netting would be pulled into a box at the end of the table, placed in a systematic fashion to allow it to be reset without getting tangled. This brought more mesh onto the table, with more flopping fish. The process was repeated until the nets had been picked clean and re-boxed.

Up in the pilot house resided what would one day be my mother's prized possession - the ship's wheel. It was handmade at the kitchen table by Grampa Ole and Uncle John. One *spoke* still has a rope knotted to it, which, when facing upward told who ever was steering the boat that the rudder was straight.

The *Ione* was powered by a Kahlenberg engine. Everyone in town knew when someone with a Kahlenberg was leaving the dock or coming home in the afternoon. The engine grumbled with a distinctive *"toogaatoogaatoogaa..."*

This was the family yacht in which Marcie was soon cruising. She had been around boats before, as her dad once owned a boat called the *Melody*. The *Melody* was used to take out sport fishermen for hire, so it smelled slightly less fishy than the *Ione*. Marcie was able to adapt and came to enjoy cruising the islands in the *Ione*, being accepted by and accepting what would become her Norwegian in-laws.

It was quite a way to get to know her future in-laws. Their favorite destination on these cruises was Presque Isle Point on Stockton Island. It was a straight shot, 15 miles out from Bayfield. Just set a course with Bass and Hermit Islands to port and Madeline Island to starboard. Then cruise past Quarry Bay and follow the shoreline to Presque Isle. At the end of the point was a natural protected harbor, a peaceful sandy beach and a hamlet of four small cabins and a fish shed. Les Cornell, Orville and Edith Powers, Ole and Uncle John made their residence here each summer.

This was our fish camp. Due to the distance from Bayfield to the fishing grounds, and the inability of a fish tug to hurry anywhere, the fishermen found that if they started their day already half way to their nets, it shortened their work day considerably. They had access to all the current necessary amenities. A pickup boat - an early version of an excursion boat - would cruise the islands, stopping at each fish camp and pick up the previous day's catch, deliver supplies and accommodate tourists who wanted to see the islands.

Ole's cabin might have been a log structure, according to Mom's recollections. I have an oil painting of the cabin, painted by Dad when he was a teenager. It is a likeness of the cabin with the log walls of the porch facing the bay, the different hues of red from the evening sunset fleeting across the sky, and the water lapping the shoreline just steps from the porch. (It had once become the family joke that if you wanted to inherit something, put your name on it. I didn't hesitate to mark my name on the back of this painting.)

The porch was home to a rocking chair, a couch and old oak ice box. The ice box had brass handles and was something today's antique hunter would cherish. To Helga it was considered a necessity; it was her only source of refrigeration. An alternative could have been sticking containers in the lake. At an average temperature of 40 degrees, the lake could work as a natural ice box, but the Frostman family was much more modern than that.

Inside were two rooms, one with a kitchen table, chairs, oil

To Mom's good fortune, there were no bears on the trail that afternoon.

The trail exited the woods and opened up onto a wide shelf of blocky sandstone ledges. The ledges stepped down to the water and were decorated with various pools of water, pieces of driftwood strewn around and the sound of water lapping at the edge of the rocks. Jim and Marcie clambered around the ledges a while, exploring in the soft light. They chose one particular ledge and sat dangling their legs over the edge, enjoying the quiet.

The teenagers watched as the calm water reflected the deepening colors of the sky as it gently lifted and settled with the waning energy of the day's waves. The pebbles at the edge of the beach made gentle shushing sounds as the lake rubbed against the beach. Gulls flew low over the water, their wings spread wide and they seemed suspended, floating above the water. Outer Island hovered low and gray a few miles to the east. Beyond Outer were the Porcupine Hills of Upper Michigan, another shade of gray framing the evening.

It was at this point that Jim lowered himself off the rock and found footing on the next ledge below. As others had done before, he began to chisel letters into the face of the sandstone ledge. What emerged was his pledge that would last a lifetime. It read "Frostman loves Cousineau."

With the light fading, they gathered the rifle, took one last look at the lake, and stepped back into the woods for the return trip to the cabin.

Terry and Jim

Not only did Marcie's world expand due to activities with Jim's family, but as a couple, Jim and Marcie were soon double dating with two of Marcie's childhood friends. Many this foursome's antics can be repeated in these pages, and as I understand it, many cannot. Their dates were not always the typical dinner and a movie.

I did not know Terry and Shirley. As growing up the middle child, I was able to stay quite oblivious to many details, and apparently tuned out when discussions turned toward anything that went on before we kids came along. Looking back, I missed out on some good stuff. As I was pumping Mom and my siblings for information, Mom, Carolyn and Jimmy all told me I would have to talk to Terry Welty.

"You got t' hear him tell about this" Jimmy would say.

"Oh Gawd, those two," Mom would say.

"He'll talk your ear off," Carolyn chimed in.

Soon I found out that Mom and Shirley worked summers as live-in domestic help for a wealthy family on Madeline Island, three miles off Bayfield. These were also the summers that Dad was dating Mom and Terry was dating Shirley. Dad and Terry soon found that they had many common interests, such as hunting, exploring the islands, and most important, spending time with "the girls." The four became close enough that they stood up in each other's weddings.

My curiosity helped me overcome my natural instinct to be an introvert, and I gave Terry a call. He answered, I explained who I was and what I was trying to write, and he agreed to tell me some stories.

We arranged to talk on a Saturday morning. I put on a pot of coffee, set up my digital recorder and got out the phone card. Shirley answered.

"Just a minute," she said and hollered for Terry. His voice came on the line and he quickly put me at ease.

He had his own coffee. "Got ta hose down the pipe, don't cha know…."

I took a sip of my own and quickly realized my role in this conversation would be to sit back and enjoy the recollections of a truly gifted storyteller.

"You all set, got that thing goin?" he asked, referring to my recorder. I pushed in the red button and smiled. He was just beginning to roll, and so was go. "Yes, fire away!" I said with anticipation.

"Okay. Anyway, Oh, yeah, I suppose that Jimmy and I were friends for a long time you know, and eh, well, I guess it started out when our wives, our girlfriends, were working on Madeline Island together and that's when I really got to know him. Cuz I'd been goin' over there a couple years, cuz I think Shirley worked there before Marcie did. Then I got pretty well acquainted on the island, and pretty well acquainted in Bayfield. I knew all the young fellows up there. You know, Jimmy Erickson, Jim Frostman and all of the guys…All those fellows I used to chum around with.

"Now, Marcie started working with Shirley, well, you know, we were young fellows and we were on a'courtin'. And we used to take lots of trips over to that island, heh! Well, neither of us had a nice little slick boat. I had a little cabin boat, the name was *Little Hilda.* Well, I used to keep that down at Soo River. And I'd go across to the island in *Little Hilda.*

"Jimmy said, 'Well, we've got a pond boat, we could row across from here. It's a lot shorter way from Soo River.' [Note: The distance from Bayfield to Madeline Island is 3 miles.]

"So, well we go up there, and I says, 'Well, what kind of a motor have ya got?' He says, 'It doesn't have a motor on it.' You know, I says, 'Well I ain't goin t' row that big tub!' That big tub boat was 20 feet long! And it felt like it was about 8 feet wide. Anyway, I said my dad had a little 3 1/2-horse power *Champion* engine. Well, that thing pushed that great big pond boat about a mile and a half an hour you know. It was just a little bit better than rowing.

"Well, we went across there lots of times in that damn pond boat with that little motor. It did pretty well. But we always carried extra gasoline, and it was a long slow trip. After a couple times doin' that, you know I thought we got to make this a little more comfortable. So I took the back seat out of my car. And we put one on the floor and one leaned against the back and one on the seat and it was quite comfortable! We sat there and we rode back and forth. When we went over there we'd throw the seats in the boat and go back and forth.

One time we were comin' back and it was a beautiful night. It was just gorgeous. In the middle of the summer you know. We were sittin' there on the way home, visited, and visited and finally we fell asleep! And what woke us up, the darn engine run out of gas! I said, 'Where in the hell are we?' We couldn't see any lights or nothin' you know, it's blacker than inside of a well. Jimmy finally figured out where we were.We were prt' near over t' Bass Island!

"Anyway, we filled up the gas tank and we powered on and we puddled our way back home again. We had an all right trip! We got home about time to go to work!"

It was clear that the more Terry talked about these old, wonderful times, the more fond of them he became.

"We went hunting a couple of times. I was always hunting. For deer, you know, and, I says, 'Jimmy, why don't cha' come hunting with me.' He says, 'Oh, I don't have time' Well, that was during the herring run. So they were kinda busy. Jimmy says, 'I can't go anyways, I left my rifle out on the island.' I says 'Well, that's too bad.' He says, 'I ain't goin hunting anyways. I won't go huntin' with you unless you go chokin' herring with me.'

"So I went for a boat ride with Jimmy and his brother, the whole crew. I went out there, we pulled nets. Oh God what a mess, stinkin' mess that was! Anyway, I worked all day and then finally we got back in an' we choked herring all night and got all done and by golly the herring run just about petered out towards the end of huntin' season!

"So anyway, Jimmy says, 'Well you know, we're not going to go pull nets tomorrow, I'd go huntin' with yah, if I had my rifle.' I said, 'Well, where is it?' He says, 'It's on the island [Presque Isle, at the cabin]. There's open water all the way around the island, but the lagoon is all frozen over.'

"Well we took my airplane and flew out there. I took a good look at that lagoon and it was in pretty good shape. So I swung around and I landed on the lagoon, you know and it was pretty good so I taxied all the way down to the end where the cabin was, closer to the cabin.Well we went over and picked up his rifle and it was working real fine!"

[Note: The plane was an Aeronca Champion. And I thought guys only wanted pickup trucks!]

"So I came back out there and I got back in the airplane, giver 'er the gun and we were going to get out of there. So I tried twice. I could get off the ice but I couldn't get over them damn big trees! Two big trees right in the middle of that lagoon that were growin' on kind of a little island. I says, 'Well, Jimmy, those trees got to come down or we're never going to get out of here.'

"So back down, we picked up an axe at the cabin where they stayed, and we come back and we proceeded to chop down those trees. And they were big, big, big pine trees.

"In the process, you know, it was snow on the ground, we got slippery hands and we were taking turns chopping down this damn tree, all we had was an axe. Well, it was ah, getting a little tired there, your hands, you had mittens on, mittens with snow on them, snow and they get a little slippery and you never want to stand where you're goin' to get hit with that axe, so I was all the way behind him when he was choppin'.

"And he was choppin'. He slipped, and fell forward, toward the tree, and as he was swingin' (heh!) he hit the handle of the axe on the tree, which jerked it out of his hand and went all the way around the tree and come swingin' at me. And hit me right smack in the forehead!

"Double bitted axe hit me with the butt end. Hit me right on the forehead. Just cut me wide open. Just knocked me clean out. And there was blood all over me and Jimmy was panicking. He was wild, he didn't know what the hell to do. You know, he couldn't fly. And we were out there. I think my dad knew where we were, you know but he wasn't going to worry about us, we were pretty good sized boys.

"Anyway, after a while I came around and Jimmy had me packed in snow and I was dizzy. I had a headache, oh God. And Jimmy didn't know how to start that engine, you had to spin the prop you know, by hand. It didn't have a starter on it.

"So anyway, I told him how to do it, and I says, 'Now, get the hell away from the propeller.' So finally he chopped the rest of that tree down. By golly we swing around there right, I managed to get that thing out of there, told Jimmy how to land it if I didn't make it. Just land on the ice cuz you had a lot of room, you know, by town, so you wouldn't have to walk so far. Anyway, we made it all right, we came all the way back to the airport in Washburn and I landed.

"Anyway, we managed to get home and get over that ordeal. Eah, oh God. What a headache!

"Once in a while in the summer time we'd get together with Jimmy Erickson, some of the other guys, Red Figgie, Jimmy Frostman and we'd have a couple friends from Ashland and we'd come over there and we'd go for a Sunday ride on the old *Ione*. I don't remember, you know about the *Ione?*

"It was a great big...must have been 50 feet long. It had a great big old Kahlenberg diesel in it and it would go *kullung, kullung, kullung*. It was a good old boat anyway, and we used to go take it on Sunday and go on picnics. We'd go from island to island and Jimmy'd show us all over. Of course most of the guys, you know we were runnin' around, I was flying around the islands all the time, never ventured on boats very often.

"We were out by Michigan Island, they have a light on the out-side of Madeline. God, one time we were out there and we'd go up to the lighthouse and look around the lighthouse and God dang we got to moseying around and nothin' was locked up and they had a railroad car that goes all the way from the dock all the way up the hill. And we were running the damn car up and down the hill.

"Oh, we'd go 'round, investigate all the islands, we'd visit them, have a few beers, y' know and lots to eat, the girls, they'd take care of the boys pretty well. So, we had lots of picnics on that *Ione,* like that one trip. That was a fun trip.

"Oh, let's see, what else...That Jimmy and I, we got into a lotta monkey business together.

"I'd fly over there [Madeline Island] quite a bit with my little airplane, during the summer when Shirley and Marcie were working. Land at the airport and uh, buzz the house and somebody'd see me and they'd take a ride out there, Mr. Nash, Shirley's employer, or one of the younger fellas would go out and pick me up. Sometimes I'd just get out on the road and start walkin' and walk all the way in there. I walked from the airport all the way in and then go a courtin'. And then I'd go back out there and spend too much time. There was no lights at the runway, you couldn't see. I'd spend the night in the airplane fightin' mosquitoes, and then about daylight I'd start 'er up and I'd head for home. It's time to go to work."

Soon Terry's supply of stories began to peter out a bit. And I knew, with no small reluctance, it was time to come back to the present.

He said, "Okay, I'm getting' run out of wind here. I can't think about any other things that would be really interesting, except that, I tell you what, your daddy was one hell of a good man. I think he was a good father, he was good to his wife, and you don't get much better than that. And he sure was a good friend of mine. We were in each other's wedding parties."

The phone call was coming to an end. I thanked Terry for his time and he welcomed me to call again. I hung up, transferred the recorder files to my laptop and went myself to *hose down the pipe* with some fresh coffee.

Shirley and Marcie

"I remember we used to go to lots of beach parties, and we always had a really good time. And Wednesday and Sunday were our nights off to go roller skating in Bayfield. Now we'd always complain and make a lot of noise when we'd come home (because it was supposed to be our days off or our evenings off). We always returned to a stack of dishes. We'd rattle pans and make a lot of noise when we came home."

Shirley Welty was talking to me over the phone, tattling on her activities with my mother during that summer job some 60 years ago. After hearing Terry's version of the dating days, I certainly had to hear Shirley's side.

She and Marcie grew up in Washburn and went to high school together. That is, until Walker High School burned to the ground in '47. Then they attended the DuPont Club together as classes crowded into the available but much smaller facility down on the main street.

As she graciously allowed my recorder to document her memories from her teenage years, I filled my coffee cup sat back and enjoyed the conversation.

We went back to Walker High School and 1947, the year of the big fire. It started out as just a small burn but grew to consume the entire school. As Shirley understood it, the school was at the same level as the water reservoir and therefore lacked water pressure. So when the fire took off there was no way to dampen it and the building simply went up in flames. The situation got exciting when the fire reached the chemistry room. An explosion took down an entire wall of the building. I had known this for years and had always tried to imagine the crash.

Everyone has their own perspective on different situations and for Shirley, this fire took away one of the most significant environments of her teenage life. On a much smaller scale, but just as poignant, was the lost of some of her possessions left in the school.

According to Shirley, "I remember, you know, we worked hard for our money. I had saved up enough money to get a pair of white stadium boots. They were very popular then, and I hadn't had them a week. And of course it was a beautiful day that the school burnt down. We went downtown without our boots. Down Washington Avenue and that's when the school started burning and I lost my boots. I worked so hard for them and they would not let me into the school to get them."

Hard work for Shirley and Marcie included two summers as live-in cook and maid for a wealthy family on Madeline Island. Just to the south of the little town of LaPointe, past the marina, was where for $35 a week Marcie served as maid, dusting and vacuuming, and Shirley the cook. They also earned their keep babysitting the boss' children. Off time was filled with beach parties with other local teenagers, taking the ferry to Bayfield on Wednesday and Sunday nights to roller-skate, and being courted by their boyfriends.

Life on the island was unique. They had to deal with a ferry ride to get to work, a lack of shopping and theaters, and even the old telephone system was interesting. Everyone was on one line, each having a different ring. A call from one house might be two rings, the next house might be three rings, something to that effect. If anyone wanted to know who was calling whom, all they had to do was quietly lift the receiver.

After working there a few summers, Mom knew the system well. People had a tendency to get nosy. Each call brought more than one or two people lifting up the receiver and casually listening in. Mom could tell, because the more people on the line, the weaker and fainter the signal would get. When this happened, she yelled, "Get off the line!"

The year-round island community was small, but large enough

to support a gas station, grocery store, bars, museum, marina and a small school. In addition to the scheduled ferry service, there were paved roads, farms, a state park, sandy beaches, and even an airstrip on the island. Then summer would arrive, and with the warmer weather would come the summer residents, many wealthy folks with large summer homes and the need for summer help. Enter Shirley and Marcie.

Having each other for company during those summer months gave them many opportunities to get the giggles. Shirley once got poison ivy on her feet at a beach party. She said her feet itched something terrible, but she still tried to work. She was able to cook dinner but had Marcie help her serve at the table. Shirley never told the boss of her problem, struggling to keep the urge to itch and complain and to scratch hidden with every trip out of the kitchen. She'd bring more food to the dinner table and then make another trip to clear the dirty dishes. With each return to the privacy of the kitchen, she'd have to sit down in the corner and scratch her feet. So every time the kitchen door closed behind her, Marcie and she would get the giggles. The bosses never knew how many poison ivy germs were crawling around in that kitchen.

Another time, they were babysitting the 2-year-old daughter. Things were going great until they realized the baby was nowhere in sight. Just short of panicking, they scrambled to search every possible place where the little girl may have wandered. Marcie went to the lake and did not find her. Shirley went door-to-door, asking the neighbors, but no luck. It was a double-edged sword for any babysitter: not only would this upset their boss, but they loved children. Their stomachs were churning and they were frantic, with the lake being so close in one direction and miles of woods in the other. Trying to think of where they had not searched, Shirley realized they hadn't looked behind the house. She ran back around the house and sure enough, there was the baby toddling around the tennis courts. Whew!

The 'boys' (Jim and Terry), were constantly courting the 'girls' while they were on the job during those summers. The boys would take the truck over on the ferry and visit. One time the guys came over and it rained, and it was so bad they couldn't get the truck out of the driveway. This caused them to miss the last ferry back to Bayfield, leaving them stranded for the night. Unbeknownst to the girls, Jim and Terry spent the night in the children's playhouse up by the tennis court. The boys were able to get towed out the next morning and left for work.

As Shirley talked with me on the phone, she reminisced about days off and cruising around the islands.

"We always went out on the *Ione,* to the different islands you know. That one island, I think it was Michigan Island, we got off, and you know they had a little railroad car that went up the bank, and Jimmy and Terry got in the pump house and they started that sucker up. I was scared to death that somebody would hear us. We figured we'd get in big trouble, but we didn't, they didn't catch us."

Not only were Jimmy and Terry visiting and taking them for cruises, the boys made sure there was not much time to forget them. Terry and Jimmy would fly Terry's plane over the house on Madeline. Shirley said, "I was interested in a little boy next door, he kind of had an eye on me, maybe Marcie too, I don't know. But then Terry and Jimmy would fly over and they'd holler down 'we love you!' right from the airplane. We never had the chance to go with the neighbor boys."

Wedding Bells

Jim proposed in the early fall of 1949. It was Marcie's senior year of high school, but she still said yes and the wheels started turning.

Mom had been raised Catholic, and the fact that she was engaged to a Lutheran made for an "interesting" and "in-depth" religious discussion between her parents and their priest. It happened in her parents' kitchen, during which she was sent back up to her room more than a few times. The result of this discussion was that the ceremony would not be held at Marcie's church, but instead in Bayfield at Jim's church, Bethesda Lutheran.

The date was set for November 12. The couple wanted a small and simple ceremony. Marcie's sister Dolly was chosen as the maid of honor, and Shirley Welty would be her bridesmaid. Jim's best man was Bob Shovick and Terry Welty was his groomsman.

Jim would wear a double breasted suit topped off with a white carnation. Marcie found a royal blue suit on a shopping trip to Superior and chose it for her wedding dress. Instead of a veil she wore a stylish hat adorned with a feather. Her lapel was decorated with a large boutonnière of flowers.

On the day of the wedding, the entire wedding party gathered in the narthex for the walk down the aisle. Dolly and Bob would walk down first, followed by Shirley and Terry and then Marcie and Jim would make their way together past family and friends, to present themselves to the pastor at the railing in front of the altar. As they waited for their cues, their usher, Manny Boutin, tried to be supportive.

"Jim, you got two minutes. Jim you got one minute."

1949 - *Marcie and Jim walking down the aisle after their wedding*

Eyes were rolled, elbows were jabbed, and yet Jim did not bolt and run for the door. One day from 19 years of age, he stood firm and tall and waited to walk his little blond-haired Swede down the aisle.

The wedding went off without a hitch. In the many photographs snapped before, during and after the service, the black and white prints showed that the couple wore the looks of insecurity, wonder, love and happiness.

The new in-laws, Helga and Ethel, joined efforts and provided a reception in the church basement after the wedding. A three layer cake and an abundance of cookies topped off the affair. After the reception the wedding party headed out for dinner at a restaurant at the junction of highways 2 and 63, the turn-off south toward Hayward.

After dinner, the happy couple left the bunch. Driving in style in his father's Oldsmobile, Jim took Marcie to Duluth, Minnesota to spend their wedding night at the Hotel Duluth. It would all pass too quickly. They headed back home the next day.

It was herring season and Jim had to go on the lake.

Herring Season

Through the early years of Jim and Marcie's marriage, the fall would always be remembered as their busy season. It was busy for them and for everyone else in town. Fall brought apple crops and school bus schedules. Fall brought deer hunting season. The cooler temperatures reminded everyone to stock up on firewood and fill the oil tanks in anticipation of the first snow. Storm windows were installed, outside faucets were drained and those houses without basements were banked with hay to ward off frozen pipes in the frigid months. And to the fishermen, fall meant herring season.

In sheds, basements and backyards across the Bayfield peninsula, small mesh nets were being readied for the annual herring run. Around mid-November, huge schools of this small silvery fish would rendezvous at various locations throughout the islands to spawn. The season lasted about 3 weeks. Fishermen, extra hired hands and support crews at the docks would work day in and day out, earning their Christmas money or stashing away funds to carry them through the winter.

During these 3 weeks, the fish ran so thick that the *Ione* and similar-sized boats could bring in a catch as big as ten tons in one day. With herring capable of growing to two pounds, this catch could add up to at least 10,000 fish, averaging 12 inches in length.

There was one day Orville Powers hauled in so many fish that he exceeded the displacement capacity of his boat. Inside the cabin were piles and piles of nets and within the mesh were thousands of entangled fish. Their combined weight caused the boat to ride dangerously low in the water. Orville was so close to the town dock, but if he continued on his course, water would soon pour in through the

1940s - *Jim 'picking herring'*

gangways and sink the vessel. If he dumped the nets out to save the boat, he would lose gear, the fish within and the profits not only from this day, but the rest of the herring season. The loss of a boat would be catastrophic, but the loss of a gang of nets was also a deep financial strain. Neither option was acceptable.

So in a moment of ingenuity and inspiration, Orville and his crew attached a buoy to the both ends of the net piled closest to the gangway. As the boat motored forward, they heaved the net overboard, still "loaded to the gills." It would be one of the messiest nets to re-lift, but the boat immediately rose up to a safe running level. The crew made it safely to the dock, unloaded the nets still onboard and then returned to lift the reset nets a second time that same day.

Dad, Grampa and Uncle John were known to spend their herring season at a shallow trench off Big Bay. It was an hour's run to the nets, barely even enough time for the crew to take a nap but long enough for the captain to enjoy a cup of coffee. This was shortest run from the dock and the results were some of the largest lifts of the year. The guys would leave the dock, head for the south channel between Long and Madeline islands, and then up the east side of Madeline.

The late fall runs could find the *Ione* battered by a rough northeaster, cutting through absolutely flat dense frigid water, or running a compass course through dense white vapor. The fall brought the phenomena we called "steam" rising off the lake. When the air was colder than the water, it would condense, looking like puffs of white vapor swirling upward from the surface of the water, like wisps of white smoke covering the entire lake for as far as one could see.

Once around the point, the fishermen would use binoculars through the portholes or stare out the open gangways, looking for their buoys. If the seas were rough or fog had settled in, they could still locate the buoy the old fashioned way, with compass, time and speed. Every leg of their run was marked in the log; direction, run times, course changes, engine speed. Before global positioning, loran or even radar, the fishermen relied on a well-calibrated compass, a well-tuned engine, charts, math, and intuition to navigate a course to their nets. It was amazing how well they could use these tools in a dense fog or rough seas, running down their buoys via calculations, skill and the good lord willing - and of course, a good cup of coffee.

What Dad was looking for would appear in the distance as a little stick waving a flag. The stick was actually the top of a 13 foot buoy. The *Ione* would glide up alongside the buoy, composed of a broomstick-shaped pole mounted on a thick-wooded middle, with an iron rod mounted on the lower portion. The bottom of the rod had a loop where the lead line to the net was attached. The trick was to position it flush with the starboard hatch where the lifter was located. The buoy was then dragged into the boat, the lead line clamped to the lifter, and as the line was hauled in the buoy would be carried to the stern and stored.

Meanwhile, the lifter would continue the haul. It would creak and groan as it gripped the maitre on the cork line. It would clamp down on the maitre and turn, clamp and turn, a fluid motion that would slowly pull the maitre and the attached mesh to the boat from the dark waters below. The water would become alive with the continuous flash of silvery fish twisting and turning, trying to avoid a ride into the boat.

As the net rose out of the water, the air would fill with the sounds of the fish slapping the water's surface, squawking gulls hovering overhead and the swishing of the wings as bombardier cormorants dove into the nets trying to steal the catch. In the background the Kahlenberg would purr and the crew would race to pull the mounds of fish and mesh away from the lifter and into piles along the deck.

Normally the nets left the lifter and traveled down a table where they were immediately picked clean of the fish and then re-boxed to be reset into the deep. During the peak of the herring season, the nets were so heavily laden there wasn't enough time or manpower to pick all fish out of the nets on the way back to town. Instead, the nets and their catch would be piled throughout the boat. The first pile might be 2 feet wide, running stern to bow, with another pile across the stern, and another up in the bow. They would pile until all the nets were lifted, or the boat was filled to capacity. Then the fishermen would reset fresh nets (for the next day's lift) and head for town.

When the nets were stowed and/or reset and the return to town was well underway, the support staff was getting mentally and physically ready for action. Mom would bring the kids to Gramma Frostman to baby-sit, like many other mothers around town. Other folks would finish their morning coffee break or finish up their normal "day" jobs and head for the docks. Still more workers made the drive from Washburn or Ashland to help out. The fisheries bull gang would also be preparing to weigh the fish, pay the fishermen for their catch, and process the catch for shipment.

The herring run had a huge impact on the local economy, and many times there weren't enough people to work with the fish. Because of this, high school students who were willing to work in the herring were allowed to get out of school to help pick, making up their class work later. So the late morning brought tension up the hill in the school, as students tried hard to concentrate on history and algebra before being excused to go down to the docks to earn some money.

The boats could return to town as early as noontime. The sound of the engines would herald their impending arrival. The neat thing about Bayfield is that there is a view of the lake from almost anywhere in town, and the sound of the engines carried for miles across the water, so the town kept watch and listened for the return of the fishermen. A couple of the town crew would arrive early, 11:30-ish, starting fires to warm up the sheds and using the extra time to tell some lies.

Soon they would be joined by the bull gang, wives, school kids and everyone else looking to earn Christmas and winter money. The herring season was known and participated in by most of the community.

As the boats entered the slips, the crew either jumped from the gangway onto the dock with the lines, or tossed the lines to their counterparts waiting on the docks. Half hitches, clove hitches or whatever knot worked was used to secure the boats to cleats or pilings running alongside the dock. After greetings, catch estimates and various lies, comments and compliments made their way across the water a little ahead of mooring, the engines would be shut down and the next phase of work would begin.

The process of picking the herring had evolved over time. Built next to each boat's slip was a 20 by 12-foot shed (I saw these sheds as I grew up, but never knew their purpose. I have never been known for my keen sense of observation). The sheds were only about one and a half feet from the edge of the dock, giving just enough room for a person to walk between the shed and the boat. The longest side of the shed ran parallel to the dock. There were two doors on the water side and one on each end, strategically located so that when the boat was tied up, the doors aligned with the stern and bow gangways.

Inside might be two tables, immediately in front of each door, and each running perpendicular to the dock. They were tall, a comfortable height for the workers to stand and pick fish. There was a space between the end of the table and the wall, big enough to place a net box. There was also a stove (wood or coal) to provide heat, since this was November in northern Wisconsin and it could be cold and damp outside.

The nets were fed from both the bow and the stern of the boat, across the dock, through the shed door, and laid across the tables until the nets and their contents covered the length of the table. The table was barely visible underneath a blanket of mesh plump with slippery entwined fish.

Next to this table was where Mom would position herself. She and the rest of the crew around the table, 6 to 20 of them, depending on the shed and the memory of the story teller, dressed in oilers (rubber overalls), rubber boots and possibly rubber gloves or arm gaiters (rubber sleeves with elastic on either end).

I was either not in existence, or too small to "enjoy" this event. I asked Mom for a play-by-play on picking fish in the herring sheds. She laughed and started in:

"Well, first you take your forefinger and your middle finger and you slide it over the head to get the twine off, then you grab the head, then you grab toward the tail and then you twist each one in the opposite direction and it slides the twine off."

The years had not dimmed the memories of these hand motions. The first fish to be picked were where the net and the doorway met, so the door could be shut and the warmth of the stove kept in. The crew had work to do, but they were going to be as comfortable as possible when doing it.

I asked her whether the fish were alive or dead, envisioning this table full of fish flopping around, gills pulsating and eyes staring at me. She said, "No, most of them were pretty well dead...There were a few that weren't (expired), but not many."

To my surprise she did not have any distinct memories of the fish being cold or numbing on her hands. Mostly what she remembered was "twist and slide." Over and over and over again. And again. The only complaint she gave was that her back would hurt from standing there so long. Others complained of shoulder pain, but all continued to *twist and slide.*

To make the time go by faster, cut down on the monotony a little, she and her co-workers would invent games such as "See who could pick the fastest," gauged by the speed the fish boxes were filled. As Mom retold the stories, it was clear that she enjoyed the company around the table, remembering it fondly. Who wouldn't? Mom's days were spent caring for her small children, and this gave her the opportunity for a little adult company, and to make some money. For three weeks straight they worked at the table, playing games and telling stories and cracking jokes to make the time pass, staying sometimes until 8:00 or 10:00 at night. They even worked Sundays, making the most of the run, since it only lasted three weeks and then the fish were gone.

Once all the fish were picked from a stretch, they would shove the empty portion of the net towards the box, and whoever was at the other end of the table would box that net, preparing it to be reset the next day. Of course, as they pulled the empty net they would have to open the door, as the other end of the net was still full of fish waiting on the boat. The table would be once again full of fish, a flurry of hands moving in the "twist and slide" motion. This would go on until all the nets were picked clean.

Coffee breaks were an important event in my hometown. And at 3:00 p.m. my aunt Eleanor was known to bring cake or doughnuts down to the docks. Everyone would shake the scales from their hands, take out their thermos and for a short time give their wrists a break. Cup of coffee, doughnut, tell more tales, then back to the grind. *Twist and slide.*

Working on the dock could be hard, but I don't remember hearing Mom ever complain. She seemed to make the best of each day. They were mostly neighbors or relatives there with her, and the Scandinavian heritage was the dominant feature found in most of the faces. The area was not 100% Scandinavian however. There were many locals of Chippewa Indian heritage in town doing the same job, but they were not usually part of the crew in the shed where Mom worked.

Working so close together meant they got to know each other better and sometimes in ways that were not expected. Mom reminisced about one particular night when a stranger walked into the shed.

"We always got along real good - talk, joke, what-not. And one time Corky, he was something else. He was down there pulling up (boxes) from the boat into the shack, and I'm right next to Corky. And late (in the evening), this guy came in with a red and black Mackinaw (a wool coat) for deer hunting season, and Corky says, 'Who is that Indian?' I looked at him, and said, 'Corky, that's my *dad!*'

"He didn't know what to say, he didn't believe me. It was your Grampa, he'd come up to see the fish and what's going on. Oh God that was funny."

It was an easy mistake to make. Grampa was French Canadian and had a very dark complexion. One Halloween, for a company party he dressed in buckskins and could have passed for a member of the local Chippewa tribe. Corky didn't know Burt Cousineau. He did know Mom had a bunch of tow-headed (blond) kids at home, and never made the connection between father and daughter. Mom said Corky was so embarrassed he wanted to jump in the lake!

From this, she immediately went into the "boot" story, a classic. She recalled, "We picked in the boat that night. We were trying to get some of the weight out of the boat."

In her oilers and rubber boots, Mom was picking in the boat instead of the shed. She picked and picked, tossing the fish to the side, depending on another crew later to shovel the fish from the deck and into boxes.

By the time they decided to shovel up the fish, Mom was knee deep in herring and unable to move her feet. When she tried to lift her legs and feet, her boots were stuck. Laughing, she said that the suction holding her boots down was so great that she couldn't get out of the boat. She finally slipped her feet out of the boots and crawled across the fish, out the gangway and onto the dock in her stocking feet.

The docks were part of the news hotline across the town. Mom was there for the following report: "One night we were picking fish and someone said, "Here comes S...... He just cut a boat in two!"

She went on to explain, "S....... went down to Lake Michigan and bought a great big old boat and he came into the marina and he went to put it into reverse and it died. And he went right into LaBelle's boat, cut it right in half and sunk it!"

Never a dull moment.

Newlyweds

After getting married, Jim and Marcie moved in upstairs of Ole and Helga's home in Bayfield. Not the ideal living situation, but they were young and the rent was right. It would give Marcie a wonderful opportunity to keep an eye on her in-laws. Or maybe vice versa.

The upstairs had four rooms, the two towards the back of the house already rented to another young couple, the Kinneys. Marcie and Jim had the front rooms, the bedroom above the living room and the small room above the downstairs bedroom. Luckily these couples were already friends, so the coziness wasn't too much of a problem.

Marcie and Jim also had the porch at the top of the stairs. It faced the lake, and since the house sat mid-way up the hill, it provided Marcie an expansive view of the lake and the town. Down to the left was Allwoods lumber company from where the whistle blew, marking 12:00 noon, 4:00 p.m. and 9:00 p.m. (This whistle marked the curfew that used to inform young Jim and his future children that it was time to hustle home). To the right of Allwoods was the railroad station, the beanery and the city harbor. There was the ball field, the railroad tracks and finally to the far right one would find the Black Hawk docks.

Above and beyond the town was the lake, beautiful Lake Superior, with Bass Island to the north, Madeline Island straight ahead and Long Island to the south. The porch gave Marcie a vantage point from which not only to watch the sunrise over Madeline Island but also to listen for the sound of the *Ione's* Kahlenberg engine. From here she could follow the sound until she found the fish tug with her husband within, headed down the channel each morning for a day of fishing.

As the morning wore on, Marcie could clock the ferries as they kept to their schedules crisscrossing between Bayfield and LaPointe. She could watch as huge rafts of logs were towed south, heading for Chequamegon Bay and the port in Ashland. From the porch, she could ponder whether or not to go downstairs and visit her in-laws.

In her own diplomatic words, this living arrangement was 'something else' for a while. She and Jim would share the bathroom, the kitchen, the washer and the phone with the elder Frostmans. To make the adjustment to marriage even more challenging, the call to Marcie's mother, a kind of lifeline to comfort and familiarity, may have been long distance, 13 miles away. She found herself spending a lot of time in her bedroom.

Not that she didn't like her in-laws. Ole continued to tease Marcie in a good-natured sort of way, but made sure she knew she was welcome in the family. She made cookies one time and she herself admitted that they turned out like Frisbees. Ole graciously commented, "But they're good dunkers Marcie!" He was also always mindful that she was raised Catholic and that Catholics didn't have meat on Fridays. Marcie and Jim ate many meals with them, and Ole made sure there was always fish on the dinner table Friday nights.

Helga was a bit of a challenge for the new bride. She liked things her way and had a habit of wanting to know what Marcie was up to. All these years later, Marcie wouldn't spend a lot of time reflecting on two women trying to live under one roof, but did admit it was a bit of a strain.

Luckily for Marcie, the Kinneys soon moved out, and she and Jim took over the entire upstairs. With this arrangement they would still have to share the bathroom downstairs, but they gained a kitchen, and their own exterior door. Jim soon bought her an automatic washing machine and they installed it upstairs. This was much to Helga's chagrin. She had a wringer washer in the basement, and couldn't see why Jim didn't buy a dryer to complement it...and put it downstairs, where she would have access to it.

Ah, newlywed bliss.

This first year would be a whirlwind of change in young Marcie's life. Not only was she now a married woman, she was also expecting her first child. Memories of her first pregnancy revolved not around the usual how many pounds were gained and how she felt day to day, hour to hour, but tire chains and a black eye.

The first event happened on her way to visit her mom. She recalled, "One time (that first winter) I took the truck and Jim had said in the morning, 'If you go to Washburn, and you go out on the highway, take the chains off.'"

She had never dealt with installing or removing chains before, but shrugged and said okay, figuring that she could handle it...whatever *it* was.

In the winter in snow country, these linked chains were wrapped around and fastened to tires to provide traction on the road. They worked great if the roads were icy or snow packed; they were lousy and loud if the roads were bare. Unfortunately for Marcie, the latter was the case.

It wasn't very far out of town when Jim's words rang in her head.

"I got out on the highway and it was bare. I'd never taken the chains off before. I unhooked them from the outside and they hung on the axle."

Thinking she had taken care of the problem, she slid back behind the wheel, cranked up the engine and pulled out on the highway.

Immediately an awful clanging/clinking noise wracked the wheel wells of the truck. She pulled over, got out, examined the tires and moaned. Pregnant and uncertain on how to remove the chains, she tried crawling underneath the truck to unhook the other side. She yanked and pulled and probably cursed, but the chains held fast.

Then she heard the crunching sound of tires rolling onto the snow behind her truck. A door opened and shut and feet appeared next to her tire. Bob Hadland looked under the truck and asked,

"You having a problem Marce?"

"Yes, I can't get the chains off!" She grumbled as she crawled out and dusted off her pants.

Bob crawled under, things clinked and clanked and the chains were quickly expelled from underneath the truck. Bob stood up, smiled, grabbed the chains, threw them in the back of the truck and headed on his way.

She'd never thought of unhooking them first.

The second event happened on New Years Eve. Jim and Marcie had gone out to celebrate the holiday in Ashland. It was late when they headed home and the snow had begun to fall. As they came through the main street in Washburn the snowfall was so heavy that visibility was next to zero.

"You could hardly see in front of the truck. And just like that, a whole group of people loomed up. Your dad hit the brakes, but there wasn't much he could do. In the group of people on the street was this guy they called Man Mountain Erickson. He grabbed his wife to pull her out of the way of our truck. It was close and we still hit her coat. We pulled over to the curb as soon as we could and Man Mountain Erickson came up and opened the door. As he opened the door he grabbed your dad and hauled off and hit him. Gave him a black eye.

"My cousin came running out to the truck and he says, 'Hey Marce, you got any liquor in here?' I said, 'No. Not a bit.' Well anyway, we weren't going to do anything about it. I mean, the guy was scared to death. We almost run over his wife. Dad wasn't going to do anything about it, but Gramma did. She had to go to court and press charges. That's the way it went, I don't really remember what happened, but I don't think anything came of it. This was in Washburn, right on the main street.

Dad had one heck of a black eye. But it was awful, snowing, couldn't see nothing. There had been an accident, that's why all the people were out in the road in the first place. Right where *The County Journal* was. That was the last time we went out of town on New Year's Eve. First and last."

Baby #1

It was now the summer of 1950, and Marcie was ready to pop. Jim was on the lake when she felt the first labor pains. She waddled down the stairs to find Helga. The plan was, if Jim happened to be out on the lake, Helga would bring her to the hospital over in Washburn. She searched the house, stopping to grab a chair as the pains hit her, but Helga was not there. She rolled her eyes and shuffled to the phone. She called next door to Ruthie Johnson's and luckily found her mother-in-law there.

"Ma, I'm in labor, I've started having labor pains. I need to get to the hospital!"

Helga asked, "Do you have back pains yet?"

"No."

"Well, it's not time to go yet. I'm not taking you to the hospital until you have back pains."

Marcie was dumbfounded. She and Helga didn't have the coziest relationship, and this imposed wait time did not make her a happy camper. She never did get back pains the entire time she was in labor. Thankfully Helga did not hold firm to her decision and they went to the hospital anyway, making it with plenty of time to spare.

Ethel and Bert met them at the hospital, a Dutch colonial building near the center of town. Marcie waved hello and was quickly whisked away, leaving her parents in the waiting room. This also left Marcie alone in a hospital room, in labor, with her husband on the lake and a lot of time to ponder many fears and unknowns of delivering a baby for the first time. Anything could go wrong, and sure enough it did.

1950 - *Marcie and Jim with Baby Carolyn.*

The hospital lost Marcie. Or maybe Marcie lost the hospital.

The nurses had set Mom up in the delivery room. This was during the days of giving the expectant mother ether, and apparently Mom got a pretty good dose. Then the nurse had to leave for something. Just for a moment.

That's all it took. When the nurse returned, Marcie was gone.

The nurse broke into a sweat and immediately started searching for this very pregnant, laboring young lady. She had no choice but to let Marcie's doctor, Dr. Guzzo, know about the "problem."

In no time doors and closets and corners and everywhere were being rattled. A nurse was sent out to ask the expectant grandpar-

1951 - *Jim holds up Carolyn on a winter day. The lake behind them is covered in broken ice.*

ents if they had seen Marcie. (I can only imagine that didn't go over well.) The answer was a quizzical but resounding "No!"

Finally Dr. Guzzo found Marcie across the hall, in the operating room, in a closet. He coaxed the young mother-to-be to be back to her room and posted a guard to keep her there.

It wasn't much longer before Carolyn Marie entered the world. Mom and Dad had their first daughter.

Island Babies

Summering on the island continued for Marcie after marriage and a baby. Unlike the previous summers, when she worked for another family on Madeline Island, she was now watching her own child in Ole's cabin at the fish camp on Presque Isle. With daughter Carolyn only weeks old and still small enough to sleep in a fish box (a clean one, don't stick your nose in the air!), Mom had no qualms about packing up her new family and living for the summer at the cabin with Dad. She had plenty of company, with Uncle John and Aunt Eleanor, Les Cornell, and Edith "Pete" Powers and her husband Orville also staying at the camp for the summer.

As a first-time mother, taking such a small baby to the island did have its share of anxious moments. Normally all the guys would be gone fishing during the day. This usually left Mom in the company of Edith or Eleanor, but on one particular day Mom was all alone. Carolyn was around 4 weeks old and she would not stop crying. Mom tried every trick she knew, but could not calm the baby. Little did she know, Carolyn would suffer until middle school with a severe kidney problem, but this day, there was just a terribly fussy infant, no cell phones, no marine radio, just Mom's common sense and the local Indian community to help her out.

According to Mom: "She (Carolyn) cried and she cried. Well, she was sick. And at that time we didn't know what it (the illness) was. So anyway, the Indians always camped down a little farther (down the beach towards the main part of the island). And this lady came back. She asked if she could hold her, and I said sure. She took Carolyn, wrapped her up so tight (in a blanket). She went and sat on the front porch (with the rocking chair), and started singing to her in Chippewa. And put her to sleep."

The lady was the wife of Gus Stoody. Her first name is lost to history, but she and her husband had become acquaintances of my folks living such a short distance from each other each summer. Mrs. Stoody asked if she could come back the next day. Mom was not about to turn down the help and made sure Mrs. Stoody know she was welcome.

Mom, 57 years later, spoke as though she were reliving the moment, exhausted and troubled because she couldn't soothe her baby. In a tired voice she said, "We couldn't get her to sleep. She was sick, but I suppose being held that way and bound up so tight, yah know, she must have gotten nice and warm and comfortable." It was a relief for her to have another mom nearby who had experience with infants, and on that particular day Mrs. Stoody had the magic touch that could relieve Carolyn's irritability.

Life on the island was, among other things, an escape from doing grocery runs. If the stay lasted longer than the food they brought, Mom would send a grocery order in with the pickup boat. Someone else would do the shopping for her! The pickup boat was an early version of an excursion boat. It had a route around the islands, delivering goods and picking up cargo (fish) from the camps. There were many different types of camps throughout the islands. There were five lighthouses with keepers, logging camps and other activities going on throughout all 22 Apostle Islands.

Tourists could ride the pickup boat, much as they do today on the excursion boats. However, the excursion boats these days don't pick up box after box of trout and whitefish to be delivered to the local fishery in town. I don't think today's average tourist cares to spent 8 hours on a boat with a few tons of trout.

Some tourists were not mentally prepared to visit the many fish camps. The camps had all the amenities that were absolutely essential, and that was enough for the fishermen and their families. Mom can remember Eli Hendrickson standing on the dock hearing one too many a tourist ask the question, "Do you live here all year long?" And, "Oh, you *poor* people."

He got fed up and barked, "I bet these people have better homes in town than you have!"

Mom would sometimes take the pickup boat called the *Apostle Islands* to and from town. Much as today's young parents go for a long drive to lull their infants to sleep, Mom would settle her babies into a clean - I repeat, CLEAN fish box - lined with blankets and set us next to the engine box for a nap. It was warm and the drone of the engine would put us to sleep. Some tourists thought this was just awful. They couldn't get over the fish box thing; but Mom did not let their attitude bother her. Many of these runs were made by none other than Captain Ole Frostman, who, having semi-retired from fishing, was running the pickup boat, and had no problem seeing his grandchildren put down for a nap in a fish box.

Mom recalled one memorable run on the pickup boat.

"There was one time I had to help the crew. We had some nuns on aboard. They got up on the upper deck and we got between Madeline and Stockton, in the channel there, and the water got pretty rough, and this poor one nun, she just couldn't move, it was just like she just froze right there. And I had to get her down. So, I finally got her off the upper deck and downstairs where she could sit down and then she was a little better. But, she was scared. She was just petrified."

Mom continued. "It got kinda rough just going through that channel. As you come up around the back, the outer side of Madeline, and then you go across to Stockton between Madeline and Michigan, and then there's the open stretch there."

As I listened to Mom reminisce about the day-to-day life at the fish camp, I was astounded that she never complained about the hassle of the boat rides, of being bored, about lacking for amenities or being stuck with us kids. Instead, her recollections were filled with mischief played out as practical jokes and pranks, nightly gatherings filled with conversations and games of cards, and many, many memorable moments that she remembred fondly.

Life at the camps never appeared to be boring. In fact, it seemed there was more socializing and pranks being pulled there than in my college dorm. As Mom told it, one day found her and Edith with nothing constructive to do. The guys were all out on the lake, and it seemed like a perfect time to pick on Les Cornell. So they went over to Les's cabin with a can of Crisco shortening in their hands, and greased everything that had a handle or a knob, inside and outside of the cabin.

As Mom relayed these stories to me, she'd give laugh and chuckle, "Oh, God," elongating the 'o' in God. "And then, sometime after that, your dad took a bucket of saltwater and threw it on the outside of his (Les's) cabin, right where his head was in his bed, so the deer licked on the cabin all night."

She laughed again, heartily, at the memory. The antics continued to flood across the phone wire as I pressed Mom for details.

"And then, during blueberry time, I'd have them over for blueberries (Les and his hired man), and Les would tell stories. His hired man would stand right behind him and he'd mouth the words before Les said 'em. Oh, God! We always knew what he was going to say next. We had to keep from laughing!

"I can remember another time when the smoke house burned. Well, there was a smoke house out on the beach over by Les's cabin."

Les's cabin was to the west of Mom and Dad's cabin. The smoke house was about the size of four modern day refrigerators put together. A smoldering fire of hardwood such as maple, oak or apple wood would be tended underneath racks of fish. The rule of thumb was that the fish would be slow cooked at 170 to 180 degrees for around 3 hours. Unfortunately for this smokehouse, the fire escaped the firebox and started to burn the structural elements.

Mom recalled the attempt to put out the fire.

"Yeah, somebody got backside of the smokehouse and was getting ready to throw water; and the man on the side by the lake side did throw a bucket of water. It went right through the open door and hit the other guy!

"The group finally put out the fire, but was left with the problem of an abundance of overly done smoked fish. The guys had been smoking fish in volume, meaning to sell it in town. Since the fish were over cooked, there was no option but to eat the fish themselves. All I could say was 'hurt me.' I love smoked fish!"

The smoke house in my memory was an old refrigerator stuck in our back yard in Bayfield. Dad would hang chubs on sticks, hang the sticks inside, and crank up a fire underneath. The smoked fish would always come out a deep bronze color from nose to the tip of the tail. To eat them, the head would be pulled off, then the skin slowly peeled away, then the meat carefully lifted off the bones, one bite at a time. The aroma would fill the air and the grease would permeate the fingers. It was so good. My husband does not agree, but then, he gags over Lutefisk. I think it stems from his lack of Scandinavian blood.

I have only one fleeting memory of the cabin on Stockton Island. Janis would join the family in 1953, and her overly energetic toddlerhood would soon put an end to the family spending full summers on the island. In Mom's words, "After Janis, I couldn't stay out there that long any more. She was awful. When I lay her down for a nap, I had to make sure I was right there, because she'd get out of the bed and run out into the woods, or she'd run out on the dock. And you didn't dare holler at her, or run after her, because she'd run right off the end of the dock."

"She did that?" I asked, envisioning this little girl with shoulder length straight blond hair and footie pajamas sprinting down the dock towards a finish line that ended in the drink.

"No, she didn't, but it was close!" Mom sounded weary just remembering. "You had to just walk and talk to her. You know, get near her before she decided to run. I finally gave up. I had to come back in town; I couldn't take it. Oh, God, she was, no fear. No fear of nothing. Not a thing."

Not that Jan was an angel on the mainland either.

Janise Anise

I truly believe all of us kids were precious to Mom and Dad. Jan, however, stood out as a very challenging daughter for a young mother to raise. We used to refer to her as *Janis Anise* after the hard candy Gramma Cousineau used to make every Christmas. Janis Ann could be sweet, but on more than one occasion, Mom has been heard to say that Janis started her gray hair.

In her defense, Janis once confessed to me that she felt guilty for everything she put Mom and Dad through. I told her I didn't think she should feel that way. The only thing she ever did, from day one, was be herself. In doing so, she gave Mom something to talk about over a half a century, and that is pretty impressive.

1950s - *Janis Ann with a traditional angel food cake.*

The stories started the day she was born. Her birth, like all but one of us, took place in Washburn, Wisconsin. Dr. Guzzo, our family doctor, was the attending physician. He saw my folks a lot, with so many kids. On this particular delivery, Dad was actually in attendance in the delivery room. I was surprised to learn this, since it was 1953 and birthing suites were not yet popular, if in existence at all.

He didn't stay very long however. Mom recalled that Dr. Guzzo took a look at him and saw this big strong man turning green. He rolled his eyes and barked, "You'd better get out of here. I can't handle both you and her."

The birth itself went well, but the delivery was not followed by the joyous bleating cry of a newborn. Instead Dr. Guzzo held in his hands a silent, limp, blue infant. He was prepared for this type of emergency with an interesting if not torturous procedure. In the delivery room were two tubs of water, one filled with hot water, the other cold. Guzzo grasped Janis tightly and dunked her first into one tub and then other, trying to shock her into life. Mom could hear Guzzo desperately chastising the infant, "Cry you little SOB, cry!!!"

Whether it was the shock of the hot and cold water, the unique lecture from the doctor or just Janis' zest for life, the method worked. The infant gasped for air and let out a wail. The sound of the baby crying mixed with the sound of a long exhale from each and every adult in the room.

Another oddity about Jan was that apparently during the pregnancy, her head was pressed onto her shoulder. For the first year of her life, her head would flop over on that shoulder when she got tired.

Soon after the birth, Mom and Dad asserted their own adult independence, moving out of the apartment and into a rental house across town. The couple years they spent on Second Street were made memorable by Janis' adventures through the terrible twos. Her world was not to be restricted to the house and yard, even though Mom and Dad tried every thing to make it so. She was bound and determined to explore the neighborhood.

This side of town was called Catholic Hill. The Catholic Church, school (both constructed of local sandstone) and the nun's residence (an ornate mansion) were located a block up the street, and I truly mean *up*. This hill had some of the steepest prolonged slopes (maybe steeper than Cooper Hill) in town. Being so steep allowed most houses here to have incredible views of Basswood Island, Madeline Island and Long Island. It was also a place to avoid driving in the winter.

And not an easy "walk," especially for 2-year- olds with short legs.

The Iron Bridge, up one block and to the west of the house, spanned high across a ravine, connecting Catholic Hill to the public school. For as long as I can remember it has been open only to foot traffic. The ravine below harbored a creek and trails that stretched from the back of the school to a huge culvert on Washington Street. The ravine had been the path of a nasty flood that washed through town in the 1940s. The culvert would now take the creek water from under the Iron Bridge and direct it under Washington Avenue for a couple of blocks and then release the water into the lake near the beach at the base of Washington Avenue. Back in '53, there was also a culvert at the corner of Second and Washington Avenue, only steps from our house. The new house, yard and neighborhood would be well traveled by this tiny towhead.

What was Janis like? There are times in every parent's life, when a child drives them to the brink and they (we?) do things that do not leave a feeling of pride once done. Janis pushed Mom this far.

The Mop - One night, Janis stood in the crib and shook the gate, crying and screaming and demanding to be paroled. Mom recalls: "She just fought going to bed, something awful. And I had bought a new mop. I was giving up. I put the mop up over my head and I just leaped across, around the doorway and I said (in a scary voice) 'Go ta Bed!' Jan flopped down in the bed and I never heard another sound."

Smearing the Masonic Temple - Mom had been inside fixing dinner. Jan was out in the back yard and Mom told Carolyn to bring her in for dinner. Carolyn went out the back door, and glanced around the small back yard. There was no one there.

Just as Carolyn ran back into the kitchen to report the missing sister, the phone rang. Marge Matayephski from down the next block, was on the line.

"Marcie, it's Marge. Jan is over at the Masonic Temple and she's got the paint cans all open."

The Masonic Temple was a block and a half down the street. Go half a block further and you were on the main drag. The Temple was a long brick building with a big porch across the front.

Mom took a deep breath and thanked Marge. This call happened 50 years ago, but the news was so startling that Mom never forgot the call or Marge's name. She had the table all set for dinner. Carolyn was sitting there all nice and well behaved. And Jan had run away to discover her inner artist with glossy enamel trim paint.

With Carolyn promising to behave and stay in the house, Mom ran down the street in search of daughter #2. She found Jan just as Marge had described, with hands covered in paint. Real painters were in the process of giving the window trim a new coat of paint and had gone on break. Instead of sealing the cans of paint before leaving, the guys had only laid the lids on top of each can. Janis had somehow found the paint and begun dipping her hands into each can and then pressing her hands against brick after brick after brick on the Temple's front porch. She was well into the effort before Mom arrived. Not only was Mom was furious at Jan, she was furious at the painters for leaving the cans open. She took the young artist by the arm, marched her off the porch and back up the hill, and set to the task of cleaning all the paint off the child.

Dinner had long grown cold.

News traveled fast in the small town and soon the mayor got wind of the situation. He called the house to give Mom his two cents worth of opinion on what Jan had done. Mom was none too happy about the incident herself and retorted, "Yeah, I know. You should try to get that paint off her brand new shoes and off of her!"

She made sure that the tone of her voice told the mayor that she knew exactly what condition her child was in, the condition the Masonic Temple was in, and that this little 2-year-old hadn't opened the paint cans by herself. The mayor backed off.

On the Roof - One day Garner was putting a TV antenna on top a roof a couple doors up from the house. He forgot something in his truck, so he climbed down the ladder to retrieve it. The truck was only a few paces away from the ladder that he left leaning up against the house. He rummaged around in the bed of the truck and found what he needed. He turned around to return to the job, and noticed movement on the roof. A little blond toddler was crawling across the shingles.

Janis.

It wasn't in the job description, but Garner safely extracted the child and returned her to her mother. Mom thanked him profusely. To this day she says, "Oh God, she was somethin' else."

Footsteps - The city was replacing three or four cement blocks in the sidewalk at the end of the block one summer. To keep anyone from walking through it, they roped off the wet cement. All the kids in the neighborhood were in attendance and sat or stood by watching quietly as the forms were placed, the cement poured and the ropes staked. Except for Janis. Immediately after the last rope was in place and the men stepped back, she slid under the rope and stomped footsteps through the entire length of the job.

The Culvert - Remember the storm culvert? Mrs. Smith came over one day and said to Mom, "Janis is going up the culvert." She felt helpless, saying, "I didn't want to yell at her cuz I was afraid she would get scared and go farther in and it's dark after you make the turn in there."

Jan eventually did crawl back out of it. She had a way of stressing every mother in the neighborhood.

Missing - Another day she simply disappeared. When children go missing, statistics show that they most likely travel downhill. So Marie Nelson, who lived across the alley, said to Mom, "I'll go up the hill and you go down the hill." This way Mom should find Janis first.

Marie searched as far as the Catholic Church, where repair men were working. She got their attention and asked, "Have you seen a little blond girl around here?"

The men replied, "Oh yah, we got her! We didn't think she belonged up here." They had become familiar with most of the kids in the neighborhood and this was the first time they'd seen young Jan. When they saw her strolling by, pushing her doll in a baby buggy, they figured something wasn't right, and somehow managed to corral the little Houdini until the inevitable search party showed up.

The Fence - It wasn't like Mom and Dad were not trying to keep an eye on Jan. They even fenced in the back yard to give her boundaries and themselves peace of mind. They had different opinions on how high a fortress would keep Janis home.

Mom said, "Make it 4 feet high."

Dad said, "Oh, no, we only need it 3."

They compromised at 3 1/2. Dad even put a board on the top of the fence so it faced inward, making it hard for her to get over the top. Agg, their neighbor, was sitting on her porch, listening to the argument, watching the construction and chuckling over Janis. While Dad was connecting the completed fence to the back porch, she called over and said, "Jim, Jan's going over the fence."

Jan had pushed her tricycle up against the fence, taken her shoes off, climbed on top of the tricycle, grabbed that upper board, pushed with her bare feet, and pulled her little body up and over the intended child containment device. She was gone again.

Screen Doors - Mom lamented years later, "Yah, on the hill there, our screen, the old fashioned slide screens, [inserted between the lower portion of a window and the lower window sill] was right on Bodin's driveway. So we had to make darn sure we had that screen closed or Jan would climb out. She knew how to slide the screen. And then we also had to put a hook and eye way up high, so she couldn't reach it on the door."

Oh God...!

Mom still shakes her head these 50 some years later. This was only her second child. Lucky for her, as the family grew and grew, the Lord chose not to send another one quite like Jan.

Soot on Second Street

Despite Jan's escapades, the move to Second Street was well worth it. It was $12 a month and away from the mother-in-law. No offense to my grandmother, but on an income of $40 per week, the house was affordably wonderful (except that it gave Jan new places to explore.)

Mom and Dad first moved in during the fall of 1953. The months had gone from cooler to downright cold, but their new home was heated by a Jungers oil heater in the dining room. Jungers were in many homes in the area, and to this day are still depended upon for heat in many cabins. They were economical, efficient, and attractive. They were even a Wisconsin product, made in Grafton by the Jungers Stove and Range Company. Gramma and Grampa Cousineau even had a bright and shiny Jungers in a corner of their dining room.

Second Street also had a coal stove in the kitchen. It served not only for baking, but as an alternative heat source for the house and the only heat source for the hot water tank. It was vented through a brick chimney in the kitchen. A pipe led from the stove to the chimney, taking the fumes upward until they escaped into the air above. So anytime Mom needed hot water, summer or winter, she had to crank a fire up in this stove. Two small children, a third planning his arrival, and a constant fire in the house. There was no anxiety there.

Here's a note about chimneys. Many times they had more than one vent hole in the chimney. Some would typically be located near the floor, planned for and facilitating the removal of varmints, birds, Santa Claus and whatever else might have become trapped in the chimney. The vent also allowed for cleaning out the buildup of soot on the inside walls of the chimney.

There might also be vent hole from a stove that had been replaced, from remodeling, or from stuff people won't talk about. Anyway, old vent holes that were no longer needed would be covered up by a decorative plate. The plate would have a spring loaded 'catch' on the back that held it in place. Our kitchen had one of these decorative plates.

That coal stove was in constant use that first winter. By springtime Dad was concerned about the soot build-up. It could create ideal conditions for a chimney fire.

A chimney fire was exciting. Flames would shoot out the top of the chimney above the roof. The walls of the chimney would heat the walls of the house. Unfortunately this could also lead to a house fire, the results of which could lead to all sorts of nasty experiences like having to run out of your house in the middle of the night in your jammies (or lack thereof) and watch all your possessions go up in flames. The latter certainly took priority over any potential excitement, so Dad had a valid concern. His sense of timing and preparation in this matter was lacking however.

He came off the lake one afternoon and had it stuck on his mind that today he would clean the chimney. This same day Mom had spent all morning giving the house a thorough cleaning.

There is a reason professional Chimney Sweeps dress all in black and drape tarps everywhere soot could possibly escape from the chimney to the inside of the house. Dad did not dress in black, and did nothing to prepare the interior of the (very clean) house for this cleaning operation.

When he got home, he rummaged around until he found a length of rope that was as long as the chimney was tall. To this he securely tied a brick. He got out the ladder and propped it against the house next to the chimney. He grabbed his rope and brick and climbed up the ladder, onto the roof and over to the top of the chimney. His plan was to lower the brick into the chimney, then raise and lower it, scraping the soot buildup off the interior sides of the chimney as he went. He could then go into the kitchen, remove the vent cover and clean out all the soot he had removed from the walls of the chimney. It was done all the time. Not a problem.

He did not count on air pressure changes and he didn't check the decorative plate to see how secure it actually was. After raising and lowering the brick several times, the air movement caused the plate to fall from its perch. Or maybe as the brick was banging its way up and down the chimney, it smacked the plate and sent it flying across the room. Either way, as Mom was in the kitchen putting away cleaning supplies, she noticed puffs of black smoke pouring out of the now uncovered vent hole and creating a cloud in her clean kitchen. She ran out the door screaming at Jim.

He heard her, of course, and stopped moving the brick. "What!"

"Get down here!"

With a sinking feeling in his gut, he pulled the brick out of the chimney, climbed down the ladder and followed the boss into the kitchen. Together they found black dust coating every surface on the previously spotless first floor of the house.

He had no option but to quickly volunteer to help clean up the mess. He filled a bucket with cold water and started scrubbing the walls with a wet rag. The soot was stubborn and only smeared across the walls. There was no hot water available, because the coal stove was 'turned off'. Adding insult to injury, Mom now had to heat water on the electric stove for the second cleaning operation. She was fuming, as hot as any fire that had ever sent smoke up that chimney. Jim dutifully took the heated water and started scrubbing again. He spent the rest of the afternoon and evening scrubbing and keeping his distance. He was afraid to get close to her until she'd calmed down.

The Farm

In 1955, a farm came up for sale just south of town, right off Highway 13. It was about 24 acres in size, with a barn sitting on top of a hill, a huge field in front sloping down to the highway and about five rows of apple trees in the back. Ravines bordered either side.

The asking price was around $2,400.00.

Dad heard about the property and drove out of town to take a look. He parked on the highway next to the *for sale* sign. Bending over, he looked out the passenger door window of the truck and up at the property. The field in front was sizable and had a good southern exposure.The barn looked to be in good shape. At least it wasn't leaning. He then turned to his left and gazed out the driver's window, across the highway, down the hill and towards the lake.Madeline Island, Long Island and Chequamegon Bay and the last stretch of lake that brought the *Ione* home was spreading out in front of him. He figured it was time he and Mom became homeowners.

As he drove across town, he practiced his sales pitch to Marcie. A farm would allow them to earn additional income by growing apples, strawberries, raspberries and vegetables. There would be space for chickens, dogs and whatever else they decided to take in. She could look out the window to see when he was coming off the lake. They would not be renters any more. There would be space to let the kids run.

He pulled into the driveway wondering how convincing he could be. The only way he would find out would be to tell her. Ask her. *Convince* her.

He walked through the door and yelled.

"Marce!"

She waddled into the kitchen.

"What!" She was now very pregnant with their third child and describing her as anxious to deliver was an understatement.

"Come on and sit down."

She poured a couple cups of coffee and lowered herself into a chair at the kitchen table. He commenced with his speech, describing the fields, the barn and their future if they purchased this property. She was unimpressed, but she didn't close the door to the idea. He was so bent on purchasing this piece of property that she agreed to at least look.

They got in the truck and drove across town, up the long driveway and parked in front of the barn. He was right. They were on top of a big hill, the property was cleared down to the highway, there was an orchard in back and then there was this "structure" in front of them. She hadn't yet pegged it as a house.

Nothing was locked, so they took a walk through, starting on the side facing the lake. As Dad opened the door, he excitedly described how they could do this here and that there. She stepped inside and let out a groan. They had entered the lean-to on the lake side of the structure; it was one huge unfinished room. It could be called a room, because they still had not entered the barn section of the building. Her view was filled with the work needed to make it livable. His vision was filled with the completed house and working farm. She was unimpressed, but with all his eagerness, she sighed and gave her approval.

My oldest brother Jimmy was born in September, before the move to the farm. It was on a Sunday, and Dr. Guzzo had to remind Mom of that. He said, "I think the last time you came in was on a Sunday too, 'cuz I didn't get to church."

Mom also remembers lying in her hospital room as Dr. Guzzo carried a crying infant passed her door. The doctor poked his head in and made an announcement: "Just clipped him at both ends!" Besides the usual male clipping, Jimmy (and his future brothers) would all be tongue-tied.

1955 - *James Joseph has arrived. Grampa Cousineau celebrated the arrival of his first grandson by presenting him with a football.*

Jimmy was Grampa Cousineau's first grandson. Grampa was never known as an avid football player, and I don't know if he ever set foot in Texas, but he came to the hospital bearing a football as a present, laying it in the crib next to the baby. Mom just shook her head.

She had a boy.

Back to the house. Mom and Dad went to work transforming their new property (shed, barn, shack???) into a home. They put up walls, installed windows and indoor plumbing and updated the wiring. They laid down linoleum and brushed paint on the walls. In the living room they hooked up a Junger oil heater to keep us warm.

During the renovation, Mom attacked the interior with a crowbar, ripping out the wallboards. After prying off one section of boards, she discovered 4 or 5 table leaves between the studs of a wall. The leaves had apparently been abandoned, boarded up *in* the walls. It was no big deal, but it was so odd that Mom can still recall, 50 years later, how they looked resting between the studs. I think it bothered her that someone somewhere couldn't expand their dining room table for company. She moved the leaves out and prepared to hang drywall over the studs.

The house/barn combination sat on the hillside, thereby having a walkout "basement." It was big enough that Dad would shelter the tractor inside. Just as the "house" needed rehab, the wooden foundation under the barn had also rotted, so much so that Mom and Dad replaced it. They scoured the property, gathering rocks from wherever they could find them. Once they had a pile big enough, Dad got the wheelbarrow, the hose and cement, and he and Mom commenced to replace the rotting foundation with a stone wall. The process took some time, since Mom's attention was divided between setting stones and chasing two small children. The third was thankfully asleep in the crib.

What emerged from the construction was a two-bedroom, one-bath home. It had a long driveway that was a breath away from the city limits off Highway 13. The drive climbed uphill and slowed down at the east side of the house, next to a yard with a huge black walnut tree. You could park here, level with the first floor, or continue all the way around the house and the barn, turn left down the hill and park in the front of the house, level with the basement.

Over time, the yard next to the front door developed into the parking area of choice. The front door led in to a porch (what today we would call a *foyer*) and a sewing room. Off to the right was Mom and Dad's bedroom. Their window looked east towards the front yard. The other end of the sewing room led to the living room.

The living room stretched across the middle of the house. The south-facing wall had a window overlooking the strawberry field, the highway and the lake. The back wall butted up to the barn. The final third was the kids' bedroom and the kitchen. The bedroom was off the front of the house, and the kitchen, basically an open extension of the living room, shared a wall with the barn.

As with any old house, things were not always square or level. The floor sloped a full 12 inches down from the far edge of the living room to the kitchen sink. There was a piano in the living room, next to the opening into the kitchen. Ronny Barningham always said, "One day, I'm goin' to find Marcie pinned to the wall in the kitchen by the piano!"

These were the days before anyone could afford or even thought about air conditioning, especially in northern Wisconsin. Still, it could get hot and stuffy in the house. Mom recalled, "I fixed the [kitchen] window so I could open it. Get some air in there, in the room, by just putting some slats, you know, on an angle so I could just drop the window on it. And then one night we had a storm, and it came right through the kitchen, through the living room, through our bedroom, pulled the shade right off the roller! And your dad went out in his underwear and nailed the window back up."

I didn't care to dwell on certain aspects of the picture that she painted. Instead I decided to ponder the lack of a screen over the open window. Wisconsin's second state bird is the mosquito, and it has a million buddies called house flies. I wondered how many had cruised through that window over time. But this was the era of the sticky tape that you hung from the ceiling to attract bugs. I do recall having them strung around the house - and there were bugs stuck to them.

Although the property came with an outhouse behind the barn, a friend happily brought out his bulldozer and plowed the structure off of its foundation and filled in the hole. He had so much fun he wouldn't accept payment for it. So, the final room in the house was the bathroom, a couple of steps up from the kitchen, carved out of a corner of the barn.

The barn was higher up than the house, so a couple steps were installed in the kitchen to access the bathroom. The opposite side of the bathroom had a door leading into the barn. The mice must have used this as an access route to the goodies in the kitchen, as Mom kept loaded mouse traps under the stairs. We know this because inquisitive little Jan just had to stick her hand blindly under the stairs one day. She screeched and yanked her arm back. One of her little fingers had a trap attached to it!

Our water source was a well a quarter of the way down the hill and off to the right of a row of apple trees. A tiny structure sheltered the pump. The pump house was apparently not quite as insulated as Dad intended it to be. Wisconsin winters can be numbing, and the pump froze up our first winter in the house. Frozen pipes were disheartening, created a huge inconvenience and ended with expensive repair bills. Thus, with three children under 6 years old, Dad was very motivated to fix it. If the pump stayed inoperable, caring for a bunch of little kids in a waterless house was going to be miserable. If kids were miserable, Mom was miserable. And if Mom was miserable, Dad was going to pay. So the evening Mom turned on the faucet and got no water, Dad bundled up and headed out the door.

He was gone for quite a while. When he came back in the house, stomping the snow off his feet and unzipping his parka, the pump was again operational and water was flowing. But he no longer looked like the pale, dark haired Norwegian that Mom married. All she could see were the whites of his eyes. All his skin and clothing were coated in something black. Apparently the repairs required a lot of grease and maybe a blow torch that let off a lot of smoke. Mom still giggles over the memory. After that first winter he moved the pump up to the house and rigged a light bulb in the space around it. It never froze up again.

The Orchard

Besides home construction, Mom and Dad also spent their time bringing the orchard back to life. It had become rundown, having been let go by previous owners. Dad spent a lot of time pruning the trees back into shape. An orchard also required spraying to control insects, fungus and whatever else would crawl in to eat the apples. Mom and Dad worked as a team on this job. Mom would drive the Ford tractor up and down the rows of apple trees towing the sprayer behind her. Dad would sit on the sprayer and work the hose and nozzle.

Driving this tractor/sprayer rig forward through the orchard was no problem for Mom. Backing up was another story however. She just could not figure out how to back up the tractor when the sprayer was attached. Once she managed to back Dad right into a tree. Another backing attempt got her so frustrated and angry that she stopped, shut the tractor down, jumped off the tractor and stormed into the house.

"He always wanted me to drive the tractor when he sprayed the apples. We'd go around and have to come back around and I'd have to back it up little bit more to straighten it up. He kept telling me how and I couldn't do it and I finally just backed it up into a tree and left."

Dad, for all his relentless teasing about how Mom was a stubborn Swede or dumb Frenchman, loved her dearly. While she was cooling off in the house, he climbed on the rig, turned it around and got it ready for the next forward movement, then went in the house to find her. Dad could be abrupt and oblivious to everything but what he had going on. This time he must have realized how frustrated and upset Mom was (the storm that careened off the tractor and pounded into the house must have been pretty awesome). He approached her quietly and hesitantly, saying, "All right, it's straight now."

Meaning, would she please come back out and help him finish the job?

He also developed an incredible sense of timing when it came to spraying. Mom made the most wonderful homemade oatmeal bread (I remember the big ceramic bowl she used to mix it in and let it rise under a white dishtowel), and every time she would be up to her elbows in bread dough, Dad would get the sprayer ready to go, then he'd come in and holler, "Come on let's go."

She'd look up at him, flour on the table, the dough ready to knead and just glare at him. I can just see the pursed lips and the tension in her face. He was oblivious. She told me, "I didn't just leave all the time. He had to wait. It never failed. It just got to the point that I would ask him when he was going to spray so I wouldn't start mixing up bread."

Dad definitely did not have a good grasp of the time, effort and complexity baking could require. Once, during herring season, he was down at the dock and Mom was home baking in the kitchen, using an electric hand mixer to make cookie dough. Finishing the mixing, she turned the mixer off, but hadn't yet pulled the plug out of the outlet. As luck would have it, her hand slid against the beaters and at the same time she bumped the on/off switch. The motor revved up and immediately sounded strained. That was because her left thumb had become entangled in the beaters. She ripped the plug out of the wall and stared at her thumb. It hurt, but not that bad; the problem was that when she tried to free her thumb by pulling out the beaters, they would not come out of the mixer. Her thumb had spread them slightly out of alignment and they would not disengage. She was stuck.

Dad was the first person she thought to call for a rescue. The docks were only a mile away and he could be home in minutes. The problem was the distance from the mixing bowl to the phone, which was in the sewing room on the other side of the house.

She needed the truck to get there but Dad had the truck, and her thumb was beginning to throb. So Mom scooped up the mixer, cradled it in the crook of her right elbow, and with the cord dragging across the linoleum, and batter and chocolate chips clinging to the beaters, she crossed the room to call for help.

These were the days before 9-1-1 and possibly before rotary dial. When they moved to the farm, the phone was still a crank model (Mom was so glad when she got rid of it and installed a rotary dial phone!). You had to lift the receiver, crank the turn handle and wait for the operator to answer; once she came on the line you told her the number you wanted her to dial. So, Mom either cranked away or used the old rotary phone to dial the four digit number to get Dad. It wasn't until somewhere around 1970's that we had to dial both the exchange and the number.

Today she wishes she still had that crank phone.

Either way, she got connected to Otto L. Kean's fishery. Danny the secretary answered, receiving what was probably the most exciting news in Bayfield that day. Mom said Danny sounded so scared. He quickly yelled out the window for Dad to come to the phone.

Dad walked over, picked up the receiver and, just like a knight in shining armor, snapped, "What's the matter."

"My thumb is stuck in the mixer and I can't get it out! I need you to come home and help me!"

"Well," Dad replied, "Can't you put it in reverse?"

"Jim, there is no reverse. Get home."

So Dad had to leave the dock and drive up to the farm to remove his wife's finger from the blades of a mixer. This would not go over well when the guys heard about it at coffee. They did a good amount of ribbing all around and he could just hear it now.

He found Mom sitting at the kitchen table, eating dough with her right hand and resting her left hand on the table, entangled in the mixer. To Mom's credit, Dad confirmed that she was truly stuck. Trying to prove he was stronger and smarter than a hand mixer took away a bit of his pride; it actually took a while for him to free her thumb, and to that end it was not exactly a he-man macho type of success. But it was still difficult enough that he might bring it up in conversation when he went back to the docks to finish picking her-ring.

The Barn

The barn butted up to the backside of the house. You'd go up a set of steps in the kitchen, through the bathroom and then enter the barn. Mom told me, "The barn had that great big door, and they used to haul hay into it and I always told him, I says, you'd better nail that door down. It's going to fall down some day."

"Yeah, yeah, yeah..." Dad would always reply.

Mom continued, "Well, one night … I heard such a horrible bang and startled I said, 'What was that?' Your dad calmly said, 'Oh, the barn door just fell down.' I think he rolled over and went back to sleep."

There was one other entry into the barn, a very narrow door on the side facing the orchard. Just inside this entry was where a crew would grade apples during the fall. Different size apples were sold for different prices, and so, after being picked, baskets and boxes of apples would be brought into the barn and sorted by size.

Mom recalled Ronny Barningham hauling in apples, because he'd cuss every time he had to come through that door. The doorway was so narrow that he'd have to hold the box of apples in front of him so they went through the doorway first. Then he'd have to turn sideways himself to get through, never without complaining to Mom.

One time he said, "You got to have a bigger door than this to get the basket of apples in the barn!"

She shot back, "Well, why don't you make it bigger?"

A little while later she heard a chainsaw rev up. Ronny was 'making it bigger.'

In order to sell the apples, Dad, sometimes with Mom along

(not us), would load up the one-ton truck and head for Minnesota and North Dakota. The back was filled with sorted, boxed apples that would be offered for sale to small grocery stores along the way. The trips were filled with sometimes comical and sometimes anxious moments.

Mom recalls, "One time, we got to this fruit market or something, and Dad went in and talked to the guy. Yah, he wanted some apples. I had been talking to a woman sitting outside, and when hearing they would take apples, I looked at her and said, 'I have to go.'

"She said, 'You don't have to do anything. Just sit down, they can handle this!' Never forgot that. And she had two Chihuahuas and I was scared to death of both of them. They were awful, barkers and nippers."

Another time, "We had some Dudley's in front of the house, and they were real big. We took a bunch of those out but had a hard time selling them. On our way home, traveling through Superior, we stopped at a market. To our surprise, the man took everything we had on the truck. We went home happy campers.

"The next morning, Sunday morning, there's a knock on the front door. We thought, "Uh oh, they're bringin' them all back." To our surprise, he wanted more! We were just dumbfounded; they were terrible apples. But we were out there pickin' the rest of the Dudleys."

These trips would last three to four days at the most. Mini-vacations for Dad and Mom that were far from the norm.

In addition to the apple orchard, they plowed and planted the strawberry field stretching between the house and the highway. Jan can remember picking strawberries as a little girl. Dad and Mom had a little card going for her, which they would punch after she'd picked a box. Later, at 52 years of age, she was still proud of that card. "Yah know, cuz I got paid."

The little girl in her still relished the memory of money in her pocket.

The strawberry patch required irrigation. There was a pond down near the road. Dad had a Kahlenberg engine installed to run the irrigation system. Kahlenberg was the make of the engine Grampa had installed in the *Ione*. They were well known for their distinctive sound. Any fisherman with one in his boat could never sneak off the lake. The sound would give him away, miles in advance. Mom did not recall hearing much purring from the direction of the pump house. Apparently the structure lacked the acoustics of the hull of a fish tug.

We also had grapes on the farm. They would be ripe during apple season and Mom would sell a lot, getting $2 a bushel. She was doing great, that is, until Dad decided they needed to be pruned. According to Mom, he didn't really know how to prune them, and gave them such a haircut that we would not have grapes again for about two years.

So Mom and Dad added farming to their resume and we kids enjoyed an era of freedom and fresh country air. Not that air in town was much different. It was only 100 feet or so from our property line to the city limits. Biking, walking or even sliding distance was all that kept us from downtown.

The homestead was comfortable if quirky. With two more kids to be added to the family, it would get a bit crowded inside, but the antics were priceless. The family grew in size and personality, the farm was thriving, and life was good. Mom always commented that with all the activity that went on, she should write a book.

Oatmeal Bread

3 cups boiling water
4 teaspoons salt
2 tablespoons shortening (oleo/butter/Crisco)

Bring to boil
Stir in 2 cups oatmeal
Let stand until cool

Dissolve 1 package cake yeast in 1 1/2 cups lukewarm water
Put 1/2 cup molasses and 1/2 cup brown sugar in oatmeal

Add 10 cups flour, a little at a time until it doesn't stick to your hands.

Let rise.
Knock down
Put in loaf pans
Let rise as high as you want it
Bake at 350° for 50 minutes
Brush with melted butter after taking out of the oven
Makes 3 loaves
(Unless you have to go spray the orchard...)

The *Outer Island*

In order to make ends meet, Dad worked the farm, fished on the *Ione*, and took odd jobs painting houses. He also worked part time where the job description included deckhand, cook, cowboy and logger, all in one. He was crew on the *Outer Island*, a WWII landing barge that did salvage, transport and other kinds of work around the islands.

This work involved living on the boat, so while employed, Dad would only be home a couple nights a week. Many of the guys, except my dad, apparently spent many of these off evenings at Junior's Bar down at the base of Cooper Hill. Many of the wives would complain to them, "Why don't you go home like Frostman does?"

The guys finally cajoled Jim into accompanying them to Junior's one night. They had a plan to get the usually sober Frostman drunk. So while sitting at the bar, someone would distract him and another would add shots to his beer. The added alcohol had the desired effect. Dad got very, very drunk.

When he arrived at the house late that evening, (I have no idea how he got home), he staggered into the living room, obviously inebriated. He hollered the typical order, "Marcie, get me something to eat!"

One look at him and she snapped, "Get it yourself."

He retorted, "If you don't get it for me, I'm going to leave."

She shot back, "There's the door. Turn the knob to the right and pull the door open."

He turned around, and with a scowl on his face, marched as best he could out of the living room. Instead of heading for the front door, he turned left into the bedroom and collapsed onto the bed.

One of the guys later called to ask Mom if Dad made it home, and to find out if she was mad at him and the 'boys'. She replied, "No, and he's in bed sleeping."

He replied, "Damn it! That was a waste of money." Dad probably agreed as he nursed a headache for three days.

Dad may have been good at coming home at night, but he was still a horrible tease to his wife. While working the *Outer Island*, there was a pair of strong binoculars on board. From his vantage point on the boat, Dad would watch through the glasses as Mom worked in the berries and say, "Why weren't you in the garden?" If she were in the garden, he would say, "Why weren't you in the berries?" She was pregnant at the time, so he should have just been glad she was busy doing anything!

He didn't limit himself to watching his wife through the binoculars. Once, while passing by a beach, the boss caught him and a crew mate watching some girls sunbathing. The binoculars were quickly confiscated.

The work on the *Outer Island* almost led to Dad's demise. The crew was up in the U.P. (Upper Peninsula of Michigan) about a six-hour drive from home. They were working with a logging crew. One particular day Dad had been handling hemlock, and cut his thumb.

At the end of the day, the crew met at the bar as was the custom when the crew was away from home. Dad sat on a stool at the bar and looked down at his arm. A red line was crawling away from the cut on his thumb and working its way up his forearm. He tried to tell the guys he had blood poisoning and needed somebody to take him to the hospital. At first they laughed it off because they didn't believe him. So he laid his arm on the bar and said, "Look at this." Curiosity got to them, and they leaned over each other in the dim light to get a look at his arm. Even with a beer or two in them, they too could see the red line move as the poison crept up towards his heart.

By the time he arrived at the local hospital, the poison had almost reached his underarm. The medical term for blood poisoning is Septicemia, or Bacteremia. It occurs when bacteria or other toxic microorganisms invade the bloodstream. For Dad the suspect was debris from the hemlocks they were logging. The toxins entered the blood stream through the cut on his thumb. It created an infection that was in the process of traveling towards his heart. Depending on the advancement of the poison, he was or was about to suffer with fever, chills, a rapid heart beat, rapid respirations, and low blood pressure. While low blood pressure would have been welcome in his later years, then it was not. What would follow would be tissue injury and organ failure. Unless he was treated quickly, they could bury him under that hemlock tree.

At the hospital, the doctors immediately administered shots (which I assume were antibiotics), and got the infection under control. Dad would need shots every four hours to get rid of the poisoning. His boss approached the doctor and asked if he could be transported to a hospital closer to home, as the Washburn hospital was 13 miles from our house. The doctor replied, "If you can get him in a hospital in four hours, I'll let him go."

The boss asked the local crew if anyone could take Dad to the Washburn hospital, and do it in less than four hours, a local Finlander offered to do the driving. Eddie, one of the loggers, loaded Dad up in his truck and practically flew him to the Washburn hospital, making unbelievable time along the old two lane highways.

Meanwhile, Mom had been informed of the situation. She was anxious, but four hours was a long time, so she didn't rush down to the hospital to sit and wait.

"When he called and told me he was coming, I was in Bayfield," she recalled, "and I don't know, I did a few things, and then went down, and he was already in the hospital in Washburn." Oops.

Dad worked on the *Outer Island* two times. While he was recovering from the poisoning, they only let him cook. Other times being crew included being a cowboy. The *Outer Island* hauled not only logs from logging operations on the islands, but also cattle. The Lullaby Lumber Company did logging on Outer Island and also kept cattle out there. There was a large lumber camp on the north east end of the island and a well maintained road running from the camp, near the lighthouse, to the south end, a distance of around seven miles.

There were horses out there for rounding up the cattle. Dad said those horses were so well trained, all you had to do was flip the reins, one side to the other, and they'd go. They knew what to do. This was good, because Dad's horse experience was limited, mostly from participating in benefit donkey basketball games at the local courthouse.

So one day all he did was ride, rounding up cattle and loading them on the *Outer*. By the end of the day he had more than his share of blisters. Unfortunately for him, that was the night he and Mom had to take Carolyn to the hospital in Duluth. He wouldn't get out of the saddle until long after the sun went down.

On another trip, Dad would show off his knowledge of washing clothes. The *Outer* had on board an old oil drum with holes punched in it. Dad needed his jeans jacket washed so he threw the jacket in the oil drum. He then secured the lid, tied the oil drum to a line secured to the stern and tossed it overboard. He let the drum 'agitate' for a few miles and then hauled it up on the deck. The system had worked so well that there was nothing left of the jacket but a few scraps of denim. So much for his laundering abilities.

Life on the Farm

Meanwhile, life continued back on the farm. We moved there when Carolyn was about five, Jan about three and Jimmy just an infant in a bassinet. Before moving again, two more babies were added to the family. I would arrive, taking my time and go on record as one of Mom's longest labors, a total of six or eight hours. (She'd averaged around two to two-and-a-half hours until then). I was posterior and hanging on with a brittle umbilical cord. It couldn't be tied without breaking so Dr. Guzzo just taped it.

Anyway, the house would eventually be bursting at the seams. Carolyn, Jan and Jimmy would share the second bedroom, I would call the couch my bedroom and Billy had the crib in Mom and Dad's bedroom.

The farm represented my parents' complete independence from their parents, and the time when they settled into their own roles as parents, homeowners, adult children and contributing adults. For years I listened to Mom's stories about living on the farm. It finally dawned on me that these memories were very precious to Mom, and if they weren't written down, the details would soon be lost.

So, with an effort to not be too annoying, I would ask her to tell and retell as many of the events as she could recall so I could get all the details down on paper. With each telling another detail would sneak into the story. To her credit, each time she responded to my "interrogations" with enthusiasm. She would laugh and grumble and I could watch the memories play again in her eyes and through the expression on her face.

There was a time that Mom couldn't get the oil heater going. Dad wasn't available so she called Grampa Cousineau to help.

Over the phone he instructed her to take out the elements and clean them. She tried, but the stove still wouldn't start. Curiosity got the better of him and Grampa said to hang on, he was coming over to have a look. He jumped in the car and drove the 13 miles from Washburn to our house to unravel the mystery.

The Junger stove sat in the corner of the living room, where the front wall and the kids' bedroom met. It had two burners, a little door in front and was brown/black enamel and shiny. There may have been grates on top. It looked like a 4-5 foot tall old fashioned refrigerator, you know, with the rounded edges. Jungers ran on diesel fuel and are still well-known, a common heater used in hunting camps throughout the northland. Grampa and Gramma Cousineau even had one in their dining room. Smooth metal exterior, a window where you could see the flame, and a big exhaust pipe connecting the stove to the wall. They made the house quite cozy.

Grampa examined the inside and outside of Mom's stove. Nothing was out of place. He was perplexed until he looked behind the stove. The copper tubing that fed the stove with oil had been flattened. The biggest suspects were the numerous sets of little hands and feet that pattered around the house. Grampa replaced the piping and the heater fired up once again.

I would like to think this stove saved my life. When I was nine months old, I caught the flu. It was early spring and I was so listless that Dad told Mom to get me to the doctor. These were the days when going to the doctor was a big deal so I must have been really sick. Dr. Guzzo could only say that I had to just fight it out. So, to keep me warm, they put my crib in the living room next to this oil heater. The heat, lots of fluids and the passage of two or three days did the trick and I finally started feeling better. In fact, I think I fully recovered.

The barn was a handy space to have attached to the house. At one point we had two puppies. They would be corralled in the barn each night. Mom chuckled when telling me about a recollection with the dogs and the barn.

"We had a babysitter one night," she reminisced, "and we had

1962 - *Jimmy gets a remote control ship and Connie gets a spanking for spoiling the surprise.*

two puppies, and we forgot to tell her about them. And they were out in the barn, and they were running around like mad. It scared her half to death! She didn't know what it was!"

If I had been that babysitter, in a house outside of town, and late at night have yelps and howls start to rattle the house, I too would have been petrified.

Remember that narrow door in the barn that was remodeled using a chainsaw? We used to stand in that doorway and watch the rain. The water droplets would splatter on the gravel under the eaves, creating a shallow ditch along the edge of the barn. The orchard across the driveway would appear gray through the mist.

We stood just inside the doorway, dry and slightly chilled, listening to the pattering of the raindrops on the roof. Mom would give us glasses and we would hold them out to the streams of water pouring off the shingles. The glasses would fill and we may have sipped the water or tossed it into the wet gravel below. I don't know. I only remember how pleasant it was gathering at the door, our glasses filling, the scent of wet grass, and the gray day outside. It instilled in me a love and appreciation for rainy days.

Rain in Wisconsin can go on for days, not a quick and often intense afternoon shower as I've experienced as an adult in the Colorado mountains and on the Georgia coast. So it was very strange one day when we were all in the house and Dad came in and yelled for us to hurry outside. When Dad barked an order, there was never any negotiation, we all jumped and did what he said. (We grumbled, but never in front of him.) We ran out the door to where he was standing. He pointed to the north towards the orchard. We were standing under cloudy skies, dry as a bone. 100 feet away in the orchard it was pouring cats and dogs.

Improvements continued on the house. There was an old lean-to on the back of the barn. It was rotten and was an accident waiting to happen. Directly above the lean-to, on the roof of the barn, was the TV antenna. Mom recalled, "I wanted to tear it down, because I was afraid you kids were going to get hurt in there. Dad says, 'Yah, I'll do it. I'll get to it.'

"Well, he never got to it. So one day I decided to tear it down. So, when you all were taking your nap, or in school or something, I went up on the roof and I started tearing it down. It was so rotten. I grabbed a hold of some black tar paper and I gave it a great yank."

What Mom did not know was that an eyebolt and support wires that held up one side of that TV antenna were under the tar paper. The lean-to was so rotten that when she yanked, she pulled the eye bolt right out of a beam. It hopped up the roof a few feet, and dangled on the end of what were now visible support wires. Mom's eyes followed the wires up to the top of the roof, and gasped as she watched the TV antenna teeter precariously. A second later the antenna swayed and toppled out of sight.

"Uh, oh."

She crawled off the lean-to roof and ran around to the front of the house. The antenna could be seen dangling half way down the barn roof. The remaining support wires had stayed firmly attached and kept the antenna from crashing to the ground. There was no way she was going to crawl up on the barn roof to fix this problem.

Jim had promised to do this entire project, so the least he could do was climb up the roof to retrieve the antenna. She went back to demolishing the lean-to until it was time for coffee and checking on the sleeping babies.

Not only did Mom do house repairs, she also did a little furniture work also. As she recalled, "We had that old iron bed, and the end of it was kinda rounded. And I asked your dad, I said, 'Why can't we take that (the footboard) and put it at the head of the bed, use it for a headboard, forget the bottom, the footboard.'"

Dad replied, "You can't cut that off."

Mom retorted, "Well, of course, you don't tell me you don't do that. So I got a hacksaw and I cut it off. And I put it up for the headboard. When I went to bed that night, I said, 'The last person in bed has to shut the light off.' So I ran, jumped in bed and when he came and jumped in bed, the whole bed went sideways."

He looked at Mom and said, "Now do you see why you couldn't cut that off?"

Marcie didn't stop at renovating beds. She wanted a fence around the yard to keep us kids away from the driveway since there was always someone driving in. Dad had running poles stored at the house for ice fishing.

Side Note: A running pole was used to set gill nets under the ice. It was a series of 1x4 boards that would be nailed together. It was shoved into one of two holes cut in the ice, the second hole being cut in the ice a distance away that was equal to the length of the running pole. The pole would be directed under the ice to the second hole. Attached to the following end of the pole was the gang of gill nets. As the first end of the running pole was pulled out of the water through the second hole, the nets were pulled into and spread under the ice between the two holes.

Back to the fence. If the running pole were cut into pieces it would be the perfect material to build the fence Marcie had in mind. Jim would be furious to have his "equipment" hijacked, but since it was summer and ice fishing was 6 months away, she figured he'd get over it. Our safety was a more urgent issue.   She wouldn't worry about "Jan-Proofing" this one however. So she built herself a fence.

The fence did not sit well with some of the other fishermen. Jimmy Erickson and his wife Muriel had six kids of their own on another farm. Word had gotten out to Muriel about this fence. So one day Erickson shows up to the house and says, "Yah, Frostman, you started something, now I gotta put up a fence!"

Jippy....

We always seemed to have pets. Jippy was the most memorable from "the farm" era. He was a black lab, great with kids and smart. As a puppy he was all legs, lanky and uncoordinated. A friend of the family used to visit, and each time he'd chase and tease the puppy, apparently more than the dog preferred.

Then there were a few months between his visits, during which time Jippy had put on considerable size and weight. When our friend next visited, he parked his truck, naturally got out and walked over to Mom and attempted to start a conversation. Jippy was in the yard, and took notice. Every muscle in the dog's body began to tense as he stared down someone he considered unwelcome. He slowly rose to his feet, and every hair on his backbone rose with him. His throat rumbled with an almost inaudible growl. Our friend felt the sixth sense of something bad about to happen and bolted for the safety of his truck. Mom suppressed a smile and waited until he had secured himself in his truck, then walked over and resumed the conversation through the truck window.

Jippy grew to be a fairly large dog. We would hook him up to our sleds and have him pull us around the yard. Jimmy would ride him like a horse. Even with his size, he was still welcome in the house. Dad would wrestle him on the living room floor, arms and paws flailing all over. I hear that most of the matches ended in a draw.

Jippy's food dish was kept in the kitchen. We had one of those kitchen table sets with the chrome legs and vinyl padding on the chairs. The floor in the house was linoleum. One day Mom was knitting at the kitchen table and realized the dog was probably hungry. Carolyn was nearby so Mom asked her to please let Jippy in the house so he could eat. Carolyn opened the front door and Jippy bolted past her, his legs flailing as he ran, his nails scraping the floor but barely getting a grip. Like Fred Flintstone, he ran at top speed but did not get anywhere fast. Tongue hanging off to the side, he navigated the sewing room, made a wide right turn into the living room and readied for the left turn into the kitchen. He managed to redirect himself into the kitchen but immediately lost all traction and went into the fastest slide of his life. He slid right into, under and past the chair Mom was sitting on. The chair skidded across the kitchen, the knitting flew in the air and Mom was on her hands and knees looking for the tornado. The dog came to a stop directly in front of his food dish. He stood up, shook himself off and started to eat, oblivious to the havoc he had just created.

One day we had all gathered in the living room. Jippy sat with us, lounging between two chairs. Also residing in the house was one of Janis' many cats. This particular one, a kitten, decided to jump from one of these two chairs to the other, right in front of the dog. While she was in mid leap, directly in front of Jippy's face, he yawned. His mouth opened wide and then snapped shut. At the same time the kitten disappeared from sight.

We all saw the kitten leap. We all saw the kitten disappear. We all sat in disbelief. Yes, dogs are known for chasing cats, but how many times have they been seen swallowing them? It truly looked like Jippy had swallowed the kitten. In disbelief we started a frantic search and found the kitten, very much alive. She was entertaining herself in another part of the room, oblivious to our anguish.

Back to Mom...

Mom's activities were never limited to the house and kids. She worked outside the farm every once in a while. In town there was a bean cannery. It was a large plain building on the flat block between Allwood's Lumber Company and Bodin's Fisheries. It was a wooden 1950's version of a huge warehouse. One night a friend of hers needed someone to fill in for her and asked if Mom could help. Mom agreed and spent the evening in front of a rolling conveyer belt with thousands of beans rumbling by her station. Her job was to pick out the bad beans. Then the beans were cut up, washed and put into cans and cooked. The product was then sold to Del Monte and other companies. It probably was a more interesting job than the one she held attaching eyes to fishing rods, but less interesting than sewing underwear in Ashland for Munsingwear. She also went on to clean wildfowl at a hunting farm on Madeline Island, tend bar and a variety of other adventures.

Mom taking a job outside the home did not mean that things would not get done around the house. Once, filling in for somebody at the cannery meant leaving Dad at home to take care of the house. He decided to help Mom out by doing the wash. Unlike laundry on the *Outer Island*, the end results here were not as costly. Mom came home to find all the clothes clean and hung out on the line to dry. The shirts were pinned by their collars and the pants hung by the bottom of the legs.

He could fix things though, just like the well pump that first winter. The automatic washer broke down (I define the type of washing machine because wringer washers were still a common sight in many homes). It had mercury switches in it. Mom and Dad fixed it once at a cost of $25. At that time $25 was a huge amount of money to my folks. So the next time the switches broke Dad fixed them with a rubber band. They never broke again.

Mom once decided to take advantage of the nuts falling off the black walnut tree in the yard. She recalled, "One year we picked up all the walnuts and laid them out upstairs in the hayloft, like, to dry them off so we could get the skins off of them. When we went back up stairs to pick them up, that's all that was left was the skins. The squirrels got them."

Such a bummer, since so much hard work had gone into picking the walnuts. There was a substance on the skin of the nut that would darken the skin, just like a dye. Mom said she couldn't get the stain off her hands, it just had to wear off. And they had no nuts left to show for it.

We kept potatoes in the basement. The basement was accessed by an outside door on the highway side of the house. You had to go out the front door, turn right, and go down the hill to get inside. It was also accessible through the barn. There was a door there that led to a staircase that led to the garage portion of the basement where Dad kept the tractor. Walk across the garage and there was another inside door into the storage room. The circuitous route always left Carolyn with goose bumps. She hated going down there and hated putting her hands into that dark burlap bag, fearing snakes and other unknown terrors.

We only dabbled in farm animals. Someone once asked if they could bring their pig up for us to keep with our chickens in a chicken coop we kept out back. It was just a little pig, but once the chickens realized they had company, they freaked. The pig scared our chickens so much that they took to hanging from the ceiling and would not lay eggs for weeks. The pig was not thrilled either and immediately commenced digging underneath the fence. The little pig was sent home and Mom could only say, "Thank, God."

There was another farm to the north of our property. Carolyn loved to visit up there and did so frequently. They had three cows and she would help milking them. She never got confident at this activity, the cows were big, she was small, they kept moving and it was all a bit nerve wracking. But she loved to skim the cream off the milk and churn homemade butter.

Every now and then these cows would find their way down to our place. This upset my parents as the cows would not only eat the strawberries, but they would trample the strawberry plants. One Sunday Mom looked out the window to see the cows in the yard. She called the neighbors to tell them to come get their cows. They were not pleased that their cows were in our yard and hinted that maybe Janis had let the cows out. Mom responded that this little girl (she was around seven or eight) couldn't have let them out. She was in Sunday school when this happened. They didn't have a good comeback for her response. It was a good thing they didn't hear Dad's response. He was on the other side of the room commenting that if he caught their cows in our yard again, he was going to milk them.

Janis did have an alibi on the cow incident, but as a very energetic little girl, she did make a good suspect. She would roam the entire property and did spend time near the cows. Dad unknowingly put her up to it. There was one day that Jan decided she wanted to go to Canada. She was out in the yard and Dad was nearby. She asked Dad where Canada was and he pointed north and said, "It's that way." So she walked up to the north end of the property, went into the ravine and played, pretending she was in Canada. In fact, she started going to Canada quite often.

This was back in the early 60s when there was not the great fear that children would be snatched if left unattended. Like Jan, all us kids explored the entire property. Calling us home when needed was no problem for Dad. He would put his thumb and forefinger between his lips and let out the shrillest whistle that I swear could be heard for miles. It brought us running from every corner of the orchard. I once was so engrossed in my imaginary play world that I missed the call. All I will say is that I learned to keep my ears open after that.

Dad did believe in spankings. One year Jimmy received a remote control Texaco oil tanker for his birthday. I remember as a four-year old running down to the school bus at the end of that day.

As soon as Jimmy got off the bus, I spilled the beans about the gift awaiting him. Snitching was not a good idea. I don't remember receiving the spanking Dad gave me. I only remember that I got it and never wanted to get it again.

Sometimes the discovery of our wrongdoings was found too late to press charges. The farm provided ready access to dirt and sand. At four years old, Jimmy and one of our cousins loved to play in the sand. A week after a particularly great sand and dirt day, Dad and Mom stopped at the DX to gas up our blue Oldsmobile. These were the days of full service gas stations, so Mom and Dad sat in the car and greeted Wally as he walked up to the car and removed the gas cap to the Oldsmobile. He inserted the nozzle and began to pump the gas. After only a couple gallons gas started to spit back at his hand. He leaned over and asked Dad if he was just topping off the tank. Dad said, "No, it should be almost empty!" Dad got out of the car and together they watched as Wally tried to put more gas into the tank. The tank would not take any more. They discussed the mystery at length, and that's when Wally got a flashlight and looked down the gas pipe. He saw sand.

Jimmy and our cousin were the obvious suspects for this egregious violation. But could punishment be effective if the perpetrator couldn't remember the crime? Or connect the punishment to the crime? Or didn't understand that it was a crime? Dad and Mom gave up on that one. As they drove home, it began to really bug Mom because the imps even had the nerve to put gas cap back on when they were done filling the tank.

They drove up the driveway and into Dad's view came the one-ton truck he relied on for work.

"Oh God," he croaked, and as he pulled the Olds up to the house, he slammed the transmission into park, burst out of the door and ran over to the truck. His heart was racing as he took the gas cap off and peered down inside. Nothing but gas vapors. He let out a relieved sigh, looked back at Mom and smiled.

The Oldsmobile would suffer for quite a while. Sand had made its way through the gas line and into the carburetor. Some days the car would run, some days it wouldn't. Dad took to cleaning the carburetor regularly at night on the kitchen table. But only after we were all in bed and dogs were sent to the barn. He would take it all apart and clean each piece, hoping eventually the symptoms would go away. We ended up selling it to get rid of the problem. In an odd twist, about 10 years later Wally overlooked Jimmy's indiscretions and hired the teenager at the gas station.

It was during the Oldsmobile's post sand inoculation that Mom was pregnant with Billy. Since the car was no longer guaranteed to start, Mom did not feel it would be trustworthy for her inevitable trip to the hospital. So she decided to stay with her mother as the due date neared. This went fine until she went into labor. As soon as Ethel heard the news (remember, Ethel didn't drive) Gramma ran full throttle out of the house and next door to get Mike Vernarsky. Mom had never seen her mother run that fast before.

Meanwhile, Mom waddled down to the Oldsmobile, and sure enough, it wouldn't start. So Mike loaded her up in his car for the trip. He looked at her and asked if they (the hospital) would take her on such short notice. He never had any children, so he didn't know what to expect. She looked at him and barked, "Drive!"

Billy was born 45 minutes later.

Besides boundaries, we kids learned and experienced typical kid things at the farm. Jan wanted a bicycle. Dad said, "You learn how to ride a bicycle then you can get one." This was obviously a catch-22 since there was no two-wheel bicycle on the farm. Dad thought he was pretty clever to get himself off the hook so easily.

He forgot it was Jan he was dealing with. The little towhead took one back wheel off her tricycle and rolled down the driveway on two wheels balancing the whole way. So Mom and Dad loaded us up and went to JC Penny in Ashland to get Jan a real bike. Jan even helped pay for it. She took her piggy bank with her and cracked it open on the counter at the store. Mom and Dad paid for the rest. It was a 24-inch bike that she kept for the next 20-some years.

Jan was also the only one of us to run away. It might have been when she was around 5 years old, when, for about a 3-week period, she decided that she was adopted. Mom and Dad couldn't convince her that she wasn't. She came up to Mom and told her she'd decided she had to run away.

Mom looked down at the little blond and quickly ran all the possible outcomes of Jan's decision through her mind. Feeling fairly confident, Mom smiled and said, "O.K., wait just a minute and I'll pack you a lunch."

Mom made her a sandwich, packed it, a drink and some clothes in a bandana and tied them all on the end of a stick. She handed the stick to Jan and out the door went the runaway. Jan put the stick over her shoulder, marched all the way to the edge of the orchard and stopped, maybe trying to decide if she wanted to go to Canada or not.

Meanwhile, Mom walked back into the house, and then ran through the living room, kitchen, and bathroom and into the barn. The barn was not exactly airtight, dressed with gaps between the barn boards, some large enough to look out of and spy on the little runaway. Just as Mom suspected, Jan wasn't really ready to go very far from home. She watched as Jan sized up the different apple trees on the edge of the driveway next to the barn. Jan then took her possessions, climbed a tree in full view of the house and settled in for the afternoon. Mom too settled in for the afternoon, occasionally checking on Jan through the cracks in the walls of the barn. By late afternoon Jan had had enough and decided it was time to come home.

Jimmy never ran away, but one day as a toddler he did disappear when Mom's back was turned (shades of a search on Madeline Island 10 years earlier). She had let him outside for a short while. Just a short while. When she wasn't looking, Jimmy did the 'normal' child behavior (unlike Janis) and toddled downhill, all the way to the highway. At the same time there was a hired man working in the strawberry patch. He stood up from the berry plants to stretch his back and to his surprise, saw this little boy walking the center line of Highway 13. The man sprinted to the road and scooped the child off his feet and off the road. Jimmy was not happy about this and cried the entire way up the driveway. Mom could hear the crying and ran towards the sound. The man reached the house with the wailing child. He handed Jimmy over and told her where he had found the imp. She was much relieved but still felt like crawling in a hole.

A couple years later, Jimmy would venture again through the berry fields, setting Mom up for another heart attack. He was about 3 and I was a little over a year. Mom had left us sitting in the car, while she checked on something in the raspberry patch. Jimmy managed to get out of the car, and in the process, lock me in. To make matters worse, Mom had dressed me in a wool sweater since it was cold that morning. When Mom realized what had happened she frantically tried to get me out. Since I was only one, she couldn't make me understand how to unlock the door. Finally she ran and got a neighbor from across the road. He attempted to go through the trunk to try to push the back seat out. Jo Barningham was helping Mom that morning and started pounding on the little fin window that cars had back then, and to everyone's relief, it opened. She was able to reach in and unlock the front door. This whole process took a while and when they finally got to me I was drenched with sweat in that wool sweater.

Winter

In the winter, the strawberry field was one large white slope. This is where Dad taught Jan to ski on a little pair of red skis. He belted the skis to her snow boots and shoved her down the hill; do or die. She lived. (It was the same method he later used to teach me to ride a two-wheeler bike. He gave me a push and I biked, upright and in a straight line, right into the side of a brick garage.) He also built us an igloo one year. Impressed the heck out of Jan. She probably went to Alaska every time she entered it.

Winters, especially long, hard, cold winters, are never easy on a stay-at-home mom, no matter what century you are in. We had no videos or video games. We did have three channels with antenna on the roof and snow on the ground (only two channels without the snow). But we would rather be outside, sliding, skiing, and making snow angels.

Mom spent buckets of time knitting us hats and mittens with strings on them. The strings would connect each mitten, running from one hand, through the sleeve of the jacket, across the back, down the other sleeve and to the other mitten. That string reduced the opportunity to loose mittens by probably 90 percent.

Necessity was the mother of invention, of course, and being on a tight budget, everything was recycled. I wore hand-me-downs for years. All of us older kids could thank the Coast Guard for our snow suits. Mom got to know the local Coast Guard staff, and when they had old wool uniforms that were about to be thrown out, she would acquire them, and transform them into the warmest, driest snow-suits for us.

But Mom was not to be snowbound to the farm in the winter.

She would bundle us up, stick whoever wasn't mobile yet into a cardboard box tied atop the toboggan, and we would walk to town. Remember, the town limit was at the end of our driveway, so it wasn't far. By the time Carolyn and Jan were complaining that they were tired, we had reached the top of Cooper Hill. Everyone would load up on the toboggan, and we would scream down the hill. Mom would then park the craft outside one of at least three grocery stores in town, get what she needed, say hi to everyone, and back up the hill we would go.

She didn't always walk to town in the winter. At one point we had this big old station wagon. Boredom and a little marital "strain" made Mom decide to drive to town one day. She was mad because Dad had driven the car up the driveway, all the way around the back of the barn, down the hill and left it parked it in front of the house, under the living room window. With the snowfall, there was no way Mom could drive the car back the way it came. The drive was too steep, hard packed with snow and slippery. It put a roadblock in her plans to go to town.

This wasn't a problem in any other season. There was an old road accessible from the front of the house. It was lined with apple trees and led straight down the west side of the strawberry field and ended at the highway. We never used it in the winter and this day it was under 2 feet of snow. At the end was a huge snow bank from when the plow had cleared the highway.

Mom looked at us and snapped, "Get in the car." So we all piled in, lining up obediently in the back seat. Remember, these were the days before seatbelts were mandated. Mom warmed up the engine, put it in gear and headed for the apple trees. All her pent up frustrations slid with her as she gunned the car past the apple trees. She lost them all as she slammed through the snow bank and burst onto the road.

We peeled ourselves off the ceiling, settled back into our seats and stole silent glances at each other. Mom had white knuckles clinging to the steering wheel as she turned the station wagon into the northbound lane. Reality and rational thinking reappeared as she slowly headed to town. A strange sound was coming from under the hood. It sounded like a bunch of birds chirping. She was now going to have to explain to Dad how she managed to bend the fan belt pulleys by simply driving into town.

Dog Overboard

Having five kids under 11 years old didn't stop the Frostmans from spending time on Presque Isle during the summer. In fact, Jim and Marcie would team up with Uncle John and Aunt Eleanor, piling up to nine of us cousins on board the *Ione* for an extended stay on the island. The trips were actually pleasant, even with so many rug rats to keep an eye on. It was the dogs that needed a spanking.

This would be a memorable trip, one never to be forgotten. It started out as Mom and Aunt Eleanor finished packing enough supplies to carry us through an extended cabin stay. At each of their respective homes they yelled for the kids to grab their stuff and load up each car. Mom got behind the wheel with four kids and two dogs, and headed down to the dock. Aunt Eleanor and her three kids did likewise and soon we all met at the boat. As soon as the cars stopped, every door flew open, and seven kids and two dogs poured out. We lined up at each tail gate, unloaded and hauled all our "stuff" to the gangway of the *Ione*. Dad was already on board, warming up the Kahlenberg engine and getting mentally prepared for the invasion of his normally reserved, adult and male domain.

Once the engine was chugging steadily on its own, he turned and met us at the open gangway on the middle of the starboard side. The gangway was a large square opening with a wooden door. As Dad stood there, his belt was level with the surface of the dock. The Great Lakes fish tugs were built so that the deck many times was at or below the water line. This put the gunnels level with the dock. We dragged our boxes to the edge of the dock, and Dad reached up and slid each box across the edge of the dock, over the water, onto the gunwale and hoisted them down into the boat. His shoulders and arms were muscular and tanned, having repeated this same motion every day with heavy boxes of nets, ice and fish.

After all the boxes were loaded, car windows and doors secured, it was time to load all of us. If big enough, we grabbed the rail and swung ourselves down into the cabin. If too small, we, just like a box of fish or nets, were hoisted off our feet and handed over the water into Dad's waiting arms.

Once inside I had to adjust to suddenly darker surroundings. Even with all the gangways wide open, the reduced lighting in the fully enclosed cabin on the Ione took some getting used to. There were electric lights inside, but I just waited and blinked my eyes until I could focus.

With everything and everyone loaded, Cousin Jerry untied the lines and Dad took the boat out of the slip. He turned the rudder to take us north, around the city harbor and then head up the channel between Basswood and Madeline. As we pulled away from Bayfield, the town behind us rose up into the sky. It always surprised me how high the hill was. The abrupt rise in elevation wasn't obvious unless viewed from the lake. Looking back, we would see the streets dissect the town in perfect east-west and north-south grids. I'd always heard that a boat's compass could be calibrated by lining up with the streets and avenues.

Throughout my life, with each trip out on the lake, I would find myself looking west, searching the hillside for our house. The huge poplar trees and our steeply pitched roof were a fairly distinctive landmark even though all the streets were lined with mature elms, maples and oaks. Once I spotted the house, I could turn to the east and put my attention on what lay ahead. On this day, however, I was probably taking a nap in a clean fish box.

As we came up on the southwest point of Basswood, a small indentation in the woods became obvious. Bass was quarried years ago for sandstone. There was a natural sandstone landing there with water deep enough to safely nose up with a boat. One could nose up, tie off and go exploring around the cut stone under the overgrown forest. We would skip that opportunity on this trip.

Next up was Wilson, or Hermit Island. A couple small

sand/cobble beaches were visible on the shoreline. Wilson also boasted a natural rock bridge on the northeast point. It was another landmark that told us we were one channel away from Stockton. Unfortunately time and erosion finally took their toll and this bridge collapsed in the 1980s.

Across the channel from Hermit came the west end of Stockton Island. This point was fairly nondescript, until we came broadside of Quarry Bay. A very large bay, it was trimmed in a narrow beach and a flat area perfect for a cabin or tents. Behind the grassy area was a beaver pond and busy large rodents. In the woods to the left was the formation that gave the bay its name. A huge sandstone quarry was just a short hike off the beach.

The 15-mile trip from Bayfield to Presque Isle normally took one-and-a-half to two hours. With calm waters, the *Ione* would slide through the water creating a wake off the bow and another off the stern. The water would be dark and reflect our images back to us. At a distance it could sparkle as the sunshine dappled on it. When we got into shallow waters, we could look over the edge and see all the way to the bottom of the lake, watching the ripples of sand and piles of boulders loom up at us as Dad played in the wheel house.

The *Ione's* Kahlenberg engine hummed toogaatoogaatoogaa as Dad and his ten crew members motored along, everyone relatively peacefully settled in for the trip. Statistically the crew boasted an average age of six, few of whom needed to shave, and two even harbored an insatiable appetite for chewing bones. Aunt Eleanor, married to my dad's brother John, had brought along her son Jerry (12) and daughters Janey (9) and Josie (7). Mom was supervising Carolyn (7), Janis (5), Jimmy (2) and I (in diapers). Rounding out the crew were our dogs Snoopy and Pudgy.

The ride, even with seven children on board, was normally a very pleasant experience. With no game-boys or cell phones, we were actually well behaved and happy to sit in the cabin or on the deck, talk or pass the time feeding the gulls and watching the scenery go by. I had to confirm this with Mom, because such a pleasant atmosphere with so many kids in a confined area didn't seem possible. She said that when Dad spoke we listened. No run-

ning around, no goofing off. End of subject.

Cousin Janey remembers that Aunt Eleanor saved up old bread for these trips. She would ration it to us and we in turn would ration it to the gulls. With one piece of bread per child, per 20 minutes, we learned to rip each piece into tiny bits and toss them to the wind. The herring gulls, hundreds of them, would materialize out of nowhere to cheer us on and squabble over the offerings.

Once done with the bread, we would sit at the stern gangway. Exposed to the sun and the breezes, we were rocked gently by the boat cutting through the water. It gave us time to practice the art of enjoying the moment.

It was on the *Ione* that Carolyn learned how to braid hair. From Dad. While other kids were in town learning how to tie their shoes, she was watching Dad mend nets. If a section of maitre had frayed, he would cut it out and splice a new section in its place. Maitre was thin rope that was used as the top and bottom of a fish net. Dad saw that Carolyn took an interest in this process and took the opportunity to teach her the art of splicing. Carolyn then transferred this new talent from maitre to her own hair and started sporting braids.

The dogs let us have our space as we fed the gulls, braided hair, and otherwise occupied ourselves. Pudgy was Carolyn's big, long haired mixed breed, and Snoopy was Jan's short haired mutt. Pudgy loved the water and Snoopy was aqua phobic. They had full freedom to explore the Ione, and usually were not much of a problem. Mom remembers telling Dad to tie them up for the trip, but he chose to ignore her. Since the dogs were well behaved, content to sit, sticking their noses out the gangways as if they were in the back of the truck, Mom chose to leave the issue alone. If Dad didn't think the dogs would be a problem that was his choice. He could be responsible if they got in trouble. In hindsight, Dad should have reviewed the rules with Snoopy.

The dogs had been enjoying the view from the side stern gangway. We were half way to Presque Island. Maybe the stern full of children and a sky full of gulls distracted Snoopy. Maybe the Ione hit a wave just right. Maybe the dog was just daydreaming about chewing bones. Those details are lost to history. The facts everyone remembers vividly are of Janis' beloved water-fearing dog disappearing out the stern gangway and entering the cold dark waters of Lake Superior, a mile from land.

Pudgy, the water loving mutt, probably took a double take and backed away from the gunnels. He knew instinctively that even with his love for the water, being a mile from the nearest beach, surrounded by 50 degree water and disobeying the captain was not the thing to do. He disappeared from everyone's collective memory for the next 10 minutes.

The reality of a dog overboard panicked the young crew. The Norman Rockwell afternoon broke into pandemonium. Everyone on board remembers the yelling and screaming that exploded off the inner walls of the boat. Accounts of the event differ from child to child. Janey and Jan remember both dogs going overboard. Jan remembers me being there, others thought I as the baby, might have been on the mainland with Gramma Cousineau. Janey can remember Dad being so upset but never swearing. I'm told "Shut up!" was used quite a bit. Since I have to make a choice on whose version of the story to use, I will continue with Mom's recollections.

The boat was moving forward which meant the wet mutt was now well off the stern of the Ione. Dad hollered to Cousin Jerry to take the helm. Wise choice as he was the only child aboard who was tall enough to reach the wheel. Dad then raced to the stern from where the dog could now be seen trying to swim back to the boat. The dog was close enough to grab, so Dad curled the toes of his boots under a ledge on the gangway, hung his body over the stern and reached for the dog.

The fantail deck on the stern was three or four feet off the water, with open air underneath it. This put the propeller a few feet forward of, not directly underneath the transom. This meant that Dad could stretch down through open air under the stern to grab for the dog. The boat was still in gear, in forward motion, and the dog ended up being out of reach. Dad pulled himself back on deck and yelled for Jerry to put *Ione* into neutral. Back dangling under the stern again, Dad's expectations were that once the boat was in neutral, the dog might swim to him and he would simply grab and heave the mutt back on board.

Remember, the engine is still going "tooga-atooga-atooga". At least two little girls are still screaming at the top of their lungs. Anxiety levels are running high with the entire crew. Somewhere on board is another dog who actually likes the water. Mom, seated next to Janis (one of the screamers) was trying to concentrate on calming her daughter. Meanwhile the view out the back gangway was of her husband's toes and pant legs. The rest of his body had vanished over the edge of the boat. This didn't do her anxiety level any good.

Jerry, from the helm, was attempting to execute Dad's order to stop the boat. With a yank of his arm, he threw the Ione not into neutral, but into reverse. The boat promptly stopped all forward movement. The prop, just feet from where Dad was hanging, stopped spinning. It then reversed direction and started sucking water towards it. Water, dog and Dad were now being pulled into the prop.

This was obviously not a healthy situation and someone just had to make a remark about how Dad and the dog could get chopped up in the prop. The comment was not well received and young Janis went from just screaming to now hysterically screaming.

At this point Dad could be heard under the boat, yelling for Jerry to put the boat in neutral. In the mayhem he also grabbed the 80 pound dog with one hand, hoisted him out of the water and threw him into the cabin. Janey can still recall the muscles bulging from under Dad's shirtsleeves as the dog appeared to fly over the fantail and onto the deck. She can also remember that Dad was furious.

As he pulled himself up into a standing position, he looked at all the screaming kids and the drenched dog. He felt his adrenalin rushing and if it had been physically possible, steam would have been coming out his ears. He was mad that we "let" the dog jump overboard. He was mad that the dog jumped overboard. He was mad because he was no longer in control of his ship. These are assumptions on my part, but since I share the same genes, I know I would have entertained a little irrational thinking, just for a moment. I also know he cared deeply for his family and the responsibility of the safety of this entire crew weighed heavily on his shoulders. He hid a tender heart and would have hated to have lost the dog. He had also put himself in a very dangerous position when he hung by his toes off the stern. In summary, he too was experiencing a highly significant emotional event.

So, having lost control of his "ship" and his own temper, Dad stood on the stern and stared at his crew. His arms and shirt were dripping wet. His blood was still draining from his head back to his feet. His toes ached from being crammed under a rail. And Janis was still screaming. She just plain refused to end her extremely emotional event. Mom was sitting next to her trying in vain to calm her down. Dad stepped through the kids and over boxes until he was next to Jan's free side. He then did the only thing he could do. He gave her a sharp slap across her face. Jan's concentration broke.

Silence filled the boat. The Kahlenberg could again be heard purring in the background. Dad suddenly felt better. Jan actually felt better. Dad thought, "One down, two to go." He left the box and searched for the dogs. Once found and dragged out of their hiding places, they were sentenced to finishing the trip tied to the decking by 6-inch tethers. He wasn't taking any chances. Then he took back the wheel.

The excitement was over and we resumed our cruise. "Tooga-atooga-atooga."

Island Playground

The dog overboard trip to Stockton was a family classic, told and retold many times over many years. One more unfortunate event would close out the night. We finally reached Anderson Bay, the quiet protected west-facing bay next to the cabins. Dad brought the Ione into the bay at dusk, pulling up to what Jimmy described as a disastrous old wooden dock.

This dock was actually constructed of an old barge that, according to Mom's recollections, was towed down from Duluth by Les Cornell with his boat, and Grampa Ole with the *Ione*. Once at Presque Isle, they positioned it and sunk it in place. The fishermen then connected the barge to the beach possibly with cribbing (logs stacked in cabin fashion and sunk) and then covered them with decking. One of the characteristics that earned it the "disastrous" label was the fact that some deck planks were missing. Those that were in place were in the process of rotting. That night we were able to safety secure the Ione to the dock, but our crew still had to navigate the planking before reaching the safety of the beach.

As soon as the *Ione* was tied up, the crew crawled up, out and onto the dock. Boxes were hoisted out and piled on the dock among tired children and eager dogs. Those big enough started to carry the supplies to the cabins at the end of the dock. Somewhere between the boat and the shore, Eleanor stepped into a hole where a plank should have been, dropping all the way up to her knee. The fall twisted her ankle, caused some nasty bruises, broke the skin and gave birth to the rumor of a blood clot. The crew of children and in-laws rushed to get her to her cabin and then, with a 50/50 chance of doing the right thing, Mom and Dad applied hot packs to her ankle to reduce the swelling.

As Dad motored into the bay, he noticed lights on in our cabins. This was not unusual as there was a standing invitation to acquaintances (such as the Indians that camped down the beach) to use our cabins when we weren't there. The unwritten rule throughout the islands was if you used someone's property you left it in the same shape as you found it. Many cabins throughout the islands provided shelter to stranded fishermen, hunters, loggers and boaters. One cabin on Cat Island was used so consistently that the pantry was always well stocked with relatively fresh provisions. So, showing good cabin etiquette, when the sound of the *Ione's* Kahlenberg engine drifted to the cabin, our company quietly tidied up and left for their campsite a mile or so down the beach.

The next day they returned for a visit. Eleanor's injury was probably the biggest news on the island, and they, having a bit more experience, quickly corrected Eleanor's treatment from hot packs to cold packs. Cousin Janey was even delegated to retrieve and apply mud packs to her mother's bruises.

Even with the bum leg, Eleanor had no desire to go back to town. A couple days into the stay, she and the rest of us were enjoying the blueberry patch in Anderson Bay. This was a half mile hike from the cabin, so she must have felt pretty good. We felt good because we were anticipating her blueberry pies. Unfortunately, bad karma was still following Aunt Eleanor. After arriving in the patch, Eleanor lit a cigarette with a lumberjack match. The burning sulfur flew off the match and into some dry tinder. This started the blueberry patch on fire. Wet dogs, bruised legs and hot blueberries. Who knew an island 15 miles out into Lake Superior could be so exciting?

Mom and Dad would enjoy these family trips to Stockton until 1962. Time was spent visiting, playing cards, playing practical jokes, watching the kids and enjoying time at a slower pace. The closest thing to technology for entertainment was working on a diesel engine. Since it was light-years before Star Trek, Game Boy and cell phones, we kids filled our time with exploring the beaches and woods and thought the island was the greatest playground around.

I polled Carolyn, Jan and Jimmy for their recollections. The consistent reply was the scent of red and white pines in the forest, the smell of blueberry bushes in Julian Bay, the singing sand, the sounds of the waves on the shoreline and eating cookies.

While other kids had swing sets in their back yard in town, Carolyn's slide was a sand dune in Julian Bay. This surprised me as I always thought of my oldest sister as Miss Prim and Proper. As the oldest, she was the one who was capable of providing the rest of us with adult-like supervision. She was the older sister I sent screaming across the yard in Bayfield when I shoved a teeny tiny red bellied snake in her face. I'm not sure what she would do around a mouse. That's why it surprised me to hear Carolyn reminisce about her island slide. Once she dragged her rear end down the steep sandy slope, she'd look back and laugh at the millions of spiders that were scrambling across her slide. Laugh?

Jan remembers the smell of the pine trees. Today, whenever she happens to hug a pine tree (Jan, do we need to talk?) the scents bring back all the visions of running wild in the woods behind the cabin. Mom was never able to break her of that habit.

She also fondly remembers the scents rising from the low blueberry bushes that covered the dunes in Anderson Bay. They would be heavy with little blue-purple dusty berries. We filled containers full and returned to the cabins to await the creation of blueberry pies. Jan remembers being intrigued with Eleanor and John's cabin. That may be because she loved to watch Aunty Eleanor taking blueberry pies out of her oven and cut a piece especially for her.

Jan also connects the cabins to Oreo cookies. Mom must have stocked up on them. For me, it was sugar wafer cookies and playing on the beach in front of the cabin. That unfortunately is my only memory of Stockton.I was too young to remember much more.

Jimmy is imprinted with visions of playing outside with his sisters and cousins. There was a hammock outside the cabins and he vividly recalls gently swinging horizontally under the trees. The woods were thick, but sunbeams streamed through the canopy to give a view of hemlocks, white pines, red pines, spruces and bracken ferns. It gave an enchanting, welcoming feel.

Part of our playground included a tree down the shoreline shaped like horse. When it was a sapling it was bent to the side and then allowed to continue growing upward. It came up from the ground maybe three feet, then took a 90 degree turn horizontal for a couple sagging feet and then continued straight up to the sky. Someone told me it was an Indian marker tree. I don't know if that is true, but it was great fun. We used to ride it like a horse. Dad said he even rode it when he was a kid.

We were visited by deer, serenaded by loons and lulled to sleep by owls. We had miles of beach, trails, bright sunshine and clean crisp air. We used a hand pump for water, an icebox for refrigeration, and the luxurious (hah) outhouse for our necessities. We ate our fill of lake trout, white fish and pie. We made our own entertainment and did so passionately. If only I could have given my children the same.

These good times came to an end in the early 1960's. As families matured, there became more important reasons to not to spend the summer on Stockton. Cousins Jerry and John Ames grew old enough to put more importance on acquiring summer jobs. We would soon be moving to southern Wisconsin. Other events would have ended our paradise anyway. We never actually owned the land. We somehow had rights of use from the actual owner, which was the William F. Vilas Estate. Others were aware of the beauty, the wilderness and the importance of preserving the qualities of our island. The property would soon to be deeded to the state, a State Forest established and our rights rescinded.

The Great Lakes Waterway

The years at the farm were not marked by financial security. We always seemed to get by, but not without a struggle. One year Mom was all prepared for Christmas, except for the wrapping paper. She took her hidden jar where she collected spare change, poured it into her purse and headed to town. When she was done buying paper, tape, tags and ribbon, there was one penny left in her hand.

Most families in the area shared the same economic status as my parents. There was no extra money to be wasted and anywhere corners could be cut, they were clipped to the quick. But it didn't mean life was miserable. Many in the area took advantage of commodity goods distributed by the county out at the town hall (such as cheese and other staples). They found ways to make a little bit go far, and they shared with each other the little they had.

The gatherings would start with a phone call. "Do you have this…?" Or, "Do you have that…?" Everyone checked their pantries, and then decided who would bring this and who would bring that, who would host the pot luck and what time everyone would gather. They'd bring all sorts of dishes and have a big party. Mom recalled, "Somebody would have sugar, or make a cake or somebody would have vegetables, stuff like that. Or guys would go hunting and somebody would have some meat, yeah, it was fun." She went on to remind me that few of her neighbors had enough money to buy meat.

So Jim and Marcie lived surrounded by their own growing family, extended family, and a wide network of friends. The problem was earning a living. By the early 60's, after years of supporting a viable commercial fishing industry, there were almost no fish left in the Apostle Islands.

To grasp what was happening to Jim's livelihood and to the livelihood of all the fishermen who plied the waters of the Apostle Islands for the last hundred years, we need to review the Great Lakes ecosystem. When the glaciers receded, they left behind a watershed that was a closed system, geographically protected from deadly aquatic species that might invade from the sea.

The top of the ecosystem was and is Lake Superior, fed by over 300 rivers, the largest of which is the St. Louis River, flowing through the Duluth-Superior harbor and spilling into the lake at an elevation of 600 feet above the ocean. Lake Superior flows slowly eastward, emptying itself through the St. Mary's River into Lake Huron. It is so vast and deep that it would take 191 years to fully flush all its contents.

Lake Huron and Lake Michigan connect to each other through the wide Straits of Mackinaw. The strait is so wide that these lakes maintain the same elevation of 577 feet above sea level. Both smaller and shallower than Lake Superior, Lake Michigan has a lake retention time of 99 years and Lake Huron 22 years. Lake Huron acts as the outlet to the Atlantic, draining through the St. Clair River to Lake St Clair and then through the Detroit River into Lake Erie. An 8 foot drop takes the water down to Erie's elevation of 569 feet above sea level.

Lake Erie is much smaller and shallower, flushing itself every 2.6 years. At its eastern terminus is the most impressive drop, 326 feet down the Niagara River, over the falls and into Lake Ontario at 243 feet in elevation. To this point, the Great Lakes, in their unaltered state, were once sealed from the invasion of alien oceanic species. Those non-native creatures that might make it through the St. Lawrence Seaway and into Lake Ontario could not negotiate the formidable wall of water that was Niagara Falls.

As man began to explore this region, they found the surrounding forests to be prime habitat for beaver, bear and deer. The 1700s found French Voyageurs traversing the lakes in long canoes loaded with furs to be shipped to Europe. Later, Scandinavians, Germans, and other European immigrants would utilize the Great Lakes to transport their goods. They farmed the Midwest and sent the grain to the Port of Duluth-Superior for shipping east. Taconite would be mined from the Iron Range in Northern Minnesota and the Upper Peninsula of Michigan, and then shipped to steel mills down the lakes. Timber was being cut and needed to be delivered to mills. Commerce had come to the shores of the Great Lakes and found the waterway to be, with a few adjustments, a perfect transportation route to bring goods west to east and east to west.

In 1829, the Welland Canal opened navigation from Lake Ontario to Lake Erie by providing a shipping route around Niagara Falls. Improvements were made to the canal in 1919, allowing ships to bypass Niagara Falls and freely travel between Lake Ontario and Lake Erie. Channels were cut and widened on the St. Clair River and Detroit River between Lake Huron and Lake Erie. In 1855, the Soo Locks, between Lakes Superior and Huron, opened to allow shipping to bypass the rapids of the St. Mary's River. The Great Lakes Waterway, connecting all five lakes and the Atlantic Ocean, had been completed.

Interestingly, the waterway was deeper in the lakes than it was in the St. Lawrence River. Because of this, two classes of freighters developed for the movement of goods. The ocean "salties" have a shallow draft allowing them to traverse the St Lawrence and enter the Great Lakes. The "lakers," built specifically for the fresh water, had a deeper draft, effectively confining themselves to the Great Lakes.

Opening the Great Lakes Waterway to ocean-going vessels was a boon to commerce, but it was ecologically devastating to the lake trout. The 1919, improvements to the Welland Canal allowed the Lamprey Eel to enter the ecosystem, and by the 40's, the lamprey had established itself throughout the Great Lakes. It bred in the many streams that emptied into the lakes. It fed by attaching itself to a fish and through a sucking motion, drained the blood from its host. It found the lake trout, the dominant predatory and commer-cially viable fish in the Great Lakes, to be the perfect host. The fine scales of the trout made its skin easier to penetrate than a more heavily scaled fish, such as the whitefish.

In the early 1900s, Salmon, a prized sport fish, was introduced into inland lakes in Michigan. To feed the Salmon, another fish was introduced, the small shimmering ocean fish called "Smelt." As luck would have it, the smelt escaped the inland lakes and found the fresh water of the Great Lakes to be a wonderful environment. Just like rabbits (theoretically) they went forth and multiplied, and multiplied, and multiplied. The declining trout population left the smelt without a serious predator to keep their population in check. They began to feed on herring fry. They also began to compete with the adult herring for habitat.

Throughout the century, fishermen had practicing their trade in Lake Superior, with the lake providing relatively stable fish populations. Dad started his fishing career after the eighth grade, around 1943. Between that time and 1956, the average trout harvest per year in the Wisconsin waters of Lake Superior was 539,000 pounds. Whitefish harvest averaged 417,000 pounds and herring averaged 5,187,000 pounds. The 1962, the lake trout catch was recorded at 120,000 pounds, whitefish at 85,000 pounds and by 1963, the herring catch was down to 941,000 pounds. 1963 had no recorded trout catch. In 1962, the Wisconsin waters of Lake Superior were closed to commercial fishing of lake trout.

There was no recorded harvest of smelt in 1943. By 1963, 619,000 pounds of smelt were being harvested. (Statistics courtesy of the Great Lakes Fishery Commission http://www.glfc.org/databases/commercial/commerc.php)

Along the way Polychlorinated biphenyls (PCB's), mercury and other poisons also settled in the water. Levels of these chemicals were soon found in the food chain. The ecosystem had been disrupted.

By this time, Dad and his fellow Bayfield fishermen could no longer fish to support their families. One by one they came to the realization that they had to find another career.

Belgium

The lamprey and smelt basically ate us out of house and home-land. With the trout fishing closed, Dad had to look elsewhere to earn a living. He tried to get a job at the ore docks in Superior, but they weren't hiring. Money was getting tight. It wasn't just money for food. Hand-me downs from Carolyn and Janis would not dress my brother Jimmy (unless he liked to wear tights and jumpers, which he did not.) So in 1962 when the horticultural agent in Washburn called and asked Dad if he would be interested in run-ning an orchard in southern Wisconsin, Dad said yes.

Dad and Mom took a trip downstate and interviewed with the owner of "Appleland." This was a large orchard near Belgium, which was near Port Washington, just north of Milwaukee. The owner needed an overseer as he himself was busy with other busi-ness ventures, besides being blind. Apparently Dad interviewed well, as we soon were packing all our belongings and the new boss was adding another bedroom to the apartment we would move into.

As I look back now, the move must have been incredibly hard for Dad. He was always a sentimental person. He commented to me later in life that he didn't understand how people could buy and sell houses as investments. To him a house was a home and should be lived in and passed down from generation to generation. He was so sentimental, that it was years after Gramma Helga died before he would allow Mom to donate the wooden leg to charity. (Meanwhile, Jan had a ball with it at slumber parties.) Anyway, the need to pro-vide for his family was greater than sentiment. He sold the farm and we moved south.

Our new homestead had a huge horseshoe shaped driveway off

1963 - *Skating on the pond in Belgium. It was also a great place in the summer to find suckers stuck on the turtles.*

the county road. Driving up the right side, there was a row of tall trees to the right, a yard and then the owner's brick ranch house. At the apex of the horseshoe was a building that contained the apple coolers. These were huge insulated rooms with thick doors and heavy latches where basket after basket of apples was stored. Behind the coolers was a large garage.

On the second floor of this building was our now four bedroom apartment. It was also huge, compared to the farm in Bayfield. The floors were even level. The boys got their own bedroom, Carolyn got her own bedroom, and Jan and I moved into a large brand new bedroom Mr. George had added in the attic. We had real closets and there was space to play.

From the back of my bedroom was an access door to a long room that made up the attic. At the end was a window that looked back to Mr. George's house and looked down at an above ground pool. I used to think that if I opened the window, stepped way back, ran as fast as I could, that I could jump out the window and dive into the pool. I also thought about jumping out Mom and Dad's bedroom window while using Karen's baby receiving blanket as a parachute. Living upstairs had all these great possibilities. Thank God I couldn't unlatch the windows.

In the "foyer," which was a wide hallway at the top of the stairs, there was a window at the end where we could watch for the school bus. The room was long enough that Dad set up plastic bowling pins and taught us how to bowl. It also held the washer and dryer and provided excitement when the washing machine, which was a front loader, decided to bubble over and fill the room with suds.

The living room had a large bay window, and the view was of pavement, a row of garages for orchard equipment, our clothesline and the orchard beyond. This was the room where we would watch Ed Sullivan and the Wonderful World of Disney on our black and white TV. This was the room where we all recovered from the chicken pox. And here was where Mom made us sit still while she aimed a light at our heads to cast a small shadow on the walls. She traced each of our silhouettes onto small pieces of paper. Then she used an old fashioned black ink pen to fill in the five little pug noses, ponytails and cowlicks with black ink. The silhouettes were framed and dressed our hall walls for the next 40 years.

Behind our apartment was another massive building where the apples were processed and mountains of pallets and boxes were stored. Back out in front, the horseshoe driveway continued its curve, passing an irrigation pond and a creek before returning to the road. The orchard completely surrounded our little development and provided all sorts of opportunities for us kids to explore.

As I understood Dad's job, he was in charge of spraying, irrigating, grafting, planting, removing and otherwise tending the trees in the orchard, and also overseeing the harvest. Even as a manager, he was still an employee of someone else. This was not his preference, but even if he was not ultimately in charge, he stood up for business practices that he believed in. Mr. George was not always in agreement, but they seemed to agree to disagree.

There was one time Mr. George came into the big shed where the apples were processed. Being blind, he expected to hear machines chugging, people talking, boxes being moved and apples rolling along the tables. It wasn't. It was silent.

He searched out my dad and asked why no one was working. Dad told him, "It's a state law, 15 minute break in the morning, 15 minutes in the afternoon. Then you haven't got them all running to the bathroom all the time." It must have taken courage to make that statement to his new boss, not knowing how he would react. Apparently Dad passed muster as Mr. George never said another word.

On other occasions Dad had to alter his work practices. He would scour the orchard, looking for apple trees that were dead or not producing any more and would remove them. He would fill the empty space with a small sapling. He did this quite a bit until Mr. George got lost. The boss used to go out in the orchard with a big bamboo pole over his shoulder. He would use the pole to tap the trees, counting them so he knew where he was and how far he had to go to get back. After Dad pulled out trees without telling him, Mr. George got lost. Dad learned to coordinate with the boss before taking out any more trees.

Mom and Dad enjoyed meeting new people and developed many lasting and hard-fought friendships while we lived "down below." It was not always easy, as in the early 1960s we were still considered outsiders to the area's tight knit community. Just as in Bayfield, it took a while for newcomers to gain acceptance. During our three-year stay Mom and Dad were blessed with new experiences and new friendships developed with Mr. George and his family, with customers, orchard workers and others met through church and elsewhere.

One customer was a Jewish man who would come each year and buy a lot of apples to take home to make cider. He would return at Christmas time and bring my folks three or four big bottles of good wine. It paid to provide good customer service.

Dad would talk to anyone, and soon became friends with someone who owned a two-seater airplane, the type Snoopy flew, with the open cockpits, one in front of the other. Jimmy and I were playing in the sandbox in the yard one day when we heard this noise in the sky. We looked up to the top of our apartment and -- *neear-rrouuu!* -- this plane buzzed the top of the building and then strafed the yard. Dad looked down and waved at us from the cockpit. We sat there, dumbfounded, waving back. He was low enough that we could look him in the eye. We had no doubt who he was, we just weren't prepared for him to come out of the sky.

There were others that became more than acquaintances. One was an older man, an immigrant from Austria named Otto. He came over to this country to work and Dad was looking for someone to help in the orchard. Otto's name was brought to Dad's attention. According to Mom, "He (Dad) didn't know him from Adam" but liked what he saw and hired Otto to run the tractors, spray and irrigate the trees, work in the shed, run the grading machine and do various odd jobs.

Otto proved to be a good worker, but the women who worked in the orchard were all afraid of him. He never did anything to them. It was probably just that he never talked to them. Mom said, "You know, he'd walk right by with that ugly face he could have and they were afraid of him. I was never afraid of him."

To prove the point, she recalled the time when, after Otto had sprayed the orchard, he tried to back the sprayer into the one car garage across from our living room window. Mom was standing in the window, watching. Otto would back the sprayer up to the garage door, but it wouldn't be aligned with the door frame. So he would pull forward, turn the wheel on the tractor and attempt to back in the equipment again, and again. He just couldn't line it up. He then saw Mom watching through the window. He yelled up, "Turn around! I can't get that sonofa#*## in." Mom just laughed.

It took a while to get Otto to open up socially. My parents would beg him to come upstairs and join them for lunch, but at first he staunchly refused. After much persistence, he was finally won over. He joined them at their kitchen table, but he refused to accept a free lunch. He had to bring his own.

One day he came upstairs while Mom was making a kettle of soup. He asked, "You're making soup in that kettle for your family?" Mom's kettle was apparently a bit small for the crowd she cooked for. The next time he came up he brought with him a good size, good quality kettle. He set it on the table and said, "Here, I think you need this." Another time he brought up a brand new coffee pot. Come to find out, his wife worked for the Westbend Company and could get seconds that to us appeared flawless.

Billy was not yet in grade school, and the little tyke quickly became Otto's favorite. Otto would take Billy on the tractor with him, out in the orchard. As they rode through the trees, Otto would keep his attention by spinning tale after tale. The next day Billy would want him to tell the same stories again. Otto would start, but since the stories were always made up, they weren't the exact same story that was told the day before. Billy would look up at him and reprimand him saying, "That's not the way it went."

One day everyone was busy in the big shed grading apples. The crowd included Mom and Billy. He was playing with older brother Jimmy's pedal-powered John Deere tractor. Some of the workers had their small children with them, so Billy wasn't the only kid in the shed. Dad told Billy that he had to give another little girl a turn on the tractor. Billy got mad because he had no intention of sharing. As soon as Dad turned to go back to the grader, Billy picked up an apple and threw it at him. Dad felt the sting, and knew just where it came from. He turned around, grabbed a hold of Billy and gave him a spanking right then and there.

Otto had been watching the entire event, standing near the end of the grader. Watching Billy get spanked dug up a lot of emotions he could normally bury. He had grown children of his own, but there was some estrangement in his relationship with them. So, while he had this big soft spot for Billy, he knew Dad had to address the flying apple. He stood there and silently watched the discipline being delivered, but could not stop the tears from running down his face. He looked to Mom and murmured, "That's my boy."

So day by day we felt more at home. We were getting more familiar with the area and Dad with the operation of the orchard. Mom would join in the orchard work, surprising herself at times. Another big pole shed had been put up and all the boxes that had been stored elsewhere needed to be moved to the new shed. There was an older gentleman who was trying to move the boxes by using this big tractor that had a double gear shift and a fork lift. This poor guy just could not get the hang of it. Mom was again standing nearby. He was frustrated and finally looked at Mom and said, "Would you come and do this?" She ended up moving 10,000 boxes that day. Her time on the tractor in Bayfield had finally paid off.

Mom would also work by selling apples at the office at the top of the horseshoe. One day someone came in and asked how good the corn was. She gave him a quizzical look and said she didn't have any corn for sale. What she didn't know was that we kids had been watching this money making operation and thought it was pretty nifty. We went to a nearby field (not our own), gathered corn, and were selling it outside the door. Our operation was quickly shut down.

Jan did go on to sell some produce legally. She wanted to have a garden so Dad tilled up some space for her to plant gourds. She was pretty good at it, and was allowed to sell the little ornamental gourds without being censured.

We attended church in Random Lake. This was where we met Janet and Eddie. They had a farm and a bunch of kids whose names all started with "D." We either invited them or they invited us over and the friendship was begun. For Dad and Eddie it was a mutually helpful relationship. If Dad needed help moving pipe in the orchard, he'd call and Eddie would come over. If Eddie needed help in the field haying, Dad would go over and help him.

While adept at orchard work, Dad would embarrassingly allow Janet and Eddie to witness his lack of carpentry talent. Mom wanted to put another leaf in the kitchen table. Janet and Eddie had some stretchers that would expand the table top. They brought them over and Dad proceeded to install them. He turned the table upside down on the kitchen floor. He lined up the stretchers on the underside of the table top, set each screw and began one by one to twist the screws into the wood, solidly attaching the stretchers to the table-top. Mom was sizing up the situation.

She said, "You're going to screw that thing right to the floor."

He replied, "No, I'm not."

"Ok," she said agreeably, knowing she was absolutely right and knowing that in his mind he thought he was absolutely right.

So when he was done, he said, "Help me turn it right side up." They all grabbed a corner, and lifted, but the table wouldn't budge. Dad had screwed through the stretchers, the table top and right into the floor. Mom just smiled

There were other embarrassing moments in Belgium, and I contributed to one of them. I was with Mom and Dad and Mr. George out in the yard. I looked up at Mr. George and said, "Mr. George, you got lots of land here haven't you?" He said, "Yes, I have Connie." I said, "Well, why don't you give some to my dad?" My parents wanted to crawl in a hole.

Bayfield was known for blizzards and northeasters. Water spouts could be seen on the lake but tornados were rare. Belgium and the surrounding area were not so lucky. Tornados were more common in southern Wisconsin. Tornado warnings would come up, and Mom would race around to get her brood into shelter. There was one storm where Mom couldn't find Carolyn. She'd gone over to Fredonia on her bicycle to see a friend. Mom called but and they said she'd already left. She made more calls but could not locate the 12-year old. Worried, Mom went down to the road and with relief, saw her eldest lazily pedaling towards her, with not a worry in the world.

From Carolyn's vantage point, the skies were clear and it was a warm calm day. When she got close enough she could see that Mom was upset. She called over as she stopped her bike and asked, "What's the matter?" Mom said, "Look behind you!"

The sky behind Carolyn was as black as the ace of spades. The wind was kicking up, bending the trees as it advanced. They both raced to the house, helped pick up some storm windows next door and got ready as best they could.

Meanwhile, Dad was looking for Jimmy, who was also out on his bike. He drove down the road and soon found Jim Jr. also lazily pedaling along. Never one to sit and explain anything first, he grabbed Jimmy off his bike and as Jimmy put it, "Threw me in the car." They raced home and joined everyone else taking shelter in the brick ranch house. Dad was good at dealing with stress in the workplace, but never seemed to deal well with it when it dealt with people close to his heart.

We were lucky. The tornados did not hit near our house. They did hit in Port Washington though, and according to Mom, it was unbelievable. It went through the middle of a ranch house and left two ends. It went around a church where a wedding was being held, took out the houses around it but left the church alone. One house had been completely flattened, except for the front door which was standing and functional. A man chose to ride out the twister sitting by a window in the upstairs of his house. From this vantage point he could watch buggies, lawn chairs and everything else fly by. He said, "I figured it was too late to go anywhere; might as well just sit here."

Port Washington was a popular weekend drive for the family, and not just because of tornados. It was right on Lake Michigan and a number of commercial fishermen claimed it as their home port. So, if Dad was feeling homesick, Port Washington could give him a good dose of lake air and conversation on nets, fish catches, regulations, engines and other hot topics that commercial fishermen gossiped about.

Our Sunday drives would usually end up near the docks. Dad had become acquainted with the different fishermen and fish shops in Port Washington. So we would walk the docks or eat or window shop, anything to enable Dad to run into someone who spoke "fish." One day we waited in a fish shop, surrounded by coolers and showcases full of smoked fish and other goodies. Dad was off getting his ration of guy/fish talk. As Mom tells it, I started drooling over the bronze colored smoked herring in the showcase. I had always loved smoked fish and there wasn't much of it at the orchard.

The guy behind the counter came up and asked, "Something I can help you with?" Mom said, "Na, we're just waiting. My husband wanted to talk to someone." She then nodded her head towards Dad, who had become deeply engrossed in a conversation with another man.

I must have said something about the smoked fish, because he looked at me and then he looked at Dad, and he said, "Oh, you're a Frostman!" The fish gods were watching over me, as he then asked, "What kind of smoked fish do you like?" He ended up giving me, this little 6-year old kid, a five pound package of smoked fish to take home. Dad had developed a tighter relationship with the owners than we had realized. And I was glad!

We spent three years in Belgium. We kids roamed the orchard, skated on the irrigation pond, made up our own board games, picked apples and shucked peas, lived through school redistricting, learned to swim in the pool, drove trucks in the sandbox, rampaged the swing set that Mr. George's kids shared with us, attended church, visited with Mom and Dad's widening circle of friends and gained another sister. Karen would be the only child not born in Washburn. Maybe that's why she's the way she is (just kidding!)

Belgium was where I learned to ride a two wheeler. Dad held me upright on the driveway in front of our apartment. He gave me a shove and I stayed upright and pedaling until I ran right into the brick wall of Mr. George's garage. That's why I can so plainly remember they had a brick house.

Belgium is where I broke my pet rabbit in two. I swear! I was trying to get it out from behind a chest and it broke in two. Some adult stuck the two ends back together and it survived. The only problem was it had a bald spot on the back. For some reason Mom doesn't remember the story quite the same way.

Belgium was also where I first remember seeing Dad pray. It was in church, right after he returned from communion and sat down in the pew. We young, unconfirmed Lutheran children did not take communion, but would stay in the pew and behave while every one else went up to the front. So I watched as Dad return to our pew, sat down, clasp his hands together on his knees, bend his head down and prayed. I've never forgotten.

But times were changing. The farm was sold and Mr. George moved his family to Random Lake. The new owner allowed us to stay in our apartment in exchange for some work, but it was not enough to pay the bills. So Dad was looking for income yet again. He found a construction job in Milwaukee. Milwaukee was a big city that was socially, ethnically, and culturally very different from rural northern Wisconsin. It was a new experience for Dad to work with a crew that included African Americans. He also was not used to large construction jobs and had not learned the little tricks crew members used to make the job easier.

For example, one day the work included carrying timbers. Dad lifted one onto his shoulder and immediately this big black man hollered at him to put it down. Dad didn't know if this guy was mad at him, if he had done something wrong or what, but figured he'd do as the man said and find out why later. The black guy grabbed a gunny sack that was nearby, marched up to Dad, and grabbed him by the shirt collar. As Dad was thinking about how to react, the man proceeded to shove the gunny sack under the shoulder of his shirt. He then said, "Now pick up that thing." The guy smiled, and Dad, who was sweating and trying to slow his breathing down, gave a weak smile in return. Another friend had made himself known.

The commute to Milwaukee had its moments. One evening Dad had been working on the car. Jan's cat found the activity interesting and had fallen asleep on the back seat. The next morning Dad got in the car and headed for Milwaukee. After driving a few miles he slowed to stop at a stop sign. At this point the cat, who had spend the night shut up in the car, woke up and jumped on Dad's shoulder. As Mom said, "It scared the livin' daylights out of him. And then he had to turn around and bring the cat home!"

There was another time when working road construction, he was in a ditch, shoveling. All the sudden he heard someone squealing "oink, oink, oink, oink" at the top of the ditch. Not knowing what to expect, he slowly looked up. It was one of his Bayfield buddies, standing there looking down at him. He had also come to Milwaukee looking for work.

The two would end up working together, and on one particular day they had to move a crane through the city. Dad was on the crane, his job being to keep the boom straight as the semi maneuvered through the streets. His cohort was in the cab, and wouldn't slow the truck down for the corners. The boom would swing out as they rounded each turn. Dad struggled with the levers to keep the end of the crane from taking down a building. Meanwhile his buddy was laughing up in the cab. Somehow the trip ended successfully.

Although Dad could find enough construction jobs, it was not his calling, and the orchard was no longer a comfortable situation in which to live. So, in 1965, the family packed up and we moved back to Bayfield, home again. Maybe Dad's prayers were finally answered.

Coming Home

Fifteen years after Mom and Dad married and moved in with Gramma and Grampa Frostman, they found themselves moving into Grampa Frostman's house for a second time. It was bittersweet move. Gramma Helga had passed away at Easter time and left a gaping hole in the family hierarchy. We had traveled home many times during our stay in Belgium, and the funeral was one of those trips.

I was too young to fully understand deaths and funerals but I understood the sorrow everyone felt, and sadly felt her absence among us in the House. There was an argument on whether, at eight years old, I was old enough to go to the funeral. Dad, in his take-charge way, decided I should attend. Mom didn't think it was a good idea, but this was one of those times she couldn't make Dad see it her way.

Dad's older sister, Aunt Viola, who was not little and not shy, sided with Mom and was not going to stand for this foolishness. Carolyn described Viola as a sweet, very religious woman whom she loved dearly. I, on the other hand, called her "Mean old Gramma." But, Mean Old Gramma felt that there was little sense in having this little towhead sit through the service. Either I would get very emotional, or just the opposite, get bored. Neither reaction would help the adults with their grieving. So she puffed herself up with all the assertive attributes she inherited from her "Ma" and laid the law down on her baby brother. She stated with no uncertainty in her voice, "Jim, she is just too young to go to a funeral." I stayed home.

I was also too young at the time to remember much about

Helga. I've heard her described as being strong-willed and wanting things to be done her way. She also didn't allow you to get close to her. To put it nicely, she was someone you could love from a distance. At least that's how Carolyn put it. Being seven years older than me, she had spent a lot more time with them and knew Gramma and Grampa Frostman better. When we lived on the farm, she would often spend the night with them, not only to visit, but as another set of ears in case of a health emergency. She would sleep on the couch in the little room off the dining room. It was a neat little space behind big French doors that we then knew as the sun room. After dark she could sit there flickering a flash light out the window, sending messages to her good friend Paula next door.

Gramma might not have been the friendliest person, but she was attentive. She would make Carolyn and Paula stacks and stacks of pancakes. She was the one that taught us kids how to count in Norwegian. She could crochet, and left us with intricate doilies and tablecloths to remember her by.

Gramma also suffered from diabetes. Shortly after we moved to the farm, she lost the first leg just below the knee. She was fitted with a wooden prosthesis and was able to get around fairly well. She had a hospital stay once, and somehow got there minus the wooden leg. Grampa was tasked to bring the leg to her. He couldn't pass up the chance to startle people and, instead of wrapping the leg up in a towel or otherwise disguising it, he strutted through the waiting room with this body part under his arm. It scared half the people in the waiting room, leaving them wondering if there was an accident or something. It left him giggling in the stairway.

Gramma would lose the second leg before we left for Belgium, this time above the knee. I remember standing next to her while she lay in her bed. I wasn't much taller than the pillows propped up on the bed, and therefore my head was level with hers. Being so young, I didn't think twice about asking her what happened to her legs, as no one had explained it to me. She turned her head to look me in the eye, and with a straight face slowly said, "A woodchopper came in the middle of the night and chopped it off!" I probably gave her the expected response with bulging eyes and a gaping mouth. I was running the scenario through my mind and didn't know what to do with it. I think I just left the room.

Carolyn said that for all of Gramma's health issues, she never felt sorry for herself. She would cook at the stove from her wheel chair. They put the bathroom door on the wrong way so she could get in and out on her own. She didn't let thresholds and small steps hold her back as she would wheel herself out of the kitchen, through the back porch and out the back door, negotiating all of it alone.

The diabetes would also steal away most of her sight, leaving her in a very blurry world. She could still crochet by feel, and played cards using a deck with huge numbers on it. She and Grampa would sit in the kitchen at night and play cribbage. Play and fight and argue big time - in Norwegian. When Carolyn stayed overnight, she would sit in the sun room, listen and laugh to herself because it sounded so funny. It was just their routine to slap cards down and argue and argue and argue over whatever. Uff da!!

Grampa is remembered as being a bunch of fun. He was a sweet old guy that said what he needed to say, but always had a twinkle in his eye. He was the one that always kept the peppermints well stocked in the glass bowl on the dining room table. The pink ones with white x's on them. We'd always lift the lid quietly and sneak some every time we passed by.

Grampa was the one to teach Janis to swim. He took her down to the harbor and basically threw her off the dock. It was sink or swim. She swam back.

And Grampa was the one who made his daughter-in-law feel welcome every time they were together. So the family felt content to move back to Bayfield and invade Grampa's home. He moved upstairs into the apartment Mom and Dad had once occupied. We hauled all our stuff in and filled up every empty space, including the upstairs bedroom. The downstairs living room became Mom and Dad's bedroom, with a space reserved for Karen's crib. Carolyn, Janis and I moved into the downstairs bedroom, and Jimmy and Billy shared the bedroom at the top of the stairs. The dining room became the living room. The kitchen, at the back of the house, retained its same title and purpose.

Unfortunately for the entire family, Grampa's health also continued to fail. Carolyn came home from school one day and found him passed out on the floor. He had fallen out of bed and neither Carolyn nor Mom could get him back in. He was so bad that they called the ambulance to take him to the hospital. Mom went down to the Washburn hospital to see him and he could only apologize, saying "I'm sorry, I'm sorry" to her. Mom always had a special fondness for Ole and now responded by gently chastising him for the apology. "Dad," she said, "You didn't do it (get sick) on purpose."

He recovered from that episode, but on a visit to Ione and Eddie's in Michigan he passed away. It was only nine months after his bride had died. Aunt Ione had his body flown to Duluth and Dad took the sad trip with Mr. Merkle (the funeral director) to pick up the body and bring it back. This time I was old enough to attend the funeral, and remember the casket in the front of the church like it was yesterday. God had called another of us home.

Ione inherited the house. Since we were already occupying it and she had no intention to leave Detroit, she agreed to sell it to Dad and Mom. So they became homeowners again. All three rooms upstairs became bedroom space and we girls moved upstairs. The downstairs would soon feel Mom's touch, each room taking on her choice of paint, wallpaper, carpeting, furniture, pictures and knick knacks.

The living room was again dressed with a couch and easy chairs. The walls opposite the windows would eventually be paneled in knotty pine. Not that Dad planned to remodel, but it became a necessity after the plaster and lathe ceiling caved in along the fracture lines we had always ignored. After hacking at the walls with crowbars, exposed were not 2x4 studs, but planks at least 15 inches wide nailed crossways. They were covered with newspaper from decades before. It was great reading. The TV was moved from the center dining room and plugged in to the wall. These were still the days of the antenna on top of the roof and the absence of cable or satellite TV.

The fancy dining table was again repositioned in the dining room. It was the bane of my existence, as I held dusting duty for years, and the legs of that table were dust magnets. Our graduation pictures would slowly fill the wall behind this table, reflected in a giant mirror over the electric organ Dad just had to buy Mom.

The sun room would lose the French doors and become known as the sewing room. Inside would soon reside a knitting machine, the sewing desk, ironing board and the hutch containing the new 8-track stereo.

The kitchen would remain unchanged until years later, after I trashed it. But that story comes later.

DuPont and Trolling

For the next seven years Dad would again work at a variety of jobs, but the lake was always calling his name. During this time he worked for his brother until Uncle John retired and sold the Ione to Hermie Johnson. He then worked for Hermie until Mom's cousin found him a job at DuPont.

DuPont was the large plant hidden in the woods between Washburn and Ashland, where Grampa Cousineau had worked for years. I was told they did various things like cladding coins and making TNT. What I knew was that Dad worked a rotating shift and we didn't dare make noise if he was sleeping in the afternoons while working the night shift rotation.

He was No. 99 according to his DuPont tag. He wore dark blue *Dickies* pants with a belt and a long-sleeve button-up shirt. They were always filled with holes. Mom once pulled a thread in the seams and a whole pair of pants fell apart. Apparently clothes took a beating working the nitro line. I had visions of him standing next to beakers and test tubes filled with clear liquid acid and having them splash onto his clothes, thus eating holes in the fabric. Probably about as realistic as my bunny that broke in two.

During this time Mr. and Mrs. Frostman also became entrepreneurs. For as much as commercial fishing was in Dad's bones, you could make money sport fishing, i.e. trolling for trout. (Our high school nickname was the "Trollers.") Mom and Dad became very good at taking out loans and buying boats. They started with a 27-foot cabin cruiser named the *Jenny L*. They outfitted it with outriggers, trolling planes, spoons (the kind attached to the end of a fishing pole), coffee pots and what not, and started advertising.

Their captain was Les Cornell, the man who gave Dad his first job after completing grade school. Dad was complementing history by hiring Les into his first job after retirement.

The boat and the licenses were good for taking six people out for a half day or full day of trolling for trout and coho and other sport fish. I'm not quite sure of the whole routine, they would never take me out on a trip. I was dying to deckhand, but most of the clientele were men. That and being the boss's daughter kept me tied to the dock. I was relegated to taking reservations via the home phone and wearing a homemade jacket that advertised our charter service on the back. What luck.

Jimmy was much luckier. He got to earn a lot of money as a deckhand. The days were usually uneventful, but it was always amazing how coincidence/fate/faith/or just dumb luck came in to play.

Jimmy suffered badly from ear infections as a child. By nine years old he had lost the hearing in one ear. He spent that summer banished from the water as the doctors had inserted a tube in the ear to drain it and restore his hearing. The treatment was successful, but his ears were still sensitive to pressure changes.

While deckhanding one day, he reached over the side rail as a bolt of lightning stuck near by. The clap of thunder bounced off the water and rang mercilessly in his ears. He let out a scream and ran down into the cabin holding his head. There were six clients on board at the time, all of whom happened to be doctors. An exam was preformed (free of charge) and Jimmy was found to be physically OK and would be fine once all the bells quit ringing in his head.

Along with the Jenny, we soon owned a 14-foot skiff with a 10-horse motor. Mom and Dad tried to rent these out but the maintenance proved to be a burden. That didn't bother Jimmy or me. We would lug the gas tank and engine from the garage down to the dock to be able to take the skiff out on the lake. It was wonderful. They also purchased a 14-foot runabout (the same skiff with a steering wheel in the middle.) We were ever so grateful and willing to spend our babysitting and lawn mowing money on gas and oil.

Dad would take a bunch of us to the coal docks south of town in these skiffs, and we would fish on the spawning bed with a bunch of other locals. The coal docks were actually submerged cribbing for docks that existed years before I was born. Stripped of their decking and submerged well under the surface, they provided a perfect habitat for spawning fish, and in turn presented a perfect fishing hole.

Everyone had great luck.Everyone except me that is.It seemed that I could only get these beautiful 18-inch long fish up to the boat. Then they would twitch, twist, grin and unhook themselves. I felt as if I could hear them snickering as they swam away. It was still a great time, until the DNR closed the area to fishing. Something about preserving future generations of the fish population. We locals didn't think highly of the closure. We locals who, when we grew up, went on to study wildlife biology had to swallow our pride. But what a bummer; those were great evenings.

Business on the *Jenny* went well enough that it was soon replaced with a 31-foot Richardson cabin cruiser. Business was doing so well that lots of the town folks were buying boats and taking out parties. It became a race to name each boat for those who had daughters with same name. Our boat was going to honor (?) the youngest daughter, Karen. Unfortunately, "Karen" was painted on another stern faster than Dad could get around to it. So the stars aligned on me and the boat became the *Connie Jean*. Wow, my name would now be plastered on fishing advertisements.

Mom and Dad invited Otto and his wife to visit while we had the *Connie*. Dad took him out fishing, and he came in second for the day in the large fish department. Another day Billy, now a few years older, took Otto down to the docks and together they fished for perch. Dad filleted and froze Otto's catch so he could take them home. On the day Otto and his wife were packing to leave, Mom said, "Otto started to cry. I can still see him standing there. He's trying to hold it back. And he just couldn't." It made my folks feel good to share what was obviously a special time for the older man.

The Connie Jean lasted as long as we could stay competitive. I remember Dad saying something about too many people in the business to keep it profitable. The boat was heavily mortgaged and one reason we stayed in business was because the bank had always allowed winter payments to be deferred and made up the when the summer income rolled in. The increased number of boats in the business and the end of the ability to delay payments brought an end to our foray into the trolling business. The *Connie Jean* went away.

Chase through the Raspberries

Life was settling into a routine, with only Dad's career path in question. By now six kids filled the house. Mom would yell up the stairs each morning to get us up for grade school and high school during the week and Church and Sunday school on Sundays. We kids had chores and sought out our own summer jobs to put cash in our pockets. We tested parenting skills with all our varying hormone levels and cognitive abilities. We made Mon and Dad proud, we made them furious, we made them shake their heads in disbelief and sometimes in relief. Jimmy once even made Dad run. After him.

It was in the raspberry patch that filled our back yard. Raspberries also filled Emma's backyard and Lucy's backyard directly behind us. This meant the entire center of our block was raspberries.

Our neighbor Henry would sneak into our patch to pick his breakfast. Sneaking wasn't exactly correct. He'd walk over first thing in the morning, with his breakfast bowl and join us as we picked the day's produce. He'd say his good morning's and decorate his Cheerios as we filled our pint baskets.

It wasn't that hard a job. Dad kept the rows clean, staked, and weeded. Unfortunately he didn't keep the spiders out, so reaching deep inside the bushes always felt creepy to me. I hated spiders. It never failed that I would look inside the bushes and see this beautiful plump bright red raspberry. Then I'd see this Daddy Long Legs sitting on top of it. Oh, I would just cringe.

Anyway, we kids would say "Good Morning" to Henry and continue our sweep of the patch, sliding each berry from its cone shaped perch within the bushes and adding it to the basket. Mom would take our harvest and sometimes sell the berries to local restaurants. Mostly she made jam. The big stainless steel kettle Otto had given Mom would bubble on the stove with berries and sugar and periodically be stirred by a long wooden spoon. Once the jam was done, she'd pour the dark red, seed-laden steaming mixture into dozens of quart Miracle Whip jars, baby food jars and sometimes even real canning jars. The final act was to seal them with wax. These would then be brought down to another spider habitat in the basement room next to the oil tank. That room also creeped me out. We would stack enough jam on those shelves to last all year, just in time for the next summer's crop to ripen.

The patch could be seen from the kitchen window. The window was over the sink, and this was a position Mom often occupied. It would provide a great vantage point to watch her husband attempt to discipline his oldest son.

When Jimmy was 12 or 13, he started calling friends in Cornucopia, not realizing it was a long distance call. Long distance calls cost money. Long distance calls appeared on the phone bill that Dad happened to open. Which made Dad livid. He demanded to know who had made the calls. He quickly narrowed the suspects down to one. Jimmy.

In order to save his pride, and his hide, Jimmy absolutely denied being responsible for making the calls. He quickly realized that Dad wasn't buying his story. Discipline from Dad came swift and usually hurt the backside. Jimmy mentally ran all his options through his young brain, made a decision, then bolted out the back door and took off running. Dad took off after him, chasing him around the raspberry patch in the back yard.

Mom had witnessed the confrontation in the kitchen, but had decided to stay out of it. Now she turned and watched out the window as her husband chased her son around and around the raspberry patch. The chase itself was so unforgettable (I can't remember Dad ever running) that no one remembers how the situation was resolved.

Jimmy got into trouble a few times. Once Dad remanded him by saying, "The next time you do that you'll get a darn good spanking!" A short time later, Jimmy did the "that" again. As Dad approached him, Jimmy piped up, "Let's talk this one over Dad!" It was a gutsy, unique approach for the young man and caught everyone off guard. Maybe they did talk it over because Mom couldn't remember a spanking being delivered.

As the years went by the raspberry patch would get smaller and smaller. A fungus or blight of some sort hit the plants, reducing the number of raspberries produced. At the same time the need for parking increased as we all reached driving age. So the patch shrunk to around four short rows and gave way to a fleet of interesting vehicles. Even with the blight, there were enough berries to keep Mom and Dad in jam well after we all left the nest.

Eric and Alaska

Eric was born in 1967. He was Mom's last and most difficult delivery. His head was wedged up under her rib cage. Stuck but good. Apparently such a Mama's boy, he didn't want to leave the womb. So it ended up that the baby of the family arrived via C-Section. Mom remembered feeling the suction as Drs. Telford and Larson tried to yank him into the outside world.

Eric turned out fine, tongue tied as his older brothers had been, but fine nonetheless. Dr. Telford, however, felt that Mom had had enough. He went out to the waiting room to find Dad. He handed Dad some papers and barked, "Sign them!"

Mom recalled, "Because after you (meaning me) he told me, "No more." Everything had fallen down and wasn't normal…"

So after the seventh kid, the good doctor decided that in the interest of Mom's health, she was done having babies. She'd only been doing it for 17 years. It was sometime after that that Dad mentioned adopting a Korean baby. Mom just gave him "The Look".

I remember Carolyn politicking to name her latest brother "Eric." She thought at least one of us needed a Scandinavian name. She got her way and it was years before Mom realized her Swedish grandfather had the same name.

The first year of Eric's life included a rare event in the history of our family. Mom and Dad actually took a vacation. Without any of us. Dad had worked it out with co-workers at DuPont to switch enough shifts so that he and Mom would be gone close to three weeks. Then Mom convinced Gramma Cousineau to come over and watch us. The sticking point was that Gram, not being a licensed driver and the hospital 13 miles away, was too nervous to take care of little Eric. Our pastor and his wife were close with Mom and Dad and also willing to have the 9-month-old little shyster 'pawned' off on them. Amazingly, sitter logistics were settled.

With the major hurdle overcome, Mom and Dad packed up the car, pried a sobbing Janis off of them, and headed down the road to Canada. Their ultimate destination was Ketchikan, Alaska. This wasn't just a relaxation vacation; Dad had ulterior motives. His friend Herb had moved to Ketchikan. He had first worked in a mill of some sort. He then found employment with a new ferry service that did a circuit up the islands along the Alaskan coast. The pay was good and the potential was great. Herb would sail one week, then be home a week. He eventually worked his way up to Captain. So he had called Dad and said, "Git your butt up here." He thought Dad had the potential to have the same success. With this informa-tion, little preplanning and NO reservations, he and Mom were off. (Yes, you read correctly, no bus, train, ferry or motel reservations.)

As Mom recalled, "We got up to Winnipeg, we were going to take the train. First we needed to find a place to leave the car. So we drove up into this hotel parking lot, and we went back into the hotel to find the manager and we told him who we were, where we were from and where we were going, and asked if it were possible for us to leave the car there? He said, "Certainly, we have a watchman that goes around every so often. And I just came from Bayfield this afternoon!"

She continued, "So anyway, the bus depot was right around the corner. We couldn't get on the train, the train was on strike. So we had to take a bus. Now, the man ahead of us was quite inebriated and I walked up and I looked in the bus and came back out and I said to your dad, "There is no way I can stand up on that bus all night." And somebody heard me and they came up and said, "This guy is not getting on the bus." And he said, "There is another bus coming and it's an Express Bus." So Dad and I were the only two on this big Greyhound Bus."

"Dad went in the back, because way in the back there was one long seat. And he lay down and fell asleep and I sat up in the front and talked to the bus driver for half the night! He said, "You mind if I go home and get some clean clothes to take with me?" I said, "I don't care where you go as long as we get towards the coast!"

"So he went home and got clean clothes and stuff, got back on the bus, and it was just Dad and I. And on the way out there was some stop where you could see some animals but it was dark at night. We changed buses and we were going down, down the mountains and you could hear the grinding of the gears and I said, "There's something wrong!"

Dad said, "Na, they're just shifting down."

I said, "Like fun!" We got to the bottom, that bus was pulled aside and they put a new one on."

"And then we got to Prince Rupert on the coast, and I had heard of a dollar for a cup of coffee and maybe 50 cents for a roll. Which would have been ridiculous in Bayfield. But that's what it was. So we went to a deli and we bought some cheese and crackers and went back to our room rather than going to a restaurant."

"Oh, and then we were standing there, we didn't know where to go to get to a hotel and some guy heard us. He understood English so he told us how to get to another hotel down the street. There were a lot of French speaking people who didn't speak any English. He told us this hotel was full but he said, you go down the street and there's a hotel down there and he was sure they would have room."

"So we walked down and we did get a room. It was beautiful. You looked out the window and you could see the mountains. And we had to get to the ferry. You walk and talk to anybody, and they say, "No speaka any English." There were lots of Asian people."

"We finally got on the ferry. And the operator says, "It's about time you got here!" She was originally from Bayfield and had moved to Alaska. She heard from the Houtarys that we were coming."

"Grant. It was another one. It was Grant that worked in a big grocery store we went into. "Well, it's about time you got here!" And Herb was on the ferry. He was the captain of the ferry or close to rank of captain of the ferry."

"We got to Prince Rupert and got on the ferry. It was about an 8-hour ride. It was amazing to watch the cranes, buses, trucks, and everything. And they had a big dining room and what not. Dad was on his way back and he said, 'Watch your head!' (to me). This young guy was trying to carry this tray up over his head). Dad says, 'Watch your head…' We got in there and all of the sudden, I had the most horrible feeling that we were sinking." Mom was watching the dock being lifted up to their deck level. It made her feel like the boat was dropping down to meet the dock.

So Mom and Dad made it to Alaska and were received with open arms. The Houtarys put them up in their home on the mountainside. The front overlooked the ocean. The back door opened up into the mountain. They were served salmon hot dish and got to watch killer whales from the front deck. The Houtarys taught Marcie and Jim that halibut have to have their eye on a certain side. If it's on the other side, Herb says you have to throw it back, it's no good.

They took their company out to experience a local tavern. It had a huge ship's bell over the bar. It was the end of Salmon season and all the boats were coming in. Whenever that bell rang, someone (probably a fisherman glad to be home) bought a round for the bar. The foursome were sitting at a big round table enjoying the evening and listening to the bell ring, again and again. It wasn't very long before Herb said it was time to go. The table was full of drinks and the atmosphere of the tavern was about to change.

Mom took in all the sights, the layout and amenities of the town, and the people.

As much as Dad might have prospered in such an environment, she could not see herself living there. There were only 17 miles of black top and a plane or boat was required to get off the island. She could not see adapting to the transportation challenges the area brought.

They enjoyed their visit but when it was time to go home, Mom felt comfortable that she was heading back to where she belonged. On the return trip, they actually made train reservations, including a state room. As they boarded the train they were informed that their room had been given to another lady. The train gods were watching over them, as the room they ended up in was much bigger and had two bunks and a bathroom. Mom found it much more to her liking than the bus they traveled out on.

The trip was interesting to these Northern Wisconsin residents. Typical of the old movie scenes, they had to walk through sleeper cars with the bunks and curtains before arriving at the dining car. It was filled with tables covered in linen and made them feel special. The waiter came to take their order and left as an old friend. Dad would start up a conversation anywhere and would talk to anyone. The young man was interesting to them, as he worked the trains in the summer and attended school in the winter. It was so different from their young adulthood.

They retired to the bar and became intrigued by a man who had 10-20 little liquor bottles sitting on his table. They chuckled as they learned that the province they were traveling through was dry. The man had come prepared and brought his own refreshments for this section of the trip.

The train did stop in the middle of the night for some accident, but made it into Jasper in the morning. Mom took in the view, remembering the old-fashioned railroad station blooming with colorful flowers, the sight of a Chinese restaurant on the side of the mountain and the local town filled with houses the size of little boxes.

The views made the trip memorable, along with the people they met. Mom talked about two older men that wouldn't let them alone. Theses guys talked and talked. Two young girls were at their mercy for too long, and then the men turned around and tried to tell Dad that the biggest grain elevators were up in Canada. Dad was up for the argument. "The biggest grain elevators are in Superior." Mom stayed out of it. She said, "Oh, they would just drive you nuts. They wouldn't shut up!"

The train finally reached Winnipeg, and Jim and Marcie gathered their luggage and left the train behind them. They found their car safe and sound at the hotel where they left it. They threw their bags in the back and headed for home. Bayfield was where they would stay and finish raising their family. They would not take another major trip until we had all left the nest.

Herring Again

The herring were still a sizable catch as Carolyn and Jan traveled through the fall semesters of middle school and high school. Voluntarily and sometimes not voluntarily, they found themselves down in the shacks, delivering messages, visiting and themselves "choking" herring. Carolyn, who was always a hard worker, flat out detested the herring sheds. According to her:

"I was pretty young and I knew I had to go down to tell somebody something down at the fish shed when they were doing the herring, and I hated like heck to go down there because I was always afraid I would get stuck choking herring and Aunty Eleanor was the one that was going to make me stay there. When you open up that doggone door and there's a rock tied to a string to make the door go closed again, so when you open that up, you got to pull hard and you got to get in and get away from the door before it beats ya in the rear end and push you forward."

"And then, I got in there once and I'm going, 'Oh my god I gotta tell whoever it was something and get out of here.' Well I didn't make it. Aunty Eleanor made me go behind the table and choke herring. And the other times I when in there, I got out as quick as I could. It was just the smell and the heat and everything else, it was pretty bad.

All I know is that Aunty Eleanor standing behind that table ordering me back by her and choke the herring. And here she is, with her babushka wrapped around her head, great big rubber gloves on, it just, the whole, if you could only see the scene. The nets are comin' in, out of the boat, slopped on top the table at one end, they drag the nets with the fish down the table to the door on the other end and then they choke the herring. You know, they try to, with two hands, try to get the herring out of the nets. And throw them in the boxes. And then the net keeps traveling down and into boxes you know, from the other side and it's just loaded in there. You can't move.

And, of course, all the other hoopla, everybody in and out, getting the boxes, you know, the nets that went into the boxes after the herring was out of there. People were there trying to get those boxes out of there as well as those pulling in the nets from the other side. It was just quite the ordeal."

I asked if she remembered the color inside the herring shed.

"No, all I remember is DARK! Dreary and I didn't want to be there!"

I asked if she ever wanted to get out of school to go pick herring.

"NO! NO! Didn't want to do that!" (Tell me how you really feel Carolyn!) "I wanted to stay in school. I know it was so slimy on that table and fish scales all over the place, well, just think about it, a pot bellied stove, the smell of fish, scales all over, wet nets, it didn't add up to anything that smelled real good. I just didn't want to go in there at all." Carolyn gave her opinion to be documented for the record books.

The men who were regulars in the sheds knew very well how Carolyn felt and took great glee in pushing her buttons. Mom was in the shack one night, and quietly watched as the guys played a prank on Carolyn.

"In the shack, we had the stove, right in the middle of the shack, but up against the wall, towards the lake. Well, we picked fish in the shack, they'd pull fish from the boats up on the tables in the shack and shove them down until they stacked that high. (She raised her hand up to about 4 or 5 feet). Well, anyway, Carolyn came down to visit, and she went over by the stove to stay warm."

Hokenson was on the crew, the bull gang or what ever they called them. They came in and they had to start taking fish out of the shack and give us more boxes, but they deliberately started piling boxes (encircling Carolyn and the stove), and Carolyn didn't even notice it. They had them piled high and of course the smell of the fish along side that stove, she didn't know if she was going to get out of there! They boxed her in!"

We didn't mind the smell. Carolyn did. She (Carolyn) croaked, "You got to get me out of here!" Mom commented that when you get those fish close to the stove it will start to stink. She chuckled at the thought of Carolyn trapped behind the boxes.

I polled Janis on her opinion about choking herring, and, as I expected, she had a totally different response. Jan was one of the kids volunteering to get out of high school to pick fish. Get a note from your parents allowing you out of school, and voila! freedom! Jan remembered getting out of maybe only one hour of school, but any amount of time was fine with her.

She'd go down to the docks, walk from shed to shed until she found a crew that needed help. She recalled a U-shaped table in her shed, dim lighting, and the air warmed by the potbellied stove. The table was wet with the net and its contents filling the surface. To stay dry and warm, she wore boots and oilers over her clothes, and she tried to wear the same shirt and pants to the docks each day. She never failed to have lake water, fish scales and other slime spill and splatter on her exposed shirt and down her boots. By the end of the herring season, the outfit stunk so bad that she would burn it in the 55 gallon drum we kept in the back yard for burning trash.

Jan always seemed to enjoy everything she did, whether she should do it or not. The conversations in the sheds were great, the scent of fish was manageable, the lights were soft (like kerosene cabin lights could be), and to her it was cozy, working elbow to elbow with the crew. Fish parts, such as the air bladder, would be tangled in the nets. Some fish would be cleaned on the way into town, and guts would get stuck in the myriad of nets piled around the boats. Jan told me that for entertainment, "We would take the air sacs and throw them on the ceiling and they'd stick." Leave it to Jan.

She recalled making around $2 an hour for her time on the docks. All the money she made went to buy sweaters for her boyfriends. Oh, Jan.

Jimmy didn't pick. I didn't either. When I was born in 1957, the annual catch of herring in the Wisconsin waters of Lake Superior was recorded at 3,162,000 pounds. By 1971, when I became a high school freshman and Jimmy a sophomore, the catch was recorded at 282,000 pounds. There was no rush to get to the dock.

Richard Trimble and Edna G

Work at DuPont was sporadic, with employees laid off because of the economy or whatever. In the late 1960s Dad again found himself looking for work. He landed a job as a watchman on the *Richard Trimble*, a 600-foot ore carrier that hauled cargo such as taconite from Northern Minnesota to other ports across the Great Lakes. In local terminology, he began "sailing." This job would take him away from home for long periods of time, and Mom was left to run the house alone.

On one of his trips, Dad was scheduled to come into Two Harbors for just one night. Mom packed up Billy, Karen, Eric and me in the station wagon and headed for the north shore of Minnesota. I recall it being dusk as we drove down a gravel road to a series of ore docks. The docks were huge, with tall loading structures hovering above our heads. It was also a blustery night, windy and cold. We were early, so we sat in the car and waited. And waited. Mom had to keep the engine running to keep us warm.

Unlike the Bayfield harbor, everything here was on a massive scale. The docks were built to hold 600-foot ore carriers like the *Trimble*, not 40-foot fish tugs and recreational boats like back home. The ships needed ample steering/turning room, so the breakwater was a blur in the distance. It was also a somewhat lonely spot as darkness settled around us. Mom did not look worried about being here alone, and didn't seem concerned that boat wasn't here yet. We kept ourselves busy and continued to wait.

As we sat there with our various worries and daydreams, the sound of footsteps on the gravel crept up to Mom's door. A rap on the window made all our hearts jump. We all peered out the windows and saw this older man in work clothes standing by Mom's door. Shem rolled the window down slightly and the man asked if we were waiting for the *Trimble* to come in. Mom gave him a wary look and said yes, her husband was the watchman.

He then proudly introduced himself, "I'm Captain Adolph Ojard, of the *Edna G.*" He pointed to a large tug tied up to a nearby dock. "Come on down and wait on my boat. I have Steam Heat." (He put big emphasis on the Steam Heat.) Mom just sat there, obviously apprehensive. She wasn't going to jump out of the car and take four small children on some stranger's boat. Meanwhile, we're all bending over in our seats to look up and see the face of our visitor.

The man wasn't easily dissuaded. I can remember him saying over and over "Steam Heat. I have Steam Heat." The car was getting cold, it was dark, I loved exploring boats and he looked friendly enough to me. He then took on a different tactic and asked where we were from. It didn't take very long to find common ground, as the people who work on Lake Superior tend to know each other, or know of each other. They have fished or sailed the same waters, bought and or had their equipment maintained by the same companies, shared the same heritage, and spread their adventures across many a cup of coffee on the surrounding shorelines. Mom and Captain Ojard soon found common ground in someone named Henry.

So Mom surmounted her internal worries and accepted his invitation to board the Edna G and enjoy the "Steam Heat." We bailed out of the station wagon and followed Mom and Captain Adolph Ojard down the dock. We scampered across the gangplank and boarded the *Edna G.* to await the Trimble's arrival.

Even as a preteen, I remember the *Edna G* to be amazing. True to his word, the inside of the tug was wonderfully warm. But even more so, the tug was gleaming. The cabin had polished birch paneling and shiny brass fittings. He took us through the entire tug, showing off the cabins, passage ways, and decks. He may have shown us the engines, but as a 12-13 year old girl, they had no lasting impact on me. I was entranced with all the woodwork, and still love refinishing old furniture today.

What I didn't know that night, was that the *Edna G* was built in 1896 by the Cleveland Shipbuilding Company. It was 92.5 feet long, coal fed and, true to Captain Ojard's word, steam powered by a Fore and Aft Compound Engine with boilers by the Babcock and Wilcox Company. (Still doesn't mean much to me, but *does* sound impressive!) It was originally built with a wooden hull, but later covered in steel to allow it to break ice. It would make a career at Two Harbors, Minnesota, as a harbor tug and fire boat. For two years during World War I she had served our country by hauling coal barges along the east cost. She would become a National Historic Site in 1974. She would tow her last ore carrier in 1981. She would then become a museum, being maintained as a fully operational tug.

But that night we knew her as a safe haven, keeping us warm and adding adventure during the long wait for the *Richard Trimble* to come in. We sat inside, Mom and Captain Ojard talking and us keeping ourselves busy, waiting as darkness surrounded us.

The radio finally came to life, and Captain Ojard and the *Trimble* exchanged information and coordinated the run to guide the carrier to the docks. Mom knew he needed to get to work so she started to gather us up to return to the station wagon. Captain Ojard interrupted her with a sincere request. He said, "When we go out to bring the *Trimble* in, I'll take him with," and he pointed to Billy, who was around nine years old. Mom quickly and firmly said, "No, you won't."

Ojard was taken aback by her quick brush off. She looked him squarely in the eye and continued, "He'll get so seasick on you!" Ojard smiled with the realization that she was not being a protective mother, but instead was doing him a favor.

I, on the other hand, would have loved the trip, but in the 1960s and the male environment, again I had no offer coming. Rats! The Captain escorted us off the tug as the crew readied to leave the mooring. We returned to the car and Mom moved us to a position where we could watch the boats maneuver.

The *Edna G.* and her "Steam Heat" left the dock, her running lights and engine noise the only clue to show us her whereabouts in the darkness. An eternity later we watched as a massive hulk with lights outlining the decks high above the lake loomed out of the darkness. It slowly pushed thru the water and settled against the dock. The *Edna G.* looked like a toy as it maneuvered next to the waterline of the *Trimble*.

As tired as I was, I became aware that the dock was now alive with moving shadows. Men were moving everywhere and Dad was suddenly in the front seat of the car. The six of us were off to a motel for what was left of the night. The next morning came quickly and Mom had to return Dad to the dock. We were alone again, on our way home.

Dad's tenure on the *Trimble* would not last long. Mom, who had a marine radio at the house, called Dad on the *Trimble* one day. Across the marine airways, she gave him the order, "Come on home." The radio crackled and Dad blurted back, "You're drunk!"

A thing to note about marine radios. They do not transmit on private frequencies like a telephone does. They are like a massive party line. Normally, every boat on the Great Lakes would monitor Channel 16, calling whomever, and then agree to switch to a different frequency for conversations.

Or, they may have numerous radios, some strictly on 16 and others tuned to common conversation channels. So this conversation, or argument, like the old telephone party lines, was able to be listened in on by anyone and everyone who had tuned in to that channel.

So Mom continued, "No, I'm not drunk. Come on home now, Bud (her cousin) says you can go back to work at the plant." So Dad resigned as watchman on the *Trimble* and returned home to work at the DuPont plant outside of Washburn.

It was years later, when Mom and Dad were downtown at the Bakery taking a coffee break, that they learned just how public that conversation was. Earl was at the next table. Like Dad, he had sailed the lakes. He was telling someone, "You should have heard the guys when some woman called up and told her husband to come home. And all the guys said 'Boy I wish my wife would say that'."

Dad about choked on his coffee. Earl gave him a strange look and Dad started laughing. He pointed to Mom. "It was Marcie" he giggled.

The *Ruby Ann*

DuPont still didn't provide a stable income; in fact, the plant would soon shut down. With this inevitability hovering in the back of Dad's mind, he decided to take a giant leap of faith and become his own boss. He rented a fish tug, the *Julie Ann*, from Everett Johnson in Port Wing. He gathered up nets, secured a license, hired a couple men, took out a checkbook under the name of Frostman Fish Company and once again set nets in the lake. This time he was in control of his own destiny, which he found to be a comfortable match for his personality and passions.

By 1972 he was fully supporting himself as a commercial fisherman. Renting a boat didn't make good business sense, so he and Mom ended up traveling to Montague, Mich., to look at a tug that was for sale. It turned out to be an odd long, narrow boat and might have been named *Henry*. Mom stood inside the cabin, facing the bow. She stretched her arms straight out from her sides, and if she had leaned over, either to the left or right, she could almost have touched the cabin walls. It was obvious to both Jim and Marcie that this boat and fishing around the Apostle Islands was not a good match.

Jim looked down the dock to a metal, beat up tug resting a short ways away from them. "What about that one?"

The *Ruby Ann* sat moored to the dock, its hull solid, its design engineered for stability and well suited to fishing on the waters of Lake Superior. She was built in 1945 by Sturgeon Bay Shipbuilding Drydock Co., and was equipped with a GM 6-71 diesel. She was 42 feet long and constructed of solid ice-breaking steel. She drew 4.5 feet and her net tonnage was 16. She had a rear pilot house and a

The **Ruby Ann**

12-foot beam. Mom could stand in the center of the boat and fall flat on her face either to port or starboard and still not hit her head on the cabin walls. Good sign.

They walked around inside, looked at the engine, checked out the instruments, opened and closed hatches and basically kicked all the aquatic tires. Jim was already envisioning the modifications he wanted to make. But they had no money. It was a dream, but until they got a bank to back them there could be no purchase. So Jim and Marcie said their thanks to the man and left for home, wondering what they could do.

Jim was filled with insecurity, much to this daughter's surprise. I'd always seen him in control, but in this case he found that his future was held in the hands of someone else, namely the loan officer. Jim and Marcie had a long discussion on the way home and Mom finished the conversation by encouraging him to apply for the loan.

He agreed to apply but still had plenty of doubts. He kept moaning, "I won't get it."

It wasn't too long before the response came in the mail. Marcie waited until Jim woke up from his noon nap and then handed the envelope to him. He looked at the envelope in her hand and refused to take it.

"You read it," he said.

She didn't have any reservations. She slid her thumb under the flap, broke the seal and slipped the letter out. She held it in front of Jim but read it silently to herself. When she was finished, she broke out in a smile and said, "Well, when do you want to go get the boat?"

He was afraid to believe her. She kept smiling. He finally smiled back, took the letter from her hands and read it. The loan, for $10,200, would be finalized on April 4, 1972. It was large enough to purchase the *Ruby* and to buy additional nets. Jim would now be captain of his own rig.

The *Ruby* didn't find a port in Bayfield right away. Oliver Smith, from Smith Bros. Fisheries in Port Washington called. Dad knew him from our Belgium days. Oliver Smith said, "Git that boat over here!" Smith Bros. Fisheries needed more fish, and Oliver trusted Dad to provide. So Dad took the boat straight across Lake Michigan to Port Washington and fished there for the spring.

The boat worked well, but that didn't mean it didn't need work. The paint job could wait, but muffling the engine could not. Oliver Smith finally chastised Jim. "You got to put a box around that engine! You're waking up everybody in town."

The trip home came in early summer. It turned out to be an interesting trip. 1972 was the year global warming skipped Lake Superior. Cakes of ice floated in the Bayfield harbor well into June. A picture of Jimmy made it into the local paper. He was sitting on a mini-ice berg in the harbor. Dad knew the ice conditions in Bayfield, but figured he could still get the boat home.

The trip went well until he neared Outer Island. He was running into ice, flows taller than the Ruby. So much ice was unheard of at this late in the spring. It could prevent him from coming into Bayfield. He got on the marine radio and called Mom. He said to go climb the fire tower (a couple miles out of town and on top of the hill) to see how much ice was in sight. The fire tower, besides being a good place for underage drinking, was a great place to get a view of the inner islands and the amount of ice between them.

Mom gave him a report and then went back to her sewing. She wouldn't know the boat had reached the dock until she saw Art Grant, (one of his crew) walk by the sewing room window.

Dad would work the *Ruby* for the next 25 years. He moved the cabin from the stern to mid-ships and made all the controls left-handed. In 1975 he replaced the engine with a 220 hp. Cummins diesel. He installed radar and an automatic pilot. The boat had a governor on it, so that the speed was regulated at 7.5 miles per hour, regardless of the rpms, allowing him to track distances traveled. The basement of the house became a factory for seaming and mending nets. The garage became a warehouse for buoys, nets, a welding machine, a large chest freezer and a reel for drying nets. Every once in a while we'd make space and put the car in there just for the heck of it.

Dad soon established a daily routine that started around 4:30 a.m. An ungodly hour, and before writing this passage, I thought Mom got up, made him coffee and joined him for breakfast. I called her to confirm the details about this early morning romantic inter-lude. Boy, did she burst my bubble. Mom would "set" the coffee pot the night before (percolator type, she still prefers it to drip) and plug it into the outlet on the stove. This outlet had a timer, so there was no need for Mom to get up and romantically join her husband in the morning for breakfast.

The coffee perked itself and come to find out, Dad didn't eat breakfast. He poured the coffee into his heavy duty Stanley ther-mos, grabbed his lunch pail (the black metal type with the Dutch colonial top), and headed down to the dock. Around 10 a.m., some-where enroute to his nets, he would open his lunch box and eat one of the two sandwiches Mom made for him the night before. That's not exactly right. Some mornings all the fishermen would meet at the Pier and drink another cup of coffee, and then head out on the lake.

Fishing no longer lent itself to occupying fish camps on

Stockton or any other island in the Apostles. The *Ruby* and the rest of the fleet were now faster and more efficiently designed. Improvements in the overall process and equipment meant the fishermen were able to return to their home port most every day. There were times in the spring and fall when Dad would stay out overnight, but instead of staying at the cabin, he would anchor in a sheltered bay and settle in for the night.

He didn't stay at the cabin because the cabin was no longer ours. The property was no longer a part of the Vilas estate. Ownership had been transferred to the state of Wisconsin. The change in ownership was completely out of Dad and Mom's circle of influence or circle of control, but the way the gentleman's agreement had been broken did cause some hard feelings.

The State did call Mom and Dad and inform them of the transfer of ownership. They told them that if they wanted the contents of the cabin they could come get it. That was nice except this offer came in the middle of the winter and we were currently living down south in Belgium. There was no way we could physically get to the island, even if we had chosen to do so. The furniture and possessions left in the cabin held many memories and were hard earned. The loss was heartfelt. The cabin and its little community were a deep-rooted part of our family history. Although the loss had to be accepted, they grumbled every time the subject came up, and life moved on.

Now that Dad was back fishing again, he passed by Presque Isle all the time. There was one particularly nasty day when he and young Jim were out fishing. They were blown off the lake and took refuge on Stockton to wait for the winds to die down. With the boat secured to the dock (now a massive concrete solid structure), they took a stroll to look around and kill time. Naturally they gravitated up the hill to the old cabin. Looking through the windows at what had once been considered his property, Dad saw the furniture that we used to eat on, sleep on, and play cards on.

Jimmy peered in next to him. Dad said, "You know, that's your ma's furniture." Jimmy nodded his head, thinking back to when he ran around here as a little guy. The next think Jimmy knew, the cabin door crashed inward. He looked at Dad and hesitantly asked, "This mean we're done fishin' for the day?"

"Yeah."

Fall Fishing

Life with fishing and family fell into a routine aligned with the seasons. Fall saw us kids pose in our new school clothes for a picture before we hiked the five and a half blocks up the hill for the first day of school. Fall brought the Apple Festival, a 1-day event (back then) where we marched in the parade and manned stands where each of our classes sold pies and apple crisp that we'd baked. Fall meant taking down the screens and putting up storm windows.

Fall meant after dinner trips down to "check the fire in the boat." October through ice up could be numbing, especially if one inhabited a steel tub that was plowing through fresh water close to the freezing point. On the coldest days Dad would keep a constant fire burning in a coal stove inside the *Ruby*. It kept the boxed nets from freezing, the engine from cracking and the mornings a little more inviting as the crew pulled away from the dock.

Fall could mean long days on the lake, with the largest catches coming in the worst weather. Fall days were short, and many times darkness would fall before the work day was over. The cold was not intense enough to form ice on the surface of the lake, but the spray from the wake and sleet falling from the sky could form a dangerous layer of ice on the *Ruby*.

At the end of one of these late fall days, the sun had set, and Dad was still making his way home, hiding in the lee on the north side of Madeline Island. It got to the point where he had to face the squall and the open stretch between Madeline and Bayfield. He was only a couple miles from the dock but it was dark and the squall was relentless with a following sea and blinding sleet. The dense cold water pushed the *Ruby* from the stern, creating an odd sluggish feeling as Dad struggled to keep the bow in the direction of town. The waves would lift up the stern, and ride under the boat, pushing the stern sideways along its intended path. Dad had to concentrate on the 'feel' of the boat to keep on course. Meanwhile the sleet kept falling.

At this time Dad was renting dock space just north of the skating rink. As the harbor lights should have come into view, the pilot house windshield and every porthole were encased in a translucent layer of ice. By the time the *Ruby* reached the harbor entrance, the build up of ice had become about four inches thick and the crew was unable to see out of any portholes or even the windshield in the pilot house,.

Dad couldn't enter the harbor unless he could physically see the dock. With no visibility, (radar wasn't going to cut it in close quarters and a wind), he would run the risk of smashing into a dock or someone else's boat. He was also concerned as the extra weight of the ice meant the *Ruby* was riding low in the water. Much lower and the gangways could go below the waterline, water would rush in, and they would sink, 100 yards from the shore. Not something the guys would let him forget.

He yelled for the crew to grab crowbars and hammers and pound the inside of the hull to knock off the ice outside. He too hammered away at the hatch over his head in the pilot house. The noise inside was deafening. Clang, clang, bang, bang, metal against metal. And outside the wind was still howling. Finally, rolling in the seas just outside the harbor, the hatch popped up. Dad was able to stick his head outside and into the freezing air. He could now see the darkness and the harbor lights in front of him. He slowly brought the *Ruby* inside the calm waters of the harbor and slid it up against the dock.

I was at the dock that night to greet Dad, along with the rest of the town. There he was in that rust colored knit hat that Mom had made on the knitting machine. He was nothing but smiles. He was unloading a 42-foot ice cube, but he acted like nothing out of the ordinary had happened. With the boat tied up, the guys were busy unloading fish, stoking the fire, laughing, reliving the ride and getting ready to call it a day.

According to the calendar, fall lasted until December 21. Fishing lasted until they couldn't bust through the ice any more. Some years fall lasted until January. The lake would freeze inside the islands first, which was where many fishermen departed from each morning and returned to each night. The guys gambled with the lake on each departure. They were taking the chance that they would still be able to plow through the ice on their way home that last night. They depended on experience, weather reports, intuition, and each other when making this judgment call.

The problem with going out one last time was that nets for whitefish were lifted every three nights, and fat nets could be left for a week. So the gamble was that if they set, would they be able to lift the net? They were gambling on making a profitable lift. If they lost the gamble, they might lose their nets and all the fish entangled in them. The former was expensive, and the latter a waste.

One year Dad almost lost his bet. He, along with Jimmy Erickson on the *Cindy Marie* and the Hadland brothers on the *Vagabond*, were coming back through the North Channel, after a day of lifting chubs. It was late and they became enveloped in darkness, freezing temperatures and push ice. Push ice was a huge thick mass of ice that had formed in Chequamegon Bay and had been "pushed" north by a strong south wind.

It had traveled up the channel, and soon surrounded the three tugs. To this day Jimmy swears they could have made it in, but in a second breath admitted that the ice was getting quite thick. It closed in around them, thick and hard. Finally, on the south end of Bass, (the same area Dad and Terry woke up years ago, on their return from wooing their future wives on Madeline), the *Ruby* became stuck. (For the record, Jimmy never said anything to me about the Cindy being officially "stuck").

We, the family, friends, and fellow fishermen, were all in Bayfield, watching and nervously waiting for this last of the fleet to come in. From the top of our front porch we could see the lights on the boats across the miles of cold and ice. And then the lights started flashing.

As Mom tried to recall the incident, she said, "One fuel tank sprung a fuel leak, if I remember right. So they were having fun with that. And trying to get in and break ice at the same time. It just got too thick; he couldn't break it any more." Dad had no choice but to get on the marine radio and call for help. For him it was the ultimate last resort.

The only vessels in the area capable of breaking ice that thick were the ferries that ran between Madeline and Bayfield. And they were bound by laws, regulations, licenses and bureaucracy. Once Dad put out the call for help, the network of government and local entities (Coast Guard, ferry service, fishermen, and whoever had a say) tossed options around, made calls and quickly cut through the red tape. Soon one of the ferries received the very rare pleasure of deviating from the one route they did day in and day out. They charted a course northeast and headed out to rescue the Ruby and her crew.

They plowed through the thickening ice towards the blinking lights. The sound of the engines pushing the boat and the cakes of ice cracking and sliding off the bow filled the night air.   T h e ferry broke ice all the way to the Ruby. Then the Captain backed off, himself gambling that he would not damage his props in the huge chunks of broken ice. The ferry turned around and began the final 3-mile journey, breaking a trail that Dad, Jimmy and the Hadlands could follow into the safety of the Bayfield harbor.

Other years iced in with much less fanfare. Many times Dad would lay the boat up in Port Wing, as it was free of ice much earlier in the spring. Eric did the trip to Port Wing four or five times. It took about eight hours. The most exciting part of the trip was the last 100 or so yards that ran the distance from the harbor entrance to the cleats at the dock.

It was exciting because, after eight hours of calm clear water, with maybe just a touch of skim ice, the harbor could be completely frozen in. One year Dad and Jack Evano did the trip together, entering the frozen harbor ice side by side. One would go up, hold the throttle on so that the boat would stay on top of the ice, then the other would run up along side, and then the weight of both boats would break the ice beneath them. According to Eric, while the boats lay on top the ice, they looked like a couple of killer whales sunning themselves.

They would ram themselves up atop the ice over and over again. The path would be filled with huge floating blocks of ice. The loose ice would hit the rudder and the boat would jerk. The vibration and noise would make horrific grinding and banging noises inside the steel hulls, but Dad and Jack had to keep boats in gear or the ice could wedge in the prop.

The trip was not without a mishap. Ice pushed Jack's bow into the Ruby, crushing a rear port hole. Dad probably vehemently exclaimed a few "Oh Geez" and other slightly stronger epitaphs, and went on to ram the boat on top of the ice again. The damage was nothing that a little 2x2 steel plating and a welding machine couldn't take care of.

Once I brought my relatively new husband, Randy, home for a visit, during which time Dad was going to lay the boat up. Dad offered to take him with. Randy couldn't figure out how to refuse the offer politely. He was still recovering from a memorable trip the summer before when he got violently seasick sailing with Uncle Gene. But, being the trooper he was, he accepted the opportunity for a boat ride from Bayfield to Port Wing. It was late fall to early winter and there was some ice on the lake. But the lake was relatively calm and Dad had the coal stove inside cranked up. How bad could it be?

I drove out to Port Wing to retrieve (rescue?) my husband, arriving in time to watch as the *Ruby* rumbled around the breakwater, plowing a wake in the open water. Directly ahead were other fish tugs tied up for the season, all frozen in place with a thick layer of ice. The ice covered the entire harbor, but the Ruby didn't slow down. In fact, I could hear the engine revving up.

As I watched, Dad rammed the bow right up onto the ice and waited. The entire front half of the boat was out of the water, tipped bow up, stern down at an impressive angle. Eventually the ice cracked beneath and the *Ruby* slipped down and backwards. I watched as Dad put her in reverse long enough for a good running start, then steamed forward, again ramming the bow back on top of the ice. Eric was right, it did look like a giant beached whale as it sat on top of the ice. It was so unnatural.

This went on for what seemed like an hour. He rammed the *Ruby* on top of the ice, over and over and over again. The boat would sit there, then crash through, and then roll wickedly from side to side. The crew, my husband and Bob, would be watching from port holes and hatches. When the roll started, heads would disappear, hatches would slam shut and the Ruby would roll, I swear, 45 degrees to port, then 30 degrees to starboard and back again. Poor Randy.

When they finally arrived within 50 feet of the boats already set up for the winter, Dad simply shut the engines down. I stood on the dock and watched. Watched not only the *Ruby*, which had settled quietly in the opening it had created in the ice. I also watched the other fishermen, who were standing on the ice just a short distance from the *Ruby*. Next thing I know, the gangway opens, Dad steps out onto the ice and casually walks over to his cohorts, carrying a cup of coffee. Poor Randy was back in the boat, gripping the rails inside the gangway, rethinking his choice of in-laws.

Maitre and Men

Fall also brought northeasters. They are amazing storms that hit with a vengeance. I called home from college on the evening of November 10, 1975. The background noise on the other end of the phone was so loud that I could hardly hear Mom's voice. There was a northeaster blowing, and the full force of the storm was still evident the next time I came home. The massive waves had literally bent the breakwater that protected the city marina. This damage was insignificant compared to the loss suffered on the eastern end of the lake. This was the same storm that sank the *Edmund Fitzgerald.*

This might have been the same storm that tried to put a dent in Dad's livelihood. Late in the 1970s he rented dock space just north of the skating rink. During one nasty northeaster, the waves battered and pounded his dock so hard and for so long that the dock began to give way. On top of the dock was a shed that had seen a lot of herring in the old days. Inside was a huge heavy metal furnace that used to keep the workers warm as they picked fish. The shed now also housed much of Dad's equipment. Water was pouring in and buoys, line, and boxes of nets were in danger of being lost into the lake.

Dad's gear, as that of most of the fishermen, was made by hand. The loss of nets could not be replaced by simply placing an order with some company in a far away place. The fishermen seamed their own nets using maitre, twine, bobbers and raw lead. They filled their own needles and stitched bobbers and twine onto the maitre, knot by knot by thousands of knots. They melted the lead into the weights that would hold down the lower edge of the net. Each lead weight would then be crimped onto the bottom maitre, perfectly spaced across from the bobber on the other side. Summer evenings and winter days were filled with the chore of mending existing nets and seaming new ones.

Nets would be lost in the lake, especially during storms like this. If Dad lost a gang of nets in the lake, he didn't file an insurance claim and wait for a check. They were usually salvageable if they could be found, so he would drag for them. He would throw overboard a 6-foot chain, folded back in half, with hooks in many of the links, and drag it over the bottom of the lake, hoping to hook something. This thing would dig into and over rocks and who knows what else hundreds of feet below the surface. When something was hooked, he'd haul it up in hopes of recovering his lost equipment.

Eric was on board one day while Dad dragged for lost nets. He watched as the lifter pulled a tangled bunch of rope, mesh, branches and whatnot out of the water and through the gangway. They spread the mess across the deck, and Dad took a slow walk through it. He picked up and examined knots on the maitre, ran his finger over the lead weights, and untangled a stick or two from the twine.

He mumbled, "Huh, these are Dean's."

Eric just looked at him, wondering how the heck Dad could tell whose nets these were from such a mishmash of jumbled twine and rope. They piled Dean's nets in boxes and went back to dragging for Dad's nets.

At the end of the day they loaded Dean's nets into the truck and drove over to his house. Eric remembered the conversation went something like this:

"D'ya get them outside of Madeline?"

"Yah."

"Ok, drop dem in da yard."

Dad had guessed right. Eric quietly stood there in amazement that a bunch of rope and netting had enough character to identify its owner. He'd also had a lesson on the character of a fisherman.

When Dad recovered his own nets, they would box the tangled mess as best as they could and bring it home to the dungeon. Dad and Mom, me, or whoever was available, would then spend our free

1980s - *Dad seaming trap net down by Bodins. It was an endless job to keep the gear in shape.*

time untangling the nets (the common term was "spreading the nets"). The box would be set at one end of the room, then one person would grab the cork line, and one person would grab the lead line. We would walk the end of the net to the opposite end of the room. Together we would then pull the mess out of the box, piling our leads and corks beside us and spreading the mesh between us. Twigs and fish scales would loosen from the nylon and fall to the floor. A pseudo orderly mound of mesh would form, preparing for the next step. We would then pull the nets back across the room, and lay the net back systematically into the box.

When a stretch (the section of net "stretched" across the room) needed repair, the maitre would be hooked to nails at either end of the room, pulling the maitre so tight that the cork and lead lines could almost "twang" like a guitar string. The stretch was at waist level, a comfortable height to work with the knife. The bad mesh would have to be cut off and new mesh sewn in. Dad always had a small jackknife in his pocket for this purpose. He kept this and all his knives sharp enough that they would catch on the surface of his fingernail if he scraped the blade against it. He kept little black whetstones at the ready to transform a dull blade.

He knew just how to cut out each ripped section. Once the net was stretched across the room, he would find a hole and cut the mesh in a straight line, knot to knot, across from the cork line to the lead line. This was a difficult task with the monofilament mesh. If it wasn't cut straight, the new mesh stitched in its place would pucker and twist, and would not set straight in the depths of the lake.

He knew just where to grasp the mesh. He walked his fingers down the mesh, counting under his breath as he followed the threads across, flicking monofilament with his knife as he went. Then the stretch of ripped netting had to be stripped from the maitre. Each knot that held the twine to the maitre had to be cut from the maitre. But God forbid, do NOT clip the maitre. Dad held strict standards when working with his nets. Nicking the treads of the maitre would weaken the net and cause a catastrophe net failure when filled with fish.

I'm really not sure about that, but Dad was very particular and exacting when it came to working on the nets. A nick would require splicing the line, and that was just more work that didn't need to be done. So I learned to position the blade of the knife just at the edge of each knot and flick it just so, cutting through the seaming twine and leaving the taught maitre intact.

Then the new mesh had to be seamed. The mesh had to be balanced between the upper maitre with the cork, and the lower maitre with the leads. The number of mesh he ran the needle of twine through had to be the same from knot to knot, and the knots on the bobber line had to match the knots on the lead line. The job required skill and patience. Mom could meet the standards Dad kept for seaming, but I knew I fell way short of perfection.

He tried to teach me, but apparently I wasn't a very successful student. I was called on often to spread and strip nets, but only once did I seam. I was never invited back to do that job. He never said how bad a job I did, he just got Mom to help him strip and redo the job later when I was out of the house. Either I was deemed untrainable, or he didn't want to hurt my feelings. I'd like to think the latter.

Mom could seam, but she too found cutting out the old twine to be too much for her. She once tried to mend a section on her own, intending to surprise Dad when he got home. The seaming would not be a problem, but first the mesh had to be cut straight from cork to lead. She tried and tried and finally sat down and cried. It could be a daunting job.

So it wasn't surprising, during that huge fall storm when the winds were howling and rain was pouring down, that when someone rushed into the Community Café and yelled, "Frostman's shed is about to be washed away," seven tables cleared and trucks were soon racing down to the dock. The men worked against time as boxes floated precariously out towards the lake and the wind bit through their jackets. They pulled out the gear, loaded everything into their pickups, hauled it up the hill and piled it in our garage. The power of the storm would be evident later when the huge furnace was found separated from its footings and moved several feet away.

With the rescue complete, backs were slapped, "Oh Yah"s were said and everyone got back in their half ton and three quarter ton pickup trucks and returned to the restaurant. As they entered the front door and shook off their wet rain jackets, they looked at their tables and smiles spread across their faces. The breakfasts of eggs, white toast, bacon and coffee had long gone cold. The old plates were gone and fresh hot breakfasts were waiting for them, compliments of the chef.

Caviar in the Dungeon

Fall also brought fish guts. Dissect the guts and you come up with an egg sack. This little sack of bright orange eggs would prove to be a gold mine. In the fall of my senior year of college, Mom and Dad discovered that distributors were buying prepared fish roe (eggs) for an unbelievable price. For years Dad had been throwing away buckets of this stuff every time he came off the lake. So Dad and Mom approached a company in the region about becoming a supplier. The company was looking for quality fish guts and Mom and Dad could provide. The process was explained to Mom and Dad, and that fall Karen and Eric found themselves employed and up to their elbows in fish eggs.

I asked Eric if he remembered the process of transforming spawn into caviar. I expected to hear complaints about the hard work, the cold guts and frozen hands. He said empathically, "I can remember everything!" He then proceeded to describe the process start to finish, detail after detail. I had to slow him down so I could catch it on paper.

"Dad would collect spawn from herring. They used very little chub spawn because the eggs were too small." Eric took off on a verbal sprint revisiting a memory of a particular special herring order where the client wanted the fish butterflied. Excited, he said, "So Dad would butterfly the herring…"

"OK," I interrupted, fuzzy with confusion. "Stop, Eric! What the heck is butterflying a herring?" I was expecting spawn (egg) stories and got a lesson in cleaning fish some fancy way. "First," Eric reminisced, "the head is cut off, and then sliced down the back. This means you would break one side of the ribs." I tried to take

1981 - *Marcie being frivolous with caviar.*

notes and picture this process at the same time. My mind was getting overwhelmed with the vision of this poor fish. At least it wasn't Bambi.

"Then you lay it (the fish) open, the two sides being attached by the belly." This sounded really bizarre after seeing Dad bring home fish whole, headless, filleted or cut in steaks like you see civilly in the grocery store, but never butterflied. Apparently it only happened once in Eric's memory. It may have resulted in plenty of intact egg sacks to be thought of during our conversation, or I had just triggered some memories. Siblings can be so enjoyably distracting and wonderful to get acquainted with as adults.

When I asked Jimmy about the caviar operation, he remembered details from the boat. When cleaning the fish, Dad, Jimmy and whoever was crew, would separate the roe from the guts, throw the guts into 35 gallon drum, and throw the roe into a white five gallon bucket. If they were cleaning whitefish, the livers were put into their own bucket. Whitefish livers were a local delicacy.

Our family learned the difference between whitefish and trout livers the hard way. Dad brought trout livers home and we ate them for dinner one night. Everybody's skin broke out and started peeling. I can remember being sick as a dog. Les Cornell heard about this and bawled Dad out good. Mom can still remember his words, "What the *@!*'s the matter with you Jim! Yah aught ta know by now that you can't eat those. They are too rich in Vitamin E!"

Whitefish livers, on the other hand, are wonderful. Dredge them in flour and fry in the pan. Chicken livers don't even come close to this delicacy. That's why Dad thought brought trout home for us to try. He didn't realize there was such a toxic difference.

Anyway, cleaning fish, especially if there were literally a ton of them to clean, took a very sharp knife. Dad always carried a jackknife in his pocket the he used when seaming nets. There was a special filleting knife in the kitchen drawer, and a stash of knives on the boat. I remember him sharpening many of these, showing me how a well sharpened blade would catch on your fingernail.

The cleaning operation took place during the ride into town. The fish would be picked out of the nets and then cleaned atop long flat steel tables inside the Ruby. If the fish were cleaned on these steel tables, the constant contact between the knife blade and the table would dull the sharp edge. To avoid this, Dad would drop boards, up to an inch thick, on top of the steel table and dress fish there.

Some guys had astro turf on their boards to hold fish in place. Dad preferred to use plain wood. Astro turf would break the sack encasing the roe. With wood, Dad could scrap roe off a board, keeping the egg sack whole and avoid sending a billion little eggs bouncing around the deck. Jimmy can still hear Dad say, "That's money you know, got to get all that stuff. Don't lose that!"

Once at the dock, Dad would haul the buckets of spawn, weighing from 40 to 80 pounds, up to the house and store them in the cold garage. Other buckets strangely appeared in our garage during the fall, but Dad always knew who had delivered them. He kept an industrial scale out there and would weigh each bucket. He kept a log of these weights. Mom would calculate how much was owed and write the checks to the other fishermen.

This was the point at which Karen and Eric became involved in the process. By now they were the only kids who hadn't left the nest. With the promise of lucrative paychecks in exchange for hard work, they put on their game faces and descended into the dungeon. During the next four years, in the months of November and December they would spend their late afternoons in the basement making more money than most of their older brothers and sisters would make all year long.

Karen doesn't recall the paychecks as much as the smell. She was 14, in high school, in the band, and into boys. After working in fish eggs, it took a lot of scrubbing and the passage of time to get the aroma out of her skin. She would work the roe before dinner, eat and run up to school for basket ball games. She was a member of the pep band and played during half time. She said, "I smelled like a fish factory while trying to play the trumpet." It also put a crimp in her dating. Girls smelling like fish guts were not appealing to the guys in high school. She attempted to justify her "condition" by bragging to her classmates that she was making caviar. She recalls, "They weren't impressed."

Once Karen and Eric got home from school the cleaning process began. The buckets were brought in from the garage to the room under the kitchen. This used to be the scariest room in the house. We never went there so it always seemed dark and cluttered and cold. A large oil tank for the furnace leaned against the south wall, the west wall had a deep metal double sink (like you'd find in a laundry) and the north wall had two small windows up high, looking out under the back porch. The walls of the basement were a patchwork of sandstone, field stone and concrete block, painted white a long time ago, and the floor was cement, luckily with a working drain. The room was cluttered with a huge crock that held our ancient dolls and stuffed animals that needed to be buried, skis, bikes, old chairs, canned goods, burlap bags of potatoes, and more.

Caviar changed all that. A bright bare bulb lit the now sparkling white walls, the floor was scrubbed to its best gray shine, a radio played the Duluth pop station and everyone was down there. When the system was in operation, three screens would be piled on top of each other in the middle of the floor. The screens were sized to fit over the plastic rectangular fish boxes Dad used on the boat. They were constructed with 4-6 inch sides and window screening attached to and creating the bottom of each frame.

The three screens would be stacked on top of each other, on top of the fish box. The top screen had the largest mesh and the mesh would get smaller with each of the next two screens. The roe would be poured into the top screen. Karen and Eric's job was to push the roe down through the top screen onto the middle screen below. This would break the egg sack and separate the eggs.

Keep in mind that the goo that was poured onto the screen had just come out of Lake Superior. It was numbingly cold. Blood clots were everywhere and sharp fish scales lurked within. Sometimes both Karen and Eric would work the same screen, both wrists deep in the roe, running their hands across the screen, pushing the eggs through the screen. It could feel so cold that bumping into each other's hands felt like hitting a rock. It didn't take long before rubber gloves were introduced to the process. The paycheck and respect of our parents were big motivation for going through this ordeal.

Remember that Dad bought roe from other fishermen? One night he dumped a particular bucket of roe onto the top screen. Along with the orange roe dropped rocks or lead net weights or something of significant weight. I've heard a couple versions of this story, like the guy who sold it to us thought he could get away with it or that it was a joke and the guy couldn't wait to have coffee with

Dad at 5:00 the next morning. Either way, Dad picked out the weights, brushed the roe off of them, took them to the garage, weighed them, and subtracted it from the guy's pay.

Anyway, the second screen would separate the individual eggs and get rid of more blood and scales. It was still numbingly cold. The third screen would continue to separate the eggs and get rid of any more impurities that got through screen 2. When finished, the result would be a box of almost pure bright orange eggs. With a large ladle we would scoop up a gallon or so of eggs into a five gallon white bucket for the next phase.

The bucket was placed in the deep sink at the back wall. A board would be placed under one side, slightly tipping the bucket. A hose would be inserted and water allowed to gently rise. The roe would start to swirl around and around as the water filled the bucket. Once it reached the top it would dribble over the edge. Scales and blood clots missed in the screening process would slowly rise to the surface and slip over the edge with the dribbling water. Meanwhile the eggs would continue to do slow circles in the bottom of the bucket. It took a while before the water would run clear. This process lent itself well to dinner time. Dinner would be put on the table, everyone would go upstairs and eat, while the eggs were on auto clean cycle in the bucket.

After dinner was over and dishes done, Mom would retire to the basement, fish dip net in hand. She would scoop out splotches of blood, scales and broken eggs that didn't float with the water over the rim of the bucket. It was a search and remove operation. Inside the five gallons of clear water would spin these beautiful orange perfectly round eggs. Mom would stare into the bucket and watch for the bad stuff to swirl into view. Broken eggs were misshapen and cloudy. Blood clots would be a bright red against the orange background. The impurities were quickly scooped into net, removing the aliens from the population. It was sometimes an elusive job. Meanwhile the water bill kept climbing.

Once it was deemed clean enough (and Mom and Dad required it to be CLEAN), the hose was shut off and the bucket was poured over the final screen mounted above another plastic fish box. This screen had mesh so small that the eggs could not go through. It was allowed to drain completely on this screen.

The final process was to remove the eggs from the screen and put them into a new clean bucket. A specific amount of salt was added to the eggs. I will not give that percentage here, not because it is a trade secret, it's just that we can't remember for sure what that percentage is!

Now, others of us did help with the process. Carolyn was going through a stressful time in her life and had moved back home. During the process she would help by making dinners and cleaning up the kitchen. This was wonderful for us who had frozen hands and pants full of fish scales. We could just walk up the stairs, wash up, sit down and have steaming roast, potatoes and corn set out and waiting for us. I know, because I was home one winter also. I rolled up my sleeves and worked the roe and remember how nice it was to be pampered with such a dinner.

I remember sharing in the paychecks at the end of my season. The money was a bit confusing for Karen and Eric. Mom and Dad didn't give them cash or even checks. They bought them Certificates of Deposit. It just didn't have the same look as cash. But it was enough for Eric to later put a down payment on a house and Karen to pay for college. Mom then handed Carolyn and me each a check for $500. Carolyn had tears well up in her eyes and tried to refuse the money because she was "only" doing housework. Since I was unemployed that winter and loved to put money in the bank, I quickly quipped, "I'm taking it!"

She looked at me, looked at Mom, and took her check.

Hauling Fish

Fall also brought another aspect of the commercial fishing business. The product had to be processed, packaged and delivered to market. For many years Dad sold fish off the *Ruby* directly to a fishery in Bayfield. He kept his boat at their dock, they bought his fish. It was a convenient arrangement.

Times changed and Dad would moor at a variety of different docks. He also expanded the market to which he sold his fish. He took orders from markets within a day's drive and even provided delivery service. Well, 'he' didn't provide all of this service. Delivery provided an excellent opportunity for Mom to try out new places for coffee and lunch, branching out from her regular haunts to sample actual franchise restaurants in the big cities (like Superior or Rhinelander in Wisconsin and Duluth across the bridge in Minnesota).

She didn't exactly do it by choice. She was the only one available to drive the truck, unless she and Dad decided to pay someone else to make the trips. This option was not likely to happen. So, while Dad was on the lake, she drove the pickup truck, loaded to the gills with boxes of herring and chubs, to various buyers around the state.

The trip from lake to market could take about 24 hours. The fish would be hauled out of the nets and, if time permitted, they would be filleted or cut into steaks on the way in to the dock. If the lift was a big one, Dad and the crew would work into the evening until the catch was processed. The fish would then be packed fresh under shaved ice in big plastic boxes with holes in the bottom. The boxes were then loaded inside the capped bed of Dad's pickup truck.

Every destination was within a day's drive, and Mom only did deliveries in the frigid days of late fall. The shaved ice and cold temperatures assured that the fish stayed fresh throughout the delivery.

What was a bit of a problem was the fact that Mom was delivering a product fresh from the lake. These were not frozen fish but very chilled fish. So fresh, that all the blood had not drained completely out of them.

Mom recalled, "These were cleaned fish. You gut them, there's still blood in them. You don't wash them, you just clean them real fast." She looked straight at me and continued, "You've seen how fast Dad, how fast he cleaned fish, well, there's still some blood left in them. And when you get a whole truck load of fish, I mean, there's bound to be some loose liquid running around."
The "loose" liquid had a lot of red blood cells in it. And as it began to "run around," it would leave a trail dripping out the back of the truck. On one trip, Mom was to rendezvous with a man driving another delivery truck and transfer the cargo to him.

As she told the story, "I was supposed to meet him there, but I didn't know who he was. And, well, there was a restaurant right across the street from Kmart, so that's where we said we'd meet him. I went in, sat down in a corner and had breakfast. And, ah, I didn't know who it was (the next driver), didn't know who to look for."

Mom continued, "A guy came up, and he says, 'Are you Mrs. Frostman?' And I say, 'Yeah' (with some uncertainty). He says who he was and I forgot the name of the fisheries that he was from, but, he says, 'Yeah, I could tell you were here, I could see the blood running out of the back of the truck!'"

With this recollection still fresh in her mind, she moaned, "Oh, God."

It was not the only time Mom dripped blood around the state. On another trip she said, "We stopped at the restaurant in Superior. Snookie (Mom's sister) was with me, and we walked out of the restaurant, and she looks and she says, "Marcie, the cops are going to stop us!" I said, "Why?" She said, "Look at the blood running out of the back of the truck!"

To this day she shakes her head in amazement that she dripped blood across the state and was never stopped by the police.

The Sunken House

Winter arrived and fishing techniques had to change with the change in the environment. Nets were still set in the lake, only they weren't set from a boat into open water. They were set under the ice. Fishermen would traverse the ice, hauling their equipment to likely spots where fish could be caught. Equipment included ice chisels (later years would bring gas powered ice augers), running boards (five or so 1x4, 20 foot long boards of fir, nailed together, end to end), short gangs of nets, two to three boxes of 350-400 foot long nets, and a shack with a pot bellied stove inside.

It was an interesting operation. A hole was chiseled through the ice (somewhere fish were likely to be swimming underneath), and a distance away, equal to the length of the nets, another hole was chopped through. The running board was shoved through the first hole and aimed at the second hole. A line was attached to the tail end of the running board, on the end of which was attached the first net. Then the front end of the running board, floating under the second hole, would be pulled from the water, pulling the line into the water. The net would follow the line which followed the running board. The line was as long as the depth the net was to be set. On the tail end of the net was another line, the same length as the first line.

The process was finished when the running board was completely removed from under the ice, and the net suspended from the lines on each end. They were fixed to the surface of the ice, and flags were set, marking the location of the net.

The nets would be lifted after a predetermined number of nights. The shack would be positioned over the hole, which had been chiseled open again, a warming fire started, and the nets would be hauled out of the lake and picked clean of their catch.

The process would remain much the same over the years, but the gear would change from memorable to undependable to fun. Dad used to make his way across the ice in a truck. I always heard that it only took four inches of ice to hold up a vehicle. But ice is not always uniform, spotted with slush holes, expansion cracks, currents underneath and who knows what.

When Mom and Dad were first married, Dad and Jack Erickson had to bring some nets and boxes to the other side of Madeline, where they had left the Ione for the winter. The ice would open earlier there in the spring, which would allow them to get on the lake earlier. Mom had agreed to join them on this trip across the ice.

Mom recalled, "So I rode with them. Well, when we got half way over, there were some planks across this one wet spot. Jack Erickson and Dad stood out on the running boards, and Dad had one foot on the gas and I'm sitting in the middle." As she sat bouncing around in the bench seat, she realized that if the unthinkable happened, the guys would be able to jump free and she was going to go down with the truck. She continued, "That's the last time I went across that ice!"

The unthinkable did happen occasionally. Dad once went down with the truck on the other side of Madeline. He shoved the door open before the truck sank below the surface, and prepared to jump to the safety of the solid ice. And then the truck quit sinking. He had landed on a sand bar. But his feet were wet, so it was just a little tragic.

As Mom recalled, "He did get the truck out. He put a long chain on it and towed it right out. Those guys were all nuts. A couple of them did go down. They said, "Well, you just look up to see a bright shining light and you head for that hole!" There weren't too many of them that went down though."

Over the years the mode of transportation evolved from trucks and old cars with the backs cut off, to powerful and sometimes dependable snowmobiles. We would own a number of makes and models of the machine. Mom kept track one winter, just for the heck of it. When the season was over she figured the cost of repairs to the snowmobiles just about equaled the profit from the catch.

As one might imagine, the machines were used for more than just work. Dad used part of the fleet one winter to take Karen and Eric on the lake to see a house that fell through the ice.

It all started around 1970 when Mom found herself employed at Port Superior, two miles south of town. "Port" was a marina, restaurant, and condo complex. Mom's job was to show and attempt to sell four model homes built along its entrance road. They were cute little two-story northwoods style vacation homes. Mom would walk potential buyers through and answer any questions they might have. Business, unfortunately, was not very brisk. In fact, it was so light that she was able to bring Eric to work with her without causing a disruption. He could sit outside and play in the sand while she waited for customers.

Economics being what they were, the houses did not sell during Mom's tenure at Port. She moved on to other endeavors and quite a few years went by before someone finally took an interest in the houses. They sold sometime in the late '70s. Not only was someone going to move into the houses, but the houses themselves were going to move. And not just up the road. Nope. They were going to move across Lake Superior to their new locations on Madeline Island.

The plan was to move the houses during the winter. Each house would be jacked up off its foundation, 12' by 12' timbers placed underneath, and dolly wheels attached at each corner. A truck would then tow them away from their foundations, slowly navigate down the road to the Port Superior marina then drop down onto the ice along a strip of beach. Next the truck would pull each house three miles across the frozen lake until regaining land near the Pub at La Pointe on Madeline Island.

This was a very viable plan, given that a road is plowed from Bayfield to Madeline Island every year. And that this road is almost always, I repeat, almost always, a safe navigable highway (during January, February and March). It would be a normal sight in town to look down on the lake and see a car, dark and small, moving across the ice to LaPointe. It looked like one of those magnetic toys, where a magnet underneath a board pushes a car across a roadway printed on top. Like the toy, if this road were backlit, you could see straight through it. The waters between Bayfield, Madeline, Bass, Hermit, and even farther out could freeze to a very drivable thickness most years.

The route to LaPointe had its seasonal cycles. Once the ice rotted enough in the spring, the ferries would break a path between Bayfield and the island, and the constant ferry schedule and warming days would keep the path clear. The spring and summer would bring open waters for normal navigation. Then in late fall the freezing temperatures would again make ice, banging on the thick hulls of ferries like the *Garhow*, the *Island Queen* and the *Nichevo*. Once the ice got to a certain thickness, the ferries would be put up for the winter, and the wind sled (a big metal box with a humongous fan on the back) would take over, ferrying high school children and others who needed to continue the commute. The wind sled could float, and with the ice not quite solid, it provided safe transportation as it blew itself noisily across the frozen lake.

It wouldn't be long before the ice thickened to the necessary four inches. Once this thickness was achieved, a route from the base of Washington Avenue in Bayfield would be plowed to the landing at LaPointe on Madeline Island. Then the road would be marked with a line of Christmas trees (paint didn't stick very well to the pavement, hah hah). For the next few months, if you didn't know the area, you might think you were driving a very icy road across an incredibly large flat field. In fact, tourists have been known to complain that the road needed to be salted because it was too slippery. But I'm not going to pick on tourists. I've become one in my old age.

Back to those houses. The plan included the creation of the road from Port to the Pub. Trucks would plow a wide swath the full distance. With the insulating blanket of snow removed from the surface of the ice, the cold could then seep down and, given time, cause this frozen roadbed to thicken even more. This would make the ice stronger and theoretically be better able to support the load of a house.

The guys did a good job. Such a good job that locals coming in from Washburn and Ashland started using this road, saving themselves the need to drive all the way into Bayfield to access the usual route.

When the ice was deemed strong enough to carry the weight of a truck and a house, the big move began. Each house was jacked up off its foundation and the timbers placed underneath. The truck was backed up and connected to the "trailer." Using the same theory as towing a jet ski or a boat or a snowmobile, the truck was put into gear and the house slowly towed away from its foundation. The truck and house lumbered down the entrance road, past the marina and out onto the ice. It must have creaked and groaned as it compressed the snow and ice under its path. The transition from road to ice would be even less smooth. I imagine every board and nail shifted while vapor barriers and vinyl flooring acted like band aids as the house inched off the pavement, across the frozen beach and onto the lake.

The trip was slow going and uneventful for the first three houses. It was also uneventful for the fourth, at least for three quarters of the trip. Remember the rule that least four inches of ice is required to support a car? Had anyone ever calculated what thickness would hold a house? Or was the thickness of the road inspected across the route? Did anyone confirm that the stars were still aligned? Ah, but hindsight is always 20-20. What happened next would be talked about for years.

Locals would compare the weight of the house on the ice to a woman walking in high heeled shoes. All the weight of the house (which was fully furnished and, according to rumor, still had dishes in the dishwasher) was concentrated on each of the four corners supported by the dollies. The rear "heels" of the house inevitably found a weak spot on the ice and pierced the frozen surface. The driver suddenly found himself stopped and felt the sickening feeling of impending "reverse." He sunk his foot into the gas pedal, but the truck was unable to bring the dolly wheels back onto solid ice. The ice continued to crack around the dolly, slowly swallowing each wheel and then started on the timbers.

As the house crashed in slow motion through the ice, it dragged the truck along with it. The driver and his buddy realized there was nothing they could do. The rig was doomed and they had no intention of going down with it. They flung the doors open and jumped free, running through the windswept snow for safer ice.

The house continued to dip towards the rear dollies, but stopped sinking after it had tipped a good 45 degrees. The truck was not so lucky. The ice continued to give way underneath the truck and it soon sank below the surface of the ice, landing upright on its wheels, on the lake bottom 70 feet below.

People in town had been watching the houses traverse the ice. Even from a distance, it was obvious that something had gone very wrong with this last trip. As word spread, coffee cups all over town were lowered, dimes thrown on tables, and cars and snowmobiles revved up, all to go check out the happenings.

The odd thing about ice is that you can stand 10 feet from open water and still be on solid ice. The driver and his companion soon had plenty of company around the house and the large dark void of broken ice. The crowd were all gathering to stare in amazement at what, from the hillside in Bayfield, looked a lot like a giant tepee on the ice.

Dad was among the curious. He must have felt the experience a valuable one to share with the kids he still had left in the nest. Create memories for them. He'd also get to see what was going on. He loaded his two youngest children onto the back of his Arctic Cat Panther. The Cat was one big snowmobile with plenty of space for all three of them.

Karen was around 12 and was dressed in her blaze orange snowmobile suit that Mom had made especially for her. Mom had recently discovered new insulated fabric and was in a winter outfit sewing phase. She made, (and got us daughters into making) ski outfits, winter jackets and outfits like Karen's blaze orange pumpkin suit. There was no way to lose this child in a crowd of snowmobiles after a fresh snowfall. Karen said she felt just a little obvious. Eric was about nine and bundled in a store-bought blue snowmobile suit with a black stripe. Karen was always a bit jealous of Eric's snowsuit. To this day she can describe its color (muted, subdued, store-bought).

There are a few good spots along the shore in town for snowmobiles to access the lake, and ice fishermen, snowmobile clubs and other types looking for off-road freedom used them quite often. Dad, Karen and Eric followed the route down Cooper Hill, past the DNR and out across the boat ramp at Black Hawk. They headed east to the scene of un-urban renewal.

There was no plowed route across this section of the lake. Dad would negotiate snowdrifts, pack ice, expansion cracks, and slush holes. Suffice it to say it was not a smooth ice rink to slide across. Also, snowmobiles are not quiet. They have this e-e-e-e-e high-pitched sound, kind of like a souped-up leaf blower. A very souped-up leaf blower. Snowmobiles really wreaked havoc with television reception in the '70s.

At the "crash" site, Karen can remember a bunch of people standing around near the sinking house. Everyone was enjoying the phenomenon. Dad was probably enjoying discussing the situation with his buddies, critiquing the driving, the way the house had been loaded and any other aspect where better decisions could have been made in hindsight.

Dad, as with probably most of the fishermen in town, was in tune with the lake. He could feel the solid sheet of ice underneath them, but still could sense the capability to the ice to expand, to crack and to roll under his feet, just as it did when he was not quite Eric's age. It was one thing for him to face the temperament of the lake on his own, but as he looked at his kids, and looked at the doomed house, he deemed it time to put distance between his little group and the hole in the lake.

With Karen in the middle and Eric in the back, Dad started the motor and aimed the Artic Cat westward for Bayfield, away from the insurance company disaster. The engine was loud and the ice was a bit rough, and with three people on the snowmobile, it was a snug fit. They bounced their way across the drifts, Dad in front, Karen hanging on behind him and Eric behind her. Half way home

Karen realized that she was suddenly more comfortable.She was able to stretch her legs. When her conscience wouldn't let her enjoy it any more, she turned her head and looked behind her. Eric was gone.

Somewhere a ways back, Eric had bounced up onto the tank at the back of the snowmobile, and then bounced off. He landed on top of a snowdrift on which he decided to sit and wait. It was just another day in northern Wisconsin. He knew it was only a matter of time before Dad and Karen would figure out that he was not there and come back. He sat there, all alone, surrounded by miles of rough flat snow-covered ice, encircled by the frozen hills of the Bayfield peninsula.

He made the best of his time, counting his fingers and toes inside his mittens and boots. He kicked the tops off snow drifts. He twirled around in circles on the tip of his boots. He was warm thanks to his store bought snowmobile suit. Unfortunately for him, the suit blended in with the shadows among the snowdrifts on this expanse of ice.

As he watched Dad become smaller and smaller in the distance, did he also contemplate the sinking house or the merits of a shadow colored snowsuit verses his sister's blaze orange snowsuit? I don't know, and he doesn't remember.

Meanwhile, Dad was hell bent on getting back to Bayfield, unknowingly putting more distance between them and his youngest child. Karen thought for a split second, and then allowed family ties to override any sense of sibling rivalry. She yelled, "Dad, Eric fell off!"

Dad yelled back, "No, he didn't!"

Karen and Dad seemed to get in a lot of these arguments over the years. "Dad, Eric fell off!" she persisted.

"No!"

It took a bit more dialog to get the facts across to Dad as they screamed across the snow. To Karen's credit, she persisted until Dad had to stop. They turned around and looked back toward the sinking house. Barely visible in the distance sat his youngest son, in his blue store-bought snowmobile suit with a black stripe, sitting on a snowdrift. He gave a weak wave. Dad finally turned around and retrieved my baby brother.

Later that year divers were hired to salvage the house. There are newspaper clippings showing them sitting in the kitchen, 70 feet under water. I'm told the truck was brought up and the owners actually got a few more years of service out of it. And then there was something about a painting surfacing from the deep. Another part of local lore…

Christmas

Of course winter meant Christmas. And Christmas at our house meant turkey, mashed potatoes, cranberry sauce made from scratch, and pies stuffed with pumpkin, apple and mince meat. Christmas meant fudge, rosettes and cookies locked in cookie jars with the lids taped shut so we wouldn't eat them before the holiday arrived.

But before all that, Christmas Eve meant Lutefisk, a Scandinavian tradition carried down by both the Frostman and Cousineau families. Lutefisk is a delicacy, a slab of cod pulled from the cold North Atlantic Ocean, filleted, soaked in lye, and then dehydrated to the consistency of a pine board. It stunk enough to draw in turkey vultures, and was so white it would make a ghost proud. We drooled at the thought of it.

Soak that board in water and the meat would reconstitute, eventually resembling a thick slab of salmon, (if you have a strong imagination). Dad was the chef, and he would boil it (Mom swears she didn't know how to cook it). When heated through it became a wonderful entrée, the meat soft, thick and flaky. The aroma would fill the house. Well, we called it an aroma anyway.

Others were not so enthralled. To them the aroma provided a stimulus/response akin to driving past a paper mill, or maybe walking by week-old road kill. Dad was oblivious. He would proudly carry it to the table and present it on a platter, in its wonderful, warm gelatinous posture. There would be wrinkled noses, but the meat would eventually settle on all the plates after we sat down at the dining room table.

We only dined at this table on major holidays, otherwise it was used for 5,000 piece puzzles, folding clothes or gathering dust. On

Christmas Eve it would transform, decked in Gramma Frostman's crocheted tablecloth, spread with boiled potatoes, lots of melted butter, corn, and rolls. If someone (like the future son-in-laws) couldn't stomach Lutefisk, there was enough of a variety that they wouldn't starve.

On special occasions, or when we begged for it, Dad would begin the meal by saying a Norwegian table prayer.

I Jesu nåvn
Gar vi til bords,
Spise og drikke
På ditt ord.
Deg Gud til ære,
Oss til gavn
Så får vimat
I Jeus navn.
Amen

(In Jesus name we go to the table to eat and drink in thy word. You, God, to honor us to benefit, so we receive this food in Jesus name, Amen)

Formalities over, we ate dinner and stuffed ourselves with dessert. Then, just before 9 p.m. we all slid into our coats, mittens and boots and headed up the street to the Christmas Eve Candlelight service. The walk was a whole two blocks in the dark, listening to our boots crunching on the hard packed snow that covered the street. The streetlights would illuminate each corner, creating shadows through trees in the ravine and on the adjacent houses.

Once at the church, we entered, climbed the stairs, took a candle from the basket and filed into our unofficially official assigned back pew, left side, Dad always at the far end.

The service was my favorite. The stained glass windows, which usually were lit with the morning light, were dark and quiet. The Christmas tree stood proudly near the alter, decorated with white ornaments and lit with dozens of small white lights. The traditional Christmas carols were sung, the story was told, and the sanctuary lights were darkened as our voices filled the air with the words to "Silent Night, Holy night." All hands, young and old, joined in the delicate and poignant finale, raising our candles high, allowing the light to flicker off the walls and ceiling above us.

After the candles were snuffed, the kids would start scraping the wax off their thumbs and all would file out of the pews. The candles would be dropped in a basket in the narthex and then each small child would be handed a small cardboard box filled with candy canes, ribbon candy, and other hard treats. We were sure to keep busy and wired until Santa came later that night. Jesus and Santa Claus. The night couldn't get any better.

Once home, we were all sent to bed as quickly as we could be shooed up the stairs. Anxiety filled each of us and our last glance would be towards the Christmas tree, which was always in the living room, to the left of the bay window. It had gone up a couple weeks earlier, a balsam fir, wide and thick. The old fashioned aluminum tinsel would glimmer from all the branches. Mom by now had passed on the ritual to us of placing the tinsel, strand by strand, all over the tree. On New Years Day she also passed on the ritual of removing the tinsel, strand by strand, so it could be reused again the next year. That night the tree would be relatively devoid of presents. Sure, there were the gifts to each other and gifts to relatives, but they all fit neatly underneath the boughs.The night would bring a dramatic change.

On Christmas morning Dad was as big a kid as the rest of us. We didn't wake up and rampage down the stairs on our own. Dad, the guy used to getting up at "O dark 30", would open the upstairs door around 6:30 and let out a holler. When Karen was in band playing the trumpet, he would confiscate the horn and "attempt" a rendition of Reveille (I recall him telling me he played trumpet when he was in school.). Either way, we didn't linger in the sack. We bailed out of bed and thundered down the stairs.

In the living room the tree would be transformed. Presents for seven kids and their parents, even on a lean year, would fill the space underneath and surrounding the tree. Mom and Dad were always able to make our Christmas magic.

When Carolyn and Janis were little, Christmas meant new patent leather shoes. Carolyn wanted the ones that had the strap that could be worn on the top like a Mary Jane, or go in back around the heel, like a "Big Girl" shoe. Holidays like Christmas and Easter also brought a new dress. Dad loved to see his little girls dressed up. Christmas also meant getting a doll, sometimes as big as the girls receiving it. Today, any time Carolyn smells that new plastic smell, memories of Christmas and that new doll wrapped under the tree come flooding back.

By the late '60's, with kids from temperamental teenagers to those only a few months old, successful planning had become complex. On top of planning, they then had to purchase, knit, sew, wrap and hide the presents while we weren't looking. The season required scouring the Sears, Penny's and Montgomery Wards catalogs, numerous trips to Ashland, and even a trip to the BIG City, Duluth, Minnesota. It was a great excuse to go out for lunch.

1968 was the year of the skis. Pieces of paper with our names were attached to the tree. Strings ran like streamers from each name tag, directing the recipient to the porch, to the coat closet under the stairs, and all over the house. At the end of each string was a pair of second-hand skis, poles and ski boots. Back under the tree was a season ticket for each of us to ski the local hill, Mt. Ashwabay. We were in seventh heaven. So were Mom and Dad. They had hit upon a way to keep us out of the house and busy every weekend all winter.

Christmas was when the first snowmobile appeared in the yard. It was not a designated toy but part of Dad's ice fishing equipment. We had some access to it, and that morning promptly buried it in the fluff of our neighbor's yard. Janis would take it one step further and drive the front ski through a basement window on the back of the house. Carolyn and her high school sweetheart one-upped Jan and took it up to the third hill above school. Unknown to them, there was a box spring abandoned under the snow. That heavy machine tore right into it and got hung up. Ah, what fun!

Christmas meant homemade presents. One year we girls all got quilted bathrobes and the label read "Sewn by Marcelline." Other years brought hand-knit sweaters. After the knitting machine arrived, hats, sweaters and mittens of a different stitch would be found wrapped under the tree.

Not every Christmas went off without a hitch.One year everyone was seated around every available space in the living room, tearing into each present dropped in our vicinity. There was usually one big gift for each of us.We would ooh and aah and smile and become happily entranced with our booty. This year was the same, but as Mom glanced around the room taking in our happy faces, her eyes fell on Jimmy, quiet and wearing a forlorn gaze. She looked at the presents he had unwrapped and realized she had forgotten to put his 'big' present under the tree. She let out a yelp, saying, "Everybody off the couch!" We looked at her in surprise, but three or four of us jumped up and she tossed off the cushions and partially pulled out the inner mattress. Underneath was a brightly wrapped present. Jimmy's Christmas was now complete. There was another year where I drove Mom's Comet around for weeks, not knowing my presents were hidden in the trunk.

By noon we would be preparing either for company or for a trip to Washburn or Ashland to share the holiday feast. With the move back to Bayfield and the passing of Gramma and Grampa Frostman, our holidays had become a Cousineau reunion. Many a Christmas we would crowd into their house in Washburn, joined by Aunt Dolly, Uncle Gene and their five kids and Aunt Snookie and John and their three kids would risk the snowy highways to join us from the Milwaukee area.

Gramma Cousineau always had angel food candy, with its chocolate exterior and middle of hard cake. There would be a bowl of ribbon hard candy and the raspberry candy with its hard outer shell shaped like a raspberry, and hidden inner soft raspberry flavoring waiting for us. There would also be green and red anise candy. Gramma made it from scratch. To harden it, she would pour the mixture into a cake pan and then, if there was snow outside, she'd put the pan in the snow to speed up the hardening process. Then, she'd cover the smooth candy with a cloth, and smack the heck out of it with a hammer. It was great stuff.

Gramma had bubble lights on her tree. They had a round bottom base, with a glass stick filled with water rising out of it. When the base got hot enough, the water would start to bubble up through the glass stick. The gathering made for lots of noise, lots of food and conversation that instilled in us a sense of family identity.

Each Christmas, Gramma Cousineau would have a gift for each of us grandchildren. For years I would get a doll, each year from a different country. I remember opening it and politely saying thank you. At least I hope I did. I was such a tomboy that I didn't grasp or appreciate the gift she was giving me. The doll was quickly put aside and I found something else to entertain me.

I still have the collection, and look at it now from an adult perspective. I have an appreciation for the thought and effort Gramma went through to shop for 15 grandchildren, finding gifts she felt held meaning and value. I can also now watch as Mom continues the ritual, either shopping or making handmade gifts for her own grandchildren. And I've watched the grandkids react with the same delayed appreciation.

As kids our Christmas was about immediate gratification, especially when it came to presents. But underneath our excitement about the day to come where we could rip open presents (we weren't a family that reused wrapping paper), our Christmas meant celebrating Jesus' birth, carrying on of traditions and gathering of extended family under one roof. We shared in conversation, the preparation and devouring of a meal and a day being surrounded by family. The day itself was a gift our parents and grandparents were giving us, another gift not fully appreciated until adulthood. I guess there's something good about getting old.

Read thru.*

Anise Candy

1. Do not stir while cooking
2. 1 or 2 tablespoon anise oil, after it's done cooking – also food coloring -- stir.

3. Pour into large buttered cake pan.
4. Do not put in refrigerator
5. Put in cold place until hard.
6. When hard. Pound into small pieces.

Cook in an enamel kettle
5 1/2 cups sugar
1 bottle Karo syrup (light) (2 cups)
1 cup water
Cook sugar and water and syrup together – stir
Put in thermometer and cook until 300 degrees.
Take off stove and put in anise oil and coloring.

Good Luck
Grams Cousineau

* I copied this from Gramma's handwritten recipe. She is very serious when she starts it with "Read thru"!

Spring

Spring brought prep time for the upcoming fishing year. This included variations on the theme of painting the *Ruby*. All the paint blisters had to be pounded and loose paint scraped off. I lucked out and got this job one year. The boat had been left in the city harbor that year, and was still frozen in next to the break wall. The ice was solid in the harbor, except around the pilings under the piers. There was a bubbler system adjacent to these to keep the ice from forming. If ice were allowed to freeze around the piers, they would be pushed upward, possibly several feet, which created a miserable maintenance problem.

So Dad handed me a crowbar and said go forth. I dropped off the edge of the dock and walked out to the boat (yes, on the ice) and started to pound every pimple (paint blister) marring the *Ruby*'s complexion. It was going fine until I got near the stern. As I banged the hull I wondered how Dad and Uncle John could stand being inside while I made such a racket. I also began to day dream about the ice beneath me breaking, falling in and saving myself by hooking the curved end of the crowbar on the rail that ran atop the edge of the *Ruby*'s roof.

Meanwhile, Jimmy Erickson was walking up to pay a visit (fishermen continuously checked on each other). He watched as I banged away at the white paint. Then he gasped as my feet broke through the soft ice and the ice swallowed me up to my belt loops.

In the time it took to splash (there was no 'slipping' about it) down to my waist, I realized my daydream about saving myself was very flawed. There was no way to swing the crowbar up to the rail when I was already three feet below the rail and falling fast. And the reality of swimming under the ice to the open water near one of those bubbler systems was not enticing. Also, I did not want to admit to Dad that I fell in. As my legs felt the shock of the ice water, holy intervention occurred. I reacted by swinging my arms and hands behind me, catching the surface of the ice, and sliding my butt up and out of the water. And I still had the crow bar.

Jimmy Erickson watched the whole thing. He started to jump down and save me from the deep, but I was out of the water before he had a chance to get off the dock. I was oblivious to his attempted heroics. I poked my head into the boat and yelled to Dad that I was going home. Not wanting to get caught having done something stupid and hear him grimace an "Oh, Geez," I then bolted from the boat and headed up the hill. As I look back on it now, I'm sure he would have given me a ride home, but at that point there was no way was I going to tell him I had fallen in.

As the harbor ice broke up, Dad would sometimes use the marina hoist to haul the boat out of the water to get various repairs done. It would sit there for a few days, suspended in the slings, exposing itself to the sunshine. The 42 foot of steel meant a lot of boat was underwater. Out of the water it was massive. The *Ruby* drew 4.5 feet (as best we recollect), so there was a lot of surface under the water line that needed to be painted.

Dad was meticulous about the boat. Our house had three different kinds of siding on it, except for the side that didn't have any siding on it, but God Forbid not doing a top notch job on the *Ruby*. You had to be careful that you didn't paint over the sonar transducer, and make sure to take the time to have the hoist straps moved so every inch could be covered with a protective coat of fresh paint. Once I worried for a whole year once thinking I had missed a spot. I feared that a hole was going to rust through, a leak was going to spring when Dad was miles from shore, and he was going to get sooo mad at me after he got back to town. It never happened, but I was good at finding something to worry about.

The *Ruby* was in the hoist one spring and Eric was scraping off the loose paint. The job either got monotonous, or Eric was daydreaming, because he scraped the name right off the hull. This was not a good thing. You don't take the name off the boat. At least you don't get caught doing it. After momentary panic, he remembered the name was on both sides of the bow. So he went to the other side, measured and copied the "typeset" and replaced the name before Dad showed up. What Dad didn't know about wouldn't upset him.

Not only was spring prep time for the boat, but the decision had to be made on when and where to go to set nets. Ice flows would come in and go out. The ice could rip the buoys from the nets. The ice packs could also trap a boat. Granted, spring was a pretty time of year to get trapped, but it could still be deadly. Dad and other seasoned fishermen knew this only too well. One year Dad tried to warn an inexperienced boater not to go out of Port Wing or Corny. The water was clear and the weather good but Dad knew that the ice pack was still floating out there, lurking just out of sight. The party chose to ignore his warning. Dad tried again to caution them against this plan. He did have a way of ordering instead of informing, but they still chose to ignore the voice of experience. Sure enough the wind shifted and their boat got stuck on top of the ice.

Jimmy recalled fishing with Dad in the spring out of Port Wing. There would be ice floating by as they headed out in the mornings. During this time of the year Dad would use ice buoys. These differed from buoys that marked the nets when the water was free of shifting ice. "Normal" buoys were eight feet long. The center of this buoy was 3/4" electrical conduit with two floats on it to the four-foot level with a chain welded to the bottom to keep it upright. On the top was a red flag.

An ice buoy lacked the sophistication just described. It was basically a 2x4. The beauty of the simplicity was that the board could slide through and under the ice. The ice couldn't grab it and drag the net away.

Jimmy remembered that the spring was a nice time to be out. The air was crisp and clear, with the promise of warmth to come. The water could be calm and ice would cast its reflection onto the surface of the lake. Spring was also the season when Jimmy watched as Dad reunited with his pet gull. They were lifting in dead calm water when suddenly Dad grinned, pointed to the roller on the lifter and called out, "Well there's my Buddy!"

On the post of the roller perched a mature gull half the size of the herring gulls that followed the boat like paparazzi after some starlet. It would stand there and watch the net go rolling by.

Jimmy stood at his post and thought, "OK, now what's going to happen?" He watched as a small fish came through the lifter. The seagull saw it and started to squawk. Dad picked the little fish out of the net and offered it gently to the gull. "Buddy" calmly and gently stretched his neck towards Dad's fingers and clamped his bill around the fish. Dad let go of his grip, Buddy settled back on his perch and with a flip of his head, sent the little fish down his gullet. Ol' Buddy stuck around long enough for Dad to feed him two or three more fish.

Buddy met Dad each spring in Port Wing. When the ice finally cleared out of Bayfield, Dad would bring the boat back to town. It was only then that the gull would move over to Jack Evano's boat to look for a meal.

Maple Syrup

Spring during the Ruby years was also when I trashed Mom's kitchen. Dad even encouraged me to do it. It all started with pancakes.

We ate a lot of pancakes growing up. Options included big thick pancakes, pancakes in the shape of our initials, or Mom's specialty, Swedish pancakes. We also called the latter "roll-up" pancakes. The batter was so thin that it spread across the entire 12-inch cast iron frying pan. Bubbles would rise and start popping, beckoning for the pancake to be flipped. There was a bit of artistry in flipping such a wide pancake with such a narrow spatula. I think the trick was to let the surface get covered with bubbles, while the bottom browned to perfection. I never paid enough attention to the details, in fact, I still burn my pancakes. Once it was firm enough Mom would flip it onto the uncooked side. Let the other side brown and then flop it onto a dinner plate.

One by one we would come to the breakfast table as each pancake was finished and our name was called. We would sit at the table, smear on a layer of margarine, sprinkle on a layer of brown sugar and then roll it up like a jelly roll, slice it and eat. Notice I said margarine, not butter. When raising seven kids, Mom needed to cut corners wherever she could with the family budget. She bought milk and "cut it" with dry milk. (She'd combine one gallon of whole milk with one gallon of dry or powdered milk. The milk went farther and was cheaper.) Oleomargarine was another cost cutting measure. It was much cheaper than butter, but was illegal in the Dairy State of Wisconsin.

It seems that the dairy industry across the United States and especially in Wisconsin felt extremely threatened by the "wholesome" oil-based spreadable product that received a U.S. patent in 1873. Originally animal fat based, it was much cheaper than butter and kept better.

The Federal Oleomargarine Act of 1886 applied a manufacturing tax to sales of margarine, gave states additional control over trade in margarine, and applied high license fees to those trading in colored margarine. Reduced license fees were allowed for those trading in uncolored margarine. In no way did dairy farmers want to lose their share of the butter market.

Wisconsin, took even greater exception to this non-dairy invasion. It passed laws making it illegal to use the word dairy or creamery in connection with margarine, applied a 15 cent tax per pound, and made it illegal to purchase colored margarine. This legislation started in 1895 and was on the books until it was legalized in 1967 and finally the tax repealed in 1973.

So, at the time, we Wisconsinites were under a Margarine Prohibition. Did that stop my family or anyone else across the state from purchasing margarine? Not all all. Dad fondly called it Oleo, and it was a good excuse to go visit his sister Viola in Bessemer, Mich., just across the border in the UP (Upper Peninsula of that state). Our margarine missions involved packing us kids in the station wagon, driving east for an hour, and crossing the border on the pretense of a visit. On our return home, in the back of the station wagon, under a towel, would be a case of 24 one-pound packets of uncolored margarine.

These packets were about the size of a one pound bag of rice. Inside would be clear margarine with the consistency and color of lard, along with a little round yellow ball. You had to break the ball in the plastic bag and then keep squeezing and squishing the bag until the contents turned yellow. Then you opened the bag and transferred the contents to a crock or other container and stuck it in the refrigerator. Yep, we were definitely margarine smugglers.

Anyway, back to pancake staples. The syrup requirement would deeply impact my life and my mother's kitchen ceiling for most of my high school years. An inhabitant of our northern woods was the sugar maple tree. One spring, early in my teens, I decided to take advantage of this fact and make maple syrup. I failed to do the proper research before embarking on this endeavor, and if Dad hadn't stepped to guide me in this project, it would have never gotten off the ground.

In front of our house and across the street was a small grove of trees. I had taken notice that: a) they were trees, and b) they were easy to get to. I figured they'd be easy to tap. End of research. That from me, the future Forestry major at the University of Wisconsin-Stevens Point. That major only lasted a semester, probably to the benefit of every forest across the United States.

I gathered my equipment. This included some sturdy dried up hollow weed stems. They came from a huge patch of this exotic weed that grew across the street in front of the house. Jimmy and I used to build forts in the patch, and called it bamboo. Bamboo was a stretch, but then we did have imaginations. Anyway, I figured these weed pipes could serve as a tap to channel the sap from the trees and into a bucket. I got a hammer and a large nail from the basement and lugged the stuff over to the trees I had picked out. I took the nail, hammered it into the tree, yanked it out and stuck the "tap" in the hole. It dripped sap!

Dad was working in the garage that day and noticed my activities. He strolled over for a closer look. I wish I had paid more attention to the expression on his face when he realized what I was doing. I don't remember his lecturing me or even casually mentioning to me that I couldn't make very good maple syrup from a White Ash tree. He just said "follow me."

We walked back across the street, through the garage filled with boxed nets, ice chisels and ski gear stuck in the rafters, and into the dungeon (basement). He rummaged through the piles of boards and metal, finally pulling out some stainless steel pipe (this basement had stores of everything). Using a hacksaw, he cut the pipe into eight inch lengths. He then went to the metal grinder.

I followed along, realizing he had a strategy in mind. I also realized that my afternoon adventure was developing into a bigger commitment than I had intended. He ground out a wedge-shaped indentation on each piece, an inch or so from one end. I watched in awe as the sparks flew and piece after piece moved deftly through his fingers.

I was then instructed to gather up empty five quart ice cream buckets (these seemed to propagate in our house). Dad grabbed a hand drill with a bit as wide as the pipes he had cut and together we left the basement. We trudged back through the garage and up the street to the ravine across from my grove of ill-suited trees.

Now, Bayfield has a number of ravines draining the hillside town. They were wonderful for us kids to explore -- steeply sloped with small creeks babbling at the bottom. They were also heavily wooded. As kids we would play in the creeks, hike the paths and explore in the cool shade. We also crawled through the culverts that connected one ravine to another. I wouldn't be caught dead in those spider web filled corrugated tubes today.

With buckets, taps and a drill, Dad and I turned left and post-holed through the melting snow and onto the upper southern edge of this ravine. Dad stopped in a small grove of trees on the top of the slope. I struggle to recall if the trees had leafed out yet. I don't think so. Dad had to know these trees by the bark, or maybe by the years spent in his childhood exploring the ravine, or passing it each day as he walked to school. Maybe his dad, Grampa Ole had taught him. I never could figure out how, but he knew these were real sugar maple trees.

He showed me how to drill a proper hole into the tree, about chest high, deep enough to access the sap superhighway, and also deep enough to hold the pipe. As I turned the handle, wet wood pulp spiraled off the drill bit and fell, piling up on the ground at my feet. I yanked the drill out of the tree and pounded a pipe into the hole. I was instructed to place the wedge end away from the tree, facing up. Once this was done, we stopped, breathed in the cool spring air, and waited. The sound of the creek in the bottom of the ravine gurgled under a blanket of melting snow and thin ice. A mat of wet leaves from last summer felt like a cushion under our feet. The pale blue sky could be seen through the naked branches of the tree tops.

It took only a moment, and then a bead of clear fluid appeared

on the inner edge of the pipe. It swelled larger and larger and finally dropped to the ground. Dad looked at me and smiled. He took a
white ice cream bucket and hooked its wire handle on thewedge cut
into the pipe. Soon I could hear the "tap, tap, tap" as the sap dripped
into the bucket. I hadn't put any thought into this part of the
process.

We put in another seven or so taps then post-holed back to the
street, up to the opposite side of the ravine and put two more taps
in an grand old maple about four feet in diameter. So began my high
school spring tradition of making maple syrup.

For weeks in the spring I would work the "sugar bush." Before
and after school I would collect the full buckets off the taps, and
replace them with empty ones. Each of my trees had a personality
of its own, a couple provided up to two buckets of sap on a good
day, others maybe only half a bucket. This meant that I had anywhere from five to maybe 12 gallons of sap between all the trees,
per day (I'm going totally on recollection here). The sap was then
stored on the back porch until the evening when I would commence
boiling it down. I had no evaporator or firebox. I did it in the
kitchen on Mom's stove.

I was oblivious to how furious Mom was. Dad must have shield-
ed me well. For two to three weeks each spring for four years running, I filled that kitchen with condensation. It takes 10 gallons of
sap to make one quart of syrup. I would boil 95 percent of it out of
the kettle and send it dripping down the cabinets, permeating the
curtains, and starting stalactites from the ceiling. It permeated the
tiles in the ceiling so much that they started to sag. Mom was so
patient. She didn't kick me out until my senior year. And then she
remodeled.

I remember setting the pots on the burners, turning on the heat,
and periodically refilling each pot as it boiled down. This probably
makes every professional syrup maker cringe, but I did end up with
thick, dark sweet syrup. Miracle Whip jar after Miracle Whip jar
was filled and took its place in the dungeon along side the raspberry jam, pickles and anything else Mom had canned that year. My
process wasn't scientific but nobody complained about the quality

of the syrup (only Mom complained -- about the mess), so I didn't look for ways to improve.

I did learn some significant effects of boiling sap. If you left the sap to boil too long, maybe getting caught up in Star Trek (the original series, spring reruns) in the living room, and did not check on the sap-now-syrup-on-its-way-to-boiling-over, you paid a dear price. Once boiling sap reaches a certain stage, it will start to bubble up in the bottom of the pot. The bubbles will continue to rise and if not checked, will boil right over the top of the pot. At this time a warning scent will travel throughout the house. Then Mom will leave no doubt as to her displeasure. All the doors will fly open to air out the kitchen and Captain Kirk will quickly become second fiddle to the job of cleaning up a sticky, charred mess in the bottom of the kettle. It was the same Kettle Otto had given Mom years ago. After I cleaned the kettle I would have to continue on and scour the stove top and under the burners. I only let this happen a few times.

It could be heart breaking: all that sap gone to waste, missing the end of an episode of Star Trek, all those trips carrying those ice cream buckets out of the ravine. I had balanced them so carefully in my hands as I drudged through the slush. I lifted them up over the stone wall, across the back yard and then to the back porch. I had positioned them atop the chest freezer to await evening and boil time. If Mom ever got mad at me because she needed to get into the freezer to pull out hamburger for dinner, I was oblivious to that too. And I missed a Trek episode.

My senior year was when Mom finally got through to Dad and me that this operation had to move outside. She was "fed up to here" with the drooping curtains, black spots on the ceiling and high humidity. From somewhere a Coleman camp stove appeared and my two kettles began to steam away, outside and under the awning by the kitchen door. It wasn't as easy to see Dr. Spock anymore. I had to stay and baby sit the sap, bundled up in a jacket, sitting on the sidewalk, leaning against the brick planters, watching the icicles melt and the sap boil.

That season marked the end of an era. I graduated in 1975. I went off to college and the trees were never tapped again. The sap did start to boil again in 2005, this time in my sister's kitchen in Washburn,12 miles down the road. Jan actually read some books. She acquired an evaporation pan system, meters to gauge the sugar content and all that scientific modern stuff. I think back and realize now that Dad had enjoyed teaching me the process of making maple syrup. He enjoyed the end product, but more so, I think he just enjoyed messing with Mom.

Summer

Summer brought all sorts of surprises and activities. One afternoon I came home from my summer job to have Dad tell me to look in the tub. The bathroom was right off the kitchen, so while standing at the kitchen sink, I could see something dark and narrow slithering around the water in the tub. He had brought home a lamprey eel. Alive. Ugh. Mom once saw a gull under the dock down at Booths. It was trying to get out but was stuck somehow. Mom looked to Dad and told him he had to do something for the poor thing. So Dad went over, laid down on the decking and reached over for the gull. He was able to grab it, but when he tried to pull it out from the crib, something pulled it back in. A tug of war commenced, and just like the cartoons, Dad pulled outward, and then was pulled inward, back and forth, in and out. Finally Dad won. He pulled the gull completely out from under the dock. To everyone's shock, latched on to the gull, and not wanting to let go, was a mink. Mom felt so bad for making Dad grab the gull, now realizing he could have been attacked by a ticked off pint sized predator!

Summer meant sharing the waters around the islands with a growing number of fiberglass sailboats and lots of Minneapolis people. Dad would complain like crazy about them and in the next breath drop everything and go to their rescue. There was once a couple on a sailboat off South Twin who couldn't get their anchor off the bottom. The man had stood on the deck and pulled and pulled, and even tried winching but to no avail. The anchor line stayed taught and the anchor stayed firmly on the bottom.

I was a Ranger on South Twin at the time, and Mom and Dad and Eric happened to be across the way at Rocky Island. I called

Dad on the radio and described the situation. He said to hold tight and he would be right over. I informed the sailor that this big 42-foot steel tug was going to pull up to his 27-foot fiberglass sailboat and see if he could help. Then I backed off and watched. The *Ruby* approached and slowed to a dead stop in the water with a gangway positioned perfectly adjacent to the stubborn anchor line and only feet from the sailboat. Dad looked up and greeted them with his impish smile.

"Hello, how yah doin'?"

The boater responded, "Hello, glad you're here. Do you have a powerful lifter?"

Dad grinned and replied, "Yah, we can pull the bottom up!"

He chuckled at his joke and then went to work. He didn't bother with the lifter. Instead, he leaned out of the opening and grasped the anchor line with his hands. He tightened his grip on the wet line, and began to pull, hand over hand. As the sailor watched, this look of amazement came over his face. He said loud enough for Mom to overhear, "Look at the muscles in his arms!"

Even though Dad had great leverage with the *Ruby*'s gangway so close to the surface of the water, there was reason for his muscles to bulge under his shirtsleeves. As the four boaters watched the sparkle on the fluted aluminum anchor as it rose from the depths, they could also see something dark and rounded appearing to pull it downward. Hooked to the lightweight modern anchor was a four-foot tall solid iron pond net anchor. From fluke to fluke it was about three feet wide. The shaft was approximately two inches in diameter. Dad grimaced and pulled and soon hoisted both anchors over the gunwale and into the *Ruby*. The boater just stared in amazement.

The guy asked, "How can I repay you?"

Dad said, "Can I keep the anchor?"

"Yes you can!" was the immediate response. Dad untangled the anchors, smiled at the man and handed his property back to him. The man thanked him, they shot the breeze for a little while and then went their separate ways. Dad brought the anchor home and placed it in the front yard at the top of the front stairs. It would stay there for the next 20-some years.

What was amazing was that Dad knew the anchor. It belonged to Lenus Jacobson, a Norwegian immigrant fisherman who had lived on the first sharp corner coming into town. The one with the garage that a few cars ran into when they didn't make the turn in time. Mom remembered Jacobson and his wife for their accent, which sounded much like her grandmother's accent. She also remembered them for the silver cream and sugar set they had given her and Dad for wedding gift. The Jacobsons never had any children and had passed away years before. That was why Dad wanted to keep the iron memento.

Another time, when Mom crewed for Dad one summer, they were waved down by another sailboat near Madeline Island. He was grounded on a sand bar. He'd tried everything he knew but couldn't get off. As soon as Dad approached, the guy threw him a line. Dad yelled over, in typical Dad fashion, "No way am I going to pull you off like that. I'll pull all those things (cleats) right out of the boat. You take that rope and wrap it all the way around the boat and then throw me the end of the line. Then I'll pull you off."

There were some slow summers, and one year a fisheries down south requested Dad to bring the *Ruby* down and fish out of Algoma, Wisconsin for the summer. He agreed, loaded up the boat and headed out. The trip did not go smoothly. There was a storm, there were equipment failures, and the boat started taking on water. Finally he was able to pull into a small marina and hunker down until the storm was over. He still hadn't called Mom.

She recalled, "He was supposed to call me when he got there, and he never called. And I called down there to Chuck, and Chuck says, "No he's not in." So I waited until the next morning, and still Chuck calls me and says he's not in. So then I called the Coast Guard. And they want to know what kind of a boat it was and all that, and did he get through the Soo yet (meaning the Soo Locks at Sault Ste Marie, Michigan). Well, then they called the Soo to find out. Yep, he had gone through the Soo. But they had had a storm. And the water pump broke. So they were bailing water. And they got above Green Bay. Someplace, Sturgeon Bay I guess. He got into there.

They sent planes out, they sent the Coast Guard out. And he never called. (Mom's voice gets a little flustered here.) Till the next day when this Coast Guardsman starts checking every port by foot. He finally finds the *Ruby*, and bangs on the hull. Dad comes out and he says, "I think you'd better call your wife, she's a little worried."

Meanwhile, Mom is at home, and feeling so worried that she called for Pastor to come sit with her. While they were visiting, Mom needed to go to the back yard for just a minute. She warned Pastor about a possible phone call. She said, "If my mother calls, maybe you'd better let Karen answer the phone."

He says, "Why?"

She replied, "Well, Ma gets, has a tendency to get pretty upset."

(Example: Grampa once wanted some fish cheeks. So Dad brought her some fish heads for Gramma to boil. He and Mom then left and went across town to visit Mabel and Frenchy. Gramma called up and said, "Jim, will you come down here and pick them apart? I can't stand to look at them with those eyes!")

Pastor was prepared for problems like this. The man of cloth looked Mom in the eye and shot back, "I can lie!"

Summer and Kids

Summers would also be filled with memories of child rearing. Four-year-old Eric came home for lunch one day as black as the ace of spades. Mom tried to wash him up but the black dirt would not come off. As she was scrubbing his arms, the phone rang. It was Ruth Ann and she said, "Marcie, do you have any rags?"

Mom replied, "Why?"

"The boys just painted Tula's white swing. They painted it black."

Mom looked at Eric's hands and the permanent dirt marks began to make sense. She found some rags and headed over to Tula's.Eric and his best friend Wilmer had painted the swing, the fence, and part of the fire place. Mom and Ruth Ann were never able to find the can of paint. The moms figured the boys got the paint out of Tula's garage, but were baffled as to how they opened the cans.

Unlike years before with Jan's painting fiasco, Mom and Ruth Ann stayed until almost all the paint had been cleaned up. Glades next door even came out and offered some help.

"You want me to tell Tula? Because," she said, "Bobbie (Tula's son) painted Cornell's garage one summer. So if someone besides you tells Tula what happened, she can't get so mad!"

Mom rolled her eyes as she recalled the scene. Then she reminisced, "Oh, God, it took forever to get all the paint out of his fingernails."

When Billy was around nine or ten, he spent an afternoon playing with Tom across the street. Mom happened to be on the upstairs porch roof deck when he came walking home. She watched him walk down the street, as fine as he could be. As soon as he got to the front steps, he started to cry. Mom didn't know what was going on. She ran into the house and down the stairs and positioned herself at the back door. Just as he reached (sobbing) for the door knob, she flung the door open. It stunned him so much that he totally forgot what he was crying about.

Just before my 16th birthday, I bought myself a 10-speed bike. I loved biking and it was my dream to step up from my banana seat bike. I paid for the new bike with my own money and couldn't wait to get it home and hit the road.

Unfortunately it wasn't long before we realized that the bike was a piece of junk. So Mom and Dad helped me return it, then they took me to Duluth and I bought what we thought was a better bike. We brought it home, I got a block and a half from the house and the gears fell apart.

Dad told Mom, "That's it. She'd better get a Schwinn." Schwinn bikes were the fanciest bikes around at that time. So we all loaded up in the station wagon and went to Bodin's on the west end of Ashland. Inside was a powder blue Schwinn *World Traveler.* Wow, was it nice, and it fit me perfectly! Dad talked to the dealer and we were soon on our way back home, with the bike in the back. I looked at Dad and said, "Gee, thanks Dad!"

Dad gave a weak smile and gave Mom an uncertain glance. I had assumed he had purchased the bike for me and I was doubly happy. We got home Dad waited until I was out of earshot before he looked at Mom and said, "What was I going to do?" Both he and Mom had intended for me to pay for the bike.

There was no mechanical dishwasher in our kitchen. There was no room for one. So we girls were the dishwasher. One week one would wash and the other would dry. Then we would switch. And there was no built-in delay. Dishes were done right after dinner. Not that we didn't make attempts to forget."

Janis once tried to go to a movie before getting the dishes done. She sneaked out of the house and walked quickly up the street. Mom figured she was up to something, and ran outside, grabbed one of our bikes and caught up with Jan at the top of Cooper Hill.

Vacationing on the **Ruby Ann.**

She looked at her daughter and said, "You better come home and do your dishes."

Jan replied, "I'll do them after the show."

Mom replied, "You go to the show and I'll come down and stand in the back of the theater and yell, Janis Frostman come home and do the dishes."

Jan stared at her in disbelief. "You wouldn't dare!"

"Just try me." Jan came home and did the dishes.

Karen had long hair as teenager. She was ready for a change and decided she wanted a Dorothy Hamill hair cut. Mom recalled, "When she came home, it was terrible. She put a scarf on her head. Dad went in the living room and he told the boys, "Don't you say one word about Karen's hair cut." Well anyway we all come for supper and Karen sits over here and Eric sits over there. And he went, "Hah, hah, hah!!! Look at her hair!" Oh, boy. That was not the right thing to say. Dad got off the chair, walked around, picked him right off the chair, went in the other room and walloped his behind. Then he brought him back in to the table and said, "Finish your dinner." Eric didn't say another word.

Eighteen was the legal drinking age in 1975. When I turned 18, I thought I should mark this coming of age by actually going to a bar. Since my best friend was 16 and obviously too young to join me, I asked Mom to go with me down to Junior's and have a beer. I was never a drinker or partier, so this was going to be new experience for me. Mom can still picture me looking at her, as we sat at the bar, with our beers in front of us. My most profound comment of the evening was, "This isn't any fun!"

Summer eventually brought more frequent island weekends. Like days of old, when Grampa Ole, Uncle John and Dad would load us all on the *Ione* and go to Presque Isle, Dad would now load a crew on board the *Ruby* and head for Rocky Island. Even though the Apostle Islands National Lakeshore had been established, encompassing all but Madeline and Long Islands, friends still had inholdings at Rocky and we would take advantage of it.

There were docks, cabins, outhouses, a quiet comfortable beach and sheltered waters. One summer, after a long weekend on the island, everyone was sitting around, waiting to board the boat and head for home. Cleone (a friend) said, "Karen, go throw a bucket of water into the outhouse to clean it up." Karen agreed, got up, and soon was seen lugging a bucket over the beach, across the grass and up to the outhouse.

The outhouse door was open, but at this particular moment, one of the guys was using it. Karen must have known he was in there because she let him have it with the entire bucket of water. Then she took off running. Down the hill, onto the dock and running as fast as she could to the *Ruby*. Big mistake. Close behind her was her victim, running after her and yelling, "Get her!"

Mom watched from her position on her lawn chair and just smiled. She was staying out of this one.

Karen jumped into the boat. Frenchy and Lenny jumped in after her. A scream drifted across the water. The next thing Mom saw was Karen flying out the gangway into the lake.

Mom didn't get up. She'd seen this scene play out on too many other weekend trips. She was confident that her youngest daughter knew how to swim.

Life was good.

First Hand Fishing

I have very little personal experience fishing on the lake. I may have mentioned by now that I wasn't allowed to deck hand on the *Jenny L*, nor the *Connie Jean*, nor, least of all, the *Ruby Ann*. I always felt a little put out about being left out. Yeah, I pouted. I was capable. I could be a worker. I was so-so company. What I didn't realize at the time was that as a 12-year-old girl, I wouldn't mix well on a trolling boat with six grown men as clients and our male captain. Most likely the guys wouldn't have had as great a day. Yah-think? But then, I was 12, and didn't understand that.

Then there was the *Ruby*. It would have been neat to spend a few days with my dad on the lake, seeing how things were done and sharing his world. But there was no bathroom on the *Ruby*. Imagine having plumbing to blame for the missed adventure. Ugh. As I look back now, I wouldn't have felt comfortable letting my young daughter go out with that crew either. I also had no idea about the hardwork, the aromatic (a.k.a. smelly) atmosphere, and whether I would or would not have gotten seasick.

So with no personal experience to draw on, I cast my line towards baby brother Eric. I was pleasantly surprised that it took very little begging and cajoling for him to enlighten me about fishing with Dad. And what was even better, my slightly keyboard phobic 'bro' got both of his index fingers moving and e-mailed me with glimpses of life on the Ruby. Eric typed the words as quickly as his two fingers could go, paying little attention to grammar and even less to spelling. Instead, he let his thoughts free flow to the screen as he reminisced about his years working for Dad. What flowed out was not only the daily grind of fishing, but the effect it had on the relationship between a father and son.

****

From: Eric
To: Connie
Subject: Dad's story
Hi, sis.

I remember when I was about nine or so, I started going out on the lake with him for a day of watching him work. When I was about twelve my father thought it was about time to start working instead of just hitchin' a ride with him daily.

On my first day of work we got me dressed in oilers, sleeves, and boots. Dad set me up across from him at the lifting table. Empty fish boxes at my right for filling during the lifting day. Standing here one will find out how fast the nets and fish and what ever else comes around the lifter.

The first thing I had to learn was to keep the nets from winding around the lifter for a second time and making a complete mess of the day, and costing my dad a load of money repairing nets in the future. Second thing to learn was to pick fish. Now me being about twelve and small in size against my 5'10" 200-plus pound dad, I listened well; as well I could with the diesel running, lifter turning and the wind coming in through the gangway. I also watched close as he took time to show me how to clear the fish gills and pick the body out of the nets. I could not get this down to a natural movement like my father could with out even thinking. I tried for a few days but could not get it!

Well one day my dad stopped the lifter and said, "now watch this closely." He grabbed the fish, well, different. He had a very hard time clearing the gills and picking the body out of the nets. I watched very close and something seemed to well click. Within the next few hours I was picking fish! Within the next few years I was picking fish with the natural movement of my father. My mom explained to me one day why dad took the time to show me a second time. I have always known my dad was left handed, when he tried to teach me he did not consider I was right handed.

Dad one day told mom that I would not ever get picking fish down and that I may not be much use to him on the lake. Mom told

Dad, "He's right handed."

I can't imagine what it took for him to take the time to stop the lifter, pick fish in a way that he had never done before to show his boy how to pick.

I am happy he took the time. Now my brothers, my father, and grandfather have something very special in common. We all worked as commercial fishermen.

****

From: Eric
To: Connie
Subject: A day not spent fishing

When growing up the son of a commercial fisherman your summers are spent fishing early in the day and a little play in the evening, but only a little play because of the early wake up call. There were never very many days when you did not go out (fishing that is) due to the wheather.

Fog and wind were the only two factors that made it difficult to get a day in, so we would take the day off to spread nets in the basement or as mom refered to it as "the dungon". One thing kind of funny is these two never came together. If there was fog it was calm but very damp. I remember water forming on the inside walls of the boat. Dad would take the time to get a fire going in the stove to dry it out. The fog made it very hard to find the buoy in the open water behind Michigan Island. Well it made it hard to find the bouy anywhere!

The buoy was only 8 ft. long and only 5ft of it was above water. The center was 3/4" electrical conduit with two floats on it to the 4' level with a chain welded to the bottom to keep it upright. On the top was a red flag and on the floats was the number 76 which was dads license number. Before dad had radar He kept his log daily and very up to date. He never made a turn or adjustment to course without writing it in to his log.

I remember how accurate his log turned out to be. Not to mention how consistant dad was at piloting his 42ft. tug. We left the dock in Bayfield on summers morn and we were blinded by the fog less than 5 mins from the dock. The gang (another term for the nets to be lifted) was outside of Michigan Island. We were out for fats. It is a 4hr. trip with several slight turns with the compass. As I said were could not see anything outside of 4' of the boat. I could hold my arm out the gangway and feel and see the water droplets of fog on my arm.

The boat idles down and dad yells "start looking for er." All front gangways are open and the boat is out of gear and gliding through the water. If you call a 42' tug able to glide this is as close to gliding as it gets. I still remember the sound of light metal hitting the bow, kind of a "ping" sound. The boat goes into reverse and full throttle for 30 sec., dad turns to the right and jumps down and grabs the bouy with the gaff. Like he ever needed to buy a radar for the boat!

Wind: With wind comes weather. Usually bad with waves and sometime rain. A heavy rain would knock down the waves but without it we would not go out right away. We would drive the truck up the hill and look to see how the lake looked out and away from the harbor. If we saw whitecaps we were staying in for the day. Only once did we not fish when the day was good for fishing.

There was a wind blowing but it was calming itself down from the night before. We did all the normal things in the am like stocking the ice on board untieing and starting out. Something was different today. I could hear dad turning up the marine radio, he never did this to listen to other boats but only for the wheather report. He was listening to the Coast Guard talking to the Carson J Callaway, not sure the size but it must be over 700' ore carrier on the lakes. It was sitting against the wind giving a small craft a little reprieve from the wind.

Dad said -- yelled, "not fishin today get the rear stern line out and run it out the rear gang way." I thought to myself we're towing someone today. Never done that before. Turns out the owner of this small craft which was a redwood (I think) Chris-Craft, took the boat out for the first time yesterday evening and the engine quit. He and his passenger stayed out in the middle of the lake between Corny *and Split Rock Lighthouse for the night. Took us about an hour to get to them. The owner had a small smile on his face, I think it was all he could do to give was a small smile. He just looked tired. The passenger was sick and cold. We tied them off and tow'd them in. Just outside of Eagle Island we spotted the Coast Guard rounding Sand Island.*

We were able to bring them to the harbor and the Coast Guard brought them to the dock. We tied up and walked over. Dad was not very happy with the Coast Guard that day. They wrote up some sort of "ticket" or fine for these poor men. Not enough of the right things for safety, I guess, but dad said "Have'nt they been through enough" just loud enough for me to hear. He left it at that and we walked back to the truck. The time is now going on noon and it was too late for us to lift. We went home.

Fog, wind, and now the welfare for another human life. Now there were three reasons for not lifting.

****

From: Eric
To: Connie
Subject: I must have been about 13.

I must have been about 13 when I learned all about the phrase "a lot of weather."

It was a windy day at the harbor but the lake did not seem all that rough. I think dad said something about a high wind. So we untied the Ruby Ann and headed towards the channel. The channel is a several mile stretch between Madeline Island to the south and the Islands of Basswood, Hermit, Stockton and ending it was Michigan to its north. Kind of gives you an Idea of the size of Madeline Island.

Crossing the open water before Bass and Madeline the water was only choppy. I was laying on the engine box trying to keep warm and to get some rest befor the day started. I knew it would not be an easy day due to the wheather. I could feel the boat start to plow through the waves. The bow would lift then run downhill and you could hear the diesel speed up in rpm's as the boat headed down the next wave. I started to get concerened when we hit the next wave hard. I just about slid right off of the engine box. I got up and climbed into the pilot house. What I saw is still with me today. I can close my eyes and it is still there picture perfect. Kind of like a nightmare that sticks with you. When friends ask about my child-hood days working with my father this is one of the stories I start with, it gets you into the mindset of a commercial fisherman and what he is willing to work through. Or in this case not.

Dad had his hand on the wheel and the other on the frame of the seat. I looked out the portholes on the pilot house and saw the sky dark black, gray and an odd color I can't even explain. The clouds where rolling against themselves in no certian pattern. I think that this was what concerned me the most. Scared? No. I could not tell you why at the time but now I know when I think back I was never scared I think dad's way on the lake, his calmness is why I had no fear. Only being able to see the skyline for a moment the boat jumped forward, the prop came out of the water, You can tell this because the old diesel speeds up something fierce, dad kills the throttle just until the prop is under water and hits 'er hard again. Just as he did this I swear to God half of the boat is now under water. In a heartbeat the black water with a white break to it rolls over the bow and all of the portholes and the pilothouse are now under water. Now that is a sight to see. The boat basically dives right through the wave.

After I guess five or six waves like this my dad asks me, "Well do ya want to lift"? A simple answer of "no" comes from my mouth. He looks at me and simply said "k." I remember giving my dad a big hug. He looked at me and said " Hang on." At the upswing of the next wave he hit the throttle turn the wheel and on the downward swing of the next wave he turned the boat around in the cradle of that wave and we were headed the other direction towards home. I saw it done but how he did it was something else. He turned a 42' tug around in the cradle of a wave no more than 70 ft wide.

On the way home on every wave the old diesel reved up on the downwared swing of every wave until we got inside of Bass when the wheather calmed down.

I remember dad saying "there is a lot of weather out there."

I have always wondered what the boat would have looked like from the view of a plane.

Maybe its a good thing I have never seen that view.

To my sister Connie who wanted another story.

Your little brother.

****

From: Eric
To: Connie
Subject: A December day.

It's a saturday in early december I was about 16 and this is how I remember the day going.

"Eric, Its time to get up!!"

If you ever heard dad yell with authority then you can hear Eric in your head as if it was yesterday, but "its time to get up" came with a sound in his voice like an apology for yelling my name. Its 5 a.m. and dad is at the kitchen table with a cup of coffee from the pot that mom had made an hour earlier. I have a glass of milk and use the bathroom. We head outside to the truck you know the one the old red 250 ford with the white stripe down the side. Dad left his keys in it again. I can't understand why he keeps the 99 tag on that key ring. Its cold out this morning.

We drive down to the pier and dad b-esses with the guys for a half hour while I have a hot coco at the counter. Ever been to the pier plaza at 5:15 a.m? The fisherman, construction workers, and retirees help themselves to the coffee behind the counter and the waitress are more than ok with it. No one has a big breakfest it seems that coffee and toast are a big order of the morning. Bob shows up at about 5:30 and we head down the dock to start our day.

The first thing on dads mind is to start the boat and fire up the stoves. It is not cold enough to light the back stove so the front stove and the exhaust from the cummings deisel will be enough to keep the boat around 50 degrees. It was problably colder but time has eased the feeling of the cold. The boat is untied the lines are pulled in and I give a push away from the dock.

We leave the saftey of the Bayfield harbour and head for the back side of stocken for herring. We have a 4-hour ride to the nets before work starts. Dad takes a quick look at his radar, Like he needs it. He has left the dock in darkness before dawn and been in nothing but a complete fog when the light of day has shown its face, you know the kind of fog that you can see

the water droplets in the air when you open the gangway and look outside. He now takes notes in his captains log and the settles in for an early morning nap.

I drift off to sleep to the "hum" of the engine under the box I am sleeping on. I awake to the change in RPM's of the engine. Dad is already in his oilers and yelling to get ready. I open the lifter gangway and set out the roller and pan, crawl under the lifting table and set up 2 boxes to my right for herring. The buoy is spotted and the work begins. The line is placed around an already turning lifter. Up the line come a couple of lead weights and here comes the bridle. Get ready for 5 to 7 boxes of nets and 1,200 pounds of herring. Lifting is slow and hard work. Picking every fish and rock,stick, dead who know what old fishing lures etc....

All of the nets are in and we are working on the inside line, the anchor comes up and now only the bouy line is left with the bouy. An anchor on a fishing gang why, because when you have several hundred feet of net stretch out in open water you have to keep it put somehow.

The nets are set as fast as we can turn around and through out the bouy. My job is to make dads and bobs job easier. I soap the nets down so they not only get clean but so they will roll over dad hands smoothly and untangly easy. The only words I will hear for the next hour are "with the sun" or "against th sun." Its either a clockwise twist in the nets when setting a counterclockwise turn of the box will untwist it, so I turn against the sun. This happens several time while setting back. Now mind you the box is somewhere around 100 to 150 pounds.I never weighed one wet.

Time for dressing out our catch. Remember when I said 1,200 pounds of herring? Well, a herring does not weigh more than a few ounces to maybe a half pound each. The next two to three hours is spent dressing the fish then cleaning up after the day of work. Now all we have to do is wait for the ride in to be over.

I have taken this time to carve this moment in stone in my memory. I open the gangway to feel the cold air on my face. Its not like november when you cannot open the gangway because of the whether and water. November is two weeks behind us and the December whether is calm and cold. When cold there are no clouds in the sky just stars. It has been a good day for making ice and the bow has about an inch or two on it. It is dark almost as dark as when we left this morning, The water is so cold you do not even think of the thought of trying to survive it We are coming inside of basswood island now and Bayfield is coming in to sight.

It is a high pressure day the smoke is rising straight up from the chimneys of Bayfield, lights are on in homes as well as the streets. I watch the wake form off of the bow and roll back as it chases the roll from the middle of the boat and then they both follow the wake from the stern. I watch as thay roll out and away into the darkness of Lake Superior. We pull into the harbour and tie up I do remember late days when mom would bring hot dinners down but this is not one of them. We unload the boat load up the 250 and a worker from Bodins will open up for us so we can deliver. Is now almost 7 p.m. and we go home.

There were several days I really did not like my father for the hard work he did and made me do, the long hours the aches and pains, the yelling, the feeling that I could never even hold a candle to him.

I would never trade a day not even my worst, of the life I have lived while growing up.

I hope this helps you see a little window into who and what I saw growing up.

Your little brother, Eric.

****

From: Eric
To: Connie
Subject: Moving day, it was a special day just for me

When growing up the son of a Commercial Fisherman I felt that there were a few days set aside just for me. This is one of them.

We were moving our nets from the summer fishing grounds outside of corny to the fall grounds of the backside of Madeline Island and the backside of Stockton Island. The day would begin as any other normal day out on the lake. Dad made plans with mom to retrieve the truck from Corny and we went out to lift the nets. We took our time lifting, which was different from every other day because we knew it would be a long day with the move. We would be storing everything on the boat for the 4 hr. ride back to the front side of Bayfield. We took care in stacking the gangs of nets in the stern for the long afternoon ride. We made sure to have a couple of extra boxes of ice to keep the fish.

After lifting the four gangs of four box nets we took off for the fall fishing grounds. The fish are all dressed and on ice. The boat is washed down and ready for the ride This is a time of water, the sun on your face through the gangway and the never changing sound of the Cummings diesel, to some it may not sound like a good time but for me it was almost peaceful. I spent my time watching the water roll off of the bow and watching the mainland slowly change in front of me.You see at cruising speed the Ruby Ann only did about 12 knots, so taking time to watch the the water and mainland was easy. The seagulls would all settle in on top of the boat almost nest down for the ride as well.

I remember a sight that that I will carry with me forever. Its not only the sight but the feeling of wind, water, sun, rain, and the emotions that went with it. I took time to open the gangway wide and look back from where we were coming from. The sky was getting dark, not scary dark but just dark enough to rain. I saw the rain start falling from the gray clouds down onto the water. It made a line in the water where sunshine faded away and the raindrops started. I watched this for more than 30 mins. It had a calming effect on me, like I said this ride was peaceful for me.

Over these 30 minutes the rain got closer and closer. When it was only a few hundred yards away the smell of fresh rain hit me. I do feel sorry for one who has never been in the right place at the right time to smell rain because that smell of Mother Nature showering herself is breathtaking. I never even closed the gangway, I let the wind then rain hit me, you can lose yourself in a moment like this, and at the age of just 17 I did.

The rain past us bye and the sun came out again. We continued past Sand Island and Little Sand Bay around the point we made our way between Hermit and Oak and out to the fall grounds of Madeline and Stockton. We set the gangs and went home. A long day it made for the travel time for now the sun is setting behind the Bayfield hill and the shade of dusk is setting in.

Sometimes it seems a day was made just for me and no one else and this one was mine.

Thanks Dad for giving me a day that will live with me forever.

I know you must have had a day like this too Connie, Maybe you know the feeling of a warm summers rain on your face while being out on the water. I hope so.

Your little brother, Eric.

****

Mom had a way of seeing the obvious, and at the same time, Dad, with health issues sneaking up on him, could no longer stay in denial. She once told me, I got to thinkin', I said to your dad, "What would happen if you had another heart attack out on the lake?" He looked at me kind of funny. And I says "Does Eric know how to take that boat in?" He didn't answer right away. Finally he says "No." That was all that was said that night.

****

From: Eric
To: Connie
Subject: Crack Of Thunder On An Uncloudy Day From Eric:

In my early teens my father had a what I call a mild heart attack. He had no surgery but carried with him at all times nitro to help him when he needed it. Not knowing what this would turn into or maybe not caring because of my age and my relationship with my "dad" as I now call him today 20 some odd years later, I never knew what was in store for me one summer day. I did not know where this came from as well, for my dad always ran his boat and no one else did, period.

One morning not unlike any other I awoke to hear his voice raise me from a good night sleep, like a crack of thunder on an uncloudy day, "Eric time to get up!!." It's summer time and we fish out of Cornucopia or as the locals call it "Corny."

Corny is a small fishing village between Bayfield/Red Cliff and Port Wing, only a small marina a general store and two bars. I spent most of my teenage summers there with only getting to know very few people. I only got to know the people dad talked to mostly because we were on his time and you did what he wanted to do on his time. We were on " the clock" and we went there to fish and to bring fish home.

The work day did not start in the morning but the evening before. We would load about 300 pounds of ice on the F250 and cover it till morning. We would take the early morning drive to Corny which is about 30 or so miles, I can still remember my head bouncing off of the passenger window as I slept most of the way out there. When you're asleep and comfortable the change of sound will wake you up every time. For me it was the sound of dad letting off the gas on the way down the hill into Corny and coasting down to the entrance to the harbour. Now awake with one eye open, the truck turns and then backs up between two local shops to the gangway of the Ruby Ann.

The local shops are only small buildings no bigger than sheds just about 18 by 20 which sell crafts and candy and ice cream. Man

I wish I had $2 to by some candy and ice cream. Dad shuts off the truck and the day begins.

I drop the tailgate and pull out the fish boxes of ice. Set them down to the slip edge which is a 12 by 12 timber and await the hook. The hook is a three-foot iron with one end rounded into an oblong circle and the other shaped as a hook. To this day I don't know why the hook needed to be pointed all we did with it was load and unload fish boxes with it. I was handed the hook and I set it into the fish box handle and dad grabbed the other end and we lowered the boxes into the boat. The hook helped greatly because I stood on the edge of the dock with dad in the boat some three to four feet below me.

My routine changed. I have been doing "my job" with this man for a few years now and I thought I knew it until today.

"Hey Eric," something I never heard before at this time of the day. Dad called me into the pilot house, "turn the key and give er some throttle" OK....... The boat fired up and I set er back to an idle. "Alright I'll get the lines" he said, I now knew something was wrong he had never done anything like this before in my lifetime. He stowed the lines and pulled himself into the pilot house. "Now turn the wheel left and put er in reverse." We backed up about 15 feet just enough to clear the cabin cruiser behind us. "Spin 'er back and go forward." Jamming the shifter forward and seeing him do this all my life I ran the bow of this 42ft. tug into the dock. That 12 by 12 timber creaked and the boat started to turn. "Give 'er more throttle," you have to keep the the bow pressed against the dock or the 32 foot fiberglass sailboat off your stern will be sitting on the bottom if you hit it.

A guess is the boat is 42 feet long, the sailboat is 10 feet wide at most, tied to the slip and the whole width of the slip possibly 56 feet wide, so yes a 14 year old has something to worry about with only four feet of clearance.

So as the boat makes the turn we jam it into reverse spin the wheel and back ourselves away from the dockm hit the forward gear and head out of the Corny harbour. I was not really nervous but I did not believe he just made me do that. "Crank 'er up to 1,200 and set the boat up to lift -- you got 10 minutes."

I think we lifted whitefish that day. Not a real money maker but it kept the bills paid and food on the table and shoes on our feet.

Most days we would just finish dressing the whitefish at the dock but today we stopped just short of the harbour and finnished dressing out the whitefish. I knew what was coming. He wanted me to bring the boat in. We entered the harbour under my controll but all of his guidance. I ran the boat straight in between two other boats dad jumped out with line in hand onto the dock and all I heard was Chubby Sincker say "Frosty, what the hell are you doing?" I think he thought that dad went out alone. I heard dad say as he tied down the stern line, "My boy brought 'er in today."

The Ruby Ann was tied and the fish loaded. I did not ask why nor did he explain. We just let it go.

I found out from my mom later that she had put him up to this. She asked him if I knew how to run the Ruby if anything happened to him out on the lake. Well this snot-nose kid gave him his answer. I was able to do something I never had to do before.

(It seems to come easy to write this to you, but reading it after I am done writing it really hurts. I have a hole in my chest where my heart used to be, he"ll never know how much those days now meant to me.) Its late and I need some sleep. So good night from your little brother, Eric.

Mr. Fish

Throughout the talks I'd had with friends and family, through all the reading of Internet pages, and reading and re-reading my notes, I realized the contents of this book had overlooked one topic. I'd literally missed experiencing this while I was growing up, and I'd missed finding it in the literature. I came to the conclusion it needed to be brought to light to fully appreciate the life of a commercial fisherman. Again, I started with a family expert.

"Hey Eric."

"Yah," Eric answered my call with the quiet voice so like my youngest son.

"What is a trout like?" I'd read a bunch of descriptions on the internet. I could recall eating a bunch of fried and boiled dinners, but this really didn't give me an inkling of the fish's personality.

"Oh, God. You have to beat the living daylights out of them......"

"Excuse me?"

"They are so strong. They can be 30 to 38 inches long. You don't want something like that flopping around the deck. It will bounce all over the floor."

He went on to say that a decent lift was 200 pounds a day. As he continued, I scribbled the math on an old receipt on my kitchen counter: 200 pounds of spotted muscle at 12 to 15 pounds per flipping wet creature. Twenty some tail fins flopping around the deck, pounding away at the metal plating. Not unlike a suburban day care center?

The thought took me back to Cumberland Island, Georgia. It was there I'd once helped try to re-float a grounded pygmy sperm whale. I'd straddled its tail for a quick moment while we tried to drag it back in the ocean. Luckily I wised up and moved my carcass. Just in time. The doomed and irritated whale flicked its tail moments after I'd stepped away. I stared in disbelief at the display of strength. He would have flicked me out to sea without a second thought. So a visual of 20 lake trout/mini-whales flopping around the deck of the Ruby was amusing.

Eric wasn't envisioning whales. He was thinking back to the trout coming off the lifter. "When they first come up they are an oddball blueish green and really pretty. They have the strength and stoutness, solid across the back…"

Eric went on in some graphic detail about processing the harvest. I'll just summarize by saying that pretty color would not last. Obviously, the fish were not to remain alive, but were destined for someone's dinner plate. They would soon expire and the brilliant colors would fade to a dullish gray.

I jumped to the next subject.

"O.K. Eric, what about whitefish?"

"They flopped around but were not as strong."

I could see him grinning as he continued, "Oh, 300 pounds of whitefish was a good day throughout the summer months. Spring whitefish were slimy. 60 fish in a box. It was like dumping in a bucket of slime. We didn't have to scale when we cleaned them. Cleaned them and kept the liver."

Whitefish livers were a delicacy. Dad would come home with his lunch box filled with the stuff. Dredged in flour, fried on the stove, oh were they good!

Eric hadn't drifted to the kitchen like I had. He continued, "If we'd hit the lake just right in the spring, we coulda caught enough and they'd be shipped out east whole and rabbis would bless them. We would have made enough money and wouldn't have to work the rest of the year."

He laughed at this thought. "Never got that. Ice flows would always come back."

He went on to say that in the summer he, Dad and Bob would fish for whitefish around Eagle Island and Squaw Bay Point, both inside the islands and out in open lake. When they fished whitefish, the trout would always be a bonus. That was, until the number of trout caught were regulated.

After the lamprey had decimated the trout population, the state closed the Wisconsin waters of Lake Superior to commercial fishing for trout, hoping to give the species a chance to make a comeback. They reopened the fishery in 1968, but the population was still struggling. So the Department of Natural Resources was soon enforcing a quota system where each fisherman was issued a specified number of tags. Each and every trout caught was required to have this tag attached to it before it came off the boat.

No tag, no trout. Vice versa, catch a trout, better have a tag. All trout caught had to be tagged. Once the quota of tags was used up, no more trout could be caught. Think about this. How do you tell the trout in the lake that you were out of tags and they had better not get stuck in your net? What happened to them if they defied the law?

According to Eric, one year the lake trout were tagged on the dorsal fin by the DNR for research purposes. The tags would hang out of the fish about an inch or so. In order to collect data, the DNR promised to give cases of Stroh's beer in exchange for tags removed from harvested fish. By the time Dad was done taking advantage of the program, the basement was filled with cases of beer.

Anyway, Dad loved it when he caught a big trout while fishing for whitefish. It was worth lots of money. He just had to make sure to tag it. The amount of whitefish caught was not regulated so no tags were required. What was great about no catch limitations was that it allowed Dad to be able to catch enough to donate to the church for the annual church fish boil. Whitefish rated right up there with lake trout in the taste department.

Moving on, I asked Eric, "How about the Fats?"

"Yup, got boxes of tags for them too."

Eric went on to discuss this oversized trout. Also known as siscowet, they were huge. When Eric was 15 or 16 he could hang on to the gills of one of these things, have his arms at his sides and the tail would drag on the floor. They would come up from the depths with their stomachs stuffed with smelt.

The Fats ran outside (of the islands), way out deep. A ton was an easy catch. They were thick with fat and could be smoked for the oil economically. Unfortunately the PCB scare stopped a lot of the sales for a while. They themselves affected the fishing industry. Eric said that Fats ate everything. It seemed that the Fats over-ran and over-ate the deep lake and came into the shallows to feed there. He noticed that at the same time the near shore populations of herring and smelt were decreasing.

We briefly touched on the herring. They were a third smaller than whitefish. Dad set one gang for herring in summer and it was set deep. Smelt would show up in these nets also, up to nine inches long. Chubs were small, half the size of a herring. In the summer you ran deep for herring and chubs. In the fall it was different. Dad would set six boxes of nets in the fall and come home with 2,500 pounds in one lift.

Eric went on about the time it took to get to the nets, the number of gangs they set, and the different configurations. I wish I understood it all.

"Four hours out to the nets, to the back side of Stockton, two or four full box gangs of nets with bridle between each box of nets. The two of us to pick, spin around, go back to town, gut fish all the way back, then clean all evening." He kind of sighed. Heck, I was worn out.

We got down to the last fish "of interest." Burbot, locally known as "lawyers." Why? Because nobody liked them? That's the joke, but I haven't found the origin of the name yet.

Eric laughed at my quest.

"Dad didn't fish for them, they just showed up. When we were out deep fishing every now and then we'd get a load of lawyers. They'd be 12 to14 inches long, wrap themselves around your hand when you tried to grab behind the gills. Try to get them out of the net and they'd wrap right around your hand. Like a snake, when they got their neck stuck in the net. Slimy, and twist and twist. You couldn't yank at them or they'd drip the net. They'd leave a pigtail left in the net. (A pigtail was a snarl or big knot in the twine. You had to pick it out or the net would rip.)

I had to get Jimmy's take on lawyers.He answered the phone and my question by blurting out, "Most god awful thing you can imagine! Just so nasty!" The recollections left him unable to speak in full sentences. I gave him a minute to collect himself.

In a moment he quit laughing and continued, "They are the worst. They look between a catfish and an eel. They're extremely slimy. There's no way to grab them. They come up and they are all over the place and they are so tangled up in the net. If they're alive you have to grab around the gills and squeeze really hard to pick the mesh off of them. If they're big they will wrap around your arm. Then at least you know where he's at. He'll fall right off when you take him off. Not that strong." He was back to incomplete sentences and out of breath.

Both Jimmy and Eric hooted about how much Mom hated lawyers. So of course I had to give her the last say. It was great because she had come for a visit, and I could watch the scowl form on her face as she blurted out her distain for the innocent fish.

She said, "The lawyers would come down the board with the nets. They were horrible looking! Awful looking! Terrible!"

She was also driven to short choppy sentences. What could be so horrible about a fish?

"…and I would just shove it back and your dad would say, "Pick it out" and I would say, "No, I'm not touching it! It's awful!" He said, "Pick that damn thing out!" I said, "No, these nets are all going to pile up, you got to come pick it out." So he'd shut the lifter off, come down and pick it out. And I'd start boxing the rest of the nets. Oh, they were awful! Slimy. They had whiskers. I told him I wouldn't pick it out. I told him I'd quit! I quit a couple times out in the lake."

Mom and Dad worked together a couple of summers before he retired. The lawyers were sparking memories.

"…like the time he was supposed to lift fats and Dad knew Lenny was down there in that area. He got on the radio and said, "What's the weather like down there?" All Lenny said was, "I wouldn't take my wife down here!" Well, guess where we went! We went down and lifted fats. I could take that (rough water), but I couldn't take lawyers."

The funny thing about burbot was that they were not a fish taken commercially, but they were known as the poor man's lobster. They had to be skinned and you'd get only a small piece of meat from the fish. It would be white with broad flakes. Boiled up, it was great. I guess the market couldn't get beyond their looks.

Then there was the sturgeon. Last but not least, because they could grow to be 11 feet long. Unfortunately neither Eric, nor Jimmy nor Mom had much experience with them. Dad didn't fish for them since commercial fishing for sturgeon was banned in 1928. The fish lives to be about 50, and doesn't reproduce until its mid-twenties. Because of this, the population couldn't recover from over-fishing and nearly went extinct.

I asked Eric if he'd ever seen a sturgeon. He said, "Yeah, small ones would get into the nets off of Corny and Squaw Bay. They were no fun at all." The plate-like scales were sharp and he'd get cut as he picked them out of the nets and tossed them back into the lake.

He'd also dealt with one that was five to six feet long. It was an ancient looking thing, with those same big plates covering its back. Eric was on the Cory with Dad, lifting a trap net set half way between Bayfield and Washburn. The fish was so big, it took everyone on board to lift it out of the pot. Luckily, the plates had dulled with age so no-one got cut. They hoisted it onto the deck, and kept it corralled while they dipped out their "normal" catch. When the lift was complete, Dad cranked up the engine and turned the Cory northward. The sturgeon was still flapping its gills on the deck.

Dad ignored it. He didn't want to deal with this pain in the butt getting in his net again. His plan was to relocate his "problem fish" just like problem bears in Yellowstone are moved to a new abode. Somewhere between Bayfield and Madeline,he brought the Cory to a stop. As the boat bobbed in the water, the three fishermen approached the Stegosaurus of the deep. Again, it took the three of them to shove the creature off the stern. No worse for the wear, the monster swam away like it was just another day in the lake.

Jimmy recalled that Dad and Jimmy Erickson had a sturgeon that frequented their trap net on Rocky Island. Every time they lifted they'd say, "Hey, it's Bob! Here's Bob again." And then they'd toss him overboard. I guess they liked this fish because there was no mention of an attempted relocation.

It is legal to sport fish for sturgeon. Jimmy reverted back to phrases when he told me about the flavor. He said, "The meat is unbelievable, smoked, the best."

There were many other fish in the lake, many that were also illegal to fish commercially. There was another day when Dad and Eric were fishing trap nets in Chequamegon Bay. Dad pulled a brown trout out of the pot. The tail of the fish almost touched the deck as Dad strained to hold it by the gills, his elbow bent at his side.

Dad hollered over to Eric, "See this kid? This is a world record fish!" Eric looked over to see Dad holding a fish half as tall as he was. He then watched in shock as Dad tossed the "World Record Brown Trout" overboard.

Eric looked at him, dumbfounded. He shot back, "Why didn't you keep it!"

Dad said simply, "I don't want to go to jail."

Car Stories

Stories of child rearing are not complete without stories of living with young inexperienced drivers and the myriad of vehicles we owned.

It was dark and very late one night when Billy finally pulled into the yard and parked the family car. He took one last despondent look around at the interior upholstery feeling his stomach turn as he panned from door to door. It was not good, not good. He was only trying to help, but Dad was going to blow up first and ask questions later.

He let out a sigh and opened the door. Dragging himself out of the driver's seat, he willed each foot to follow the other to the house. Quietly he opened the door, stepped into the porch and headed for Mom and Dad's bedroom. He knew Mom would be listening to him approach. Mom always knew when each of us came home. She always heard us and could tell by our walk which prodigal child had come to roost. So when he quietly knocked on the door and whispered for Mom to come to out, she was up in a heartbeat and curious. It wasn't usual for us to stop and announce our presence. We usually kept sneaking up the stairs.

Wrapped in her robe, she cracked open the door. He gave her a worn out look and croaked, "Help me clean the blood out of the car?" Not exactly what a mom likes to hear in the middle of the night.

Billy had come across an accident at Schindler's Corner. The guy was bloody but didn't want to go to the hospital so Bill gave him a ride home. After he dropped the man off at his house, Bill headed for home, having to pass the accident scene again. By this time there were lights and patrol cars and police all over the scene of the accident. He stopped and told them what happened. One officer started grilling him about the situation. Billy didn't always handle stress very well, and had the ability to pass out if the right buttons were pushed. Another local law enforcement officer that knew my brother was also at the scene. He stepped into the conversation and probably rescued Billy from another possible medical emergency. Bill was ordered to "Just go home!"

So Mom and Billy cleaned the evidence from the seat of the car, saving themselves from a morning of listening to Dad rant and rave. They probably saved Dad from a bout of high blood pressure in the process.

Another time Billy broke the grill on the maroon Oldsmobile Omega. It was early spring and he was pulling up behind Wilmer, Eric's best friend, at the stop sign at 5th Street and Cooper Hill. The problem was that he hit a patch of ice and couldn't stop. He slid right into the back end of Wilmer's truck. The combination of the impact and the frigid cold caused the white plastic grill in front of the hood to shatter into $250 worth of little pieces.

A year later Eric, driving the same Omega, hit yet another vehicle. It was spring and everything was both slushy and slippery again. He came home, hesitantly moved up close to the kitchen table where Mom was sitting, and dropped all the pieces of the same grill onto the table. He looked at her and croaked, "Dad's going to kill me!"

Mom sized up the situation and said, "Ah." She felt the sudden urge to practice the art of deception. She gave Eric his marching orders.

"Open up the garage door and drive the car so the front end is inside the garage." (It was early spring, cold and windy, but with all the bikes, fishing gear, skis, lawn mower, and 'stuff' that's about as much of the car that could fit in the garage.) They took the rest of the grill off, brought it into the basement and assessed the situation. Lining up all the pieces, they found that there was only one little tiny piece missing from the inside of the grill. So Mom sent Eric downtown to get some super glue. Together they spent the rest of the evening super gluing the grill back together. Dad didn't know anything about it until they sold the car.

We had a blue sedan that was allergic to winter. All the doors would freeze up and either not open or not close completely. Mom was sick of counting the times she had to plug in a long extension cord, attach the hair dryer to the end of it and drag them both across the snow to de-ice the locks.

The engine in this car could be a royal pain, but this was our ride to the ski hill every weekend during the winter. We didn't pay any attention to the fact that it would die on the way down the hill (and there were hills everywhere). We never realized that Mom had to keep one foot on the brake and one foot on the gas every time she slowed down, even with the automatic transmission. To us the car was so big that we could stick all the skis, boots and poles and kids inside the car with no problem. We thought it was great transportation to the hill.

One day Mom got so fed up with the frozen doors and the stalling out that she dropped us off at the hill then drove straight to Gruenkes Restaurant. This was where Dad was having coffee with the boys. As she pulled into the parking lot, Dad was gabbing with Jimmy Erickson in the parking lot next to the truck. She pulled up near the truck, threw the shifter into park, and listened to the engine die one last time. After she let the steam drift from her ears, she flung the door open and stormed over to the driver's door of Dad's truck. Dad and Jimmy were now well aware of her frame of mind, and glanced at each other as she stated loudly and sternly (I don't recall her ever really yelling), "I'm going to run that car off the city dock."

She then climbed into the truck and drove home.

Mom had a Corvair for a while. Dad liked it because with the weight of the engine in the back, he could pass cars going up Cooper Hill.

Mom also had a Mercury Comet. It held the record for driver door replacements. A few days before Mom and I were to drive to Stevens Point for my college orientation, she was down at Gruenke's having coffee. While she was inside, a man backed into her driver's door as he was leaving the parking lot. To his credit, the poor guy came into the restaurant and approached Mom as she sat at the counter. As much as it hurt to do so, he looked at Mom and confessed, "Marcie, I just backed into your car."

Another day, Mom parked in front of the theater on the Main Street. All the parking here was parallel to traffic. As she opened the door to get out, a passing car came by and took the door off. She was unhurt, but Dickerhoff, the local tow truck fix it guy, said he was going to put a zipper on that door.

Dad owned two brand new trucks, the green one when he was a teenager, and the red one while he fished the *Ruby*. The latter ran for 20 years. Everybody kept asking him when he was going to get rid of that battle ridden ship. It ran and it was warm but it looked like heck. We called it the cancer truck. The box was riddled with holes. In its afterlife Jimmy took it and got a few last miles out of it.

In later years the station wagons, sedans and economy vehicles gave way to a Volvo. Dad loved the status symbol. He also enjoyed going out to lunch in Duluth every time they needed to get it serviced, which was frequently.

One day Eric and Dad were working on the roof when Mom pulled into the yard. She got out of the Volvo, failing to throw the shift lever all the way into park. It waited until she had gotten the grocery bags out and stepped away from the car before it started to roll. Eric casually called down, "Mom, you'd better catch the car!" She whipped her head around, screeched, dropped the groceries and dove for the open door. She won the shifter sprint that day. Losing would have resulted in the car rolling over the stone wall before crashing into the street. But then again, they would get another trip to Duluth to get it fixed. And that meant eating out for lunch.

Health Concerns

Years after we had all moved out of the house, Mom and Dad were sitting down at the table on the front porch, having a cup of coffee. They got to talking and came to the realization that they had raised seven kids and we were all still alive and healthy. Then they stopped and took in that thought. Jim and Marcie came to the realization that they had been blessed with health themselves, and blessed with relatively healthy children. Dealing with illnesses and injuries in a small town and on a small income could prove to be a challenge. We were not without a few challenges along the way, and the illnesses and injuries were interesting topics of conversation.

Carolyn was very sick as an infant. Apparently she had a back-wash of urine from the bladder, backing up into the kidney. She would develop an infection, then the infection would break and drain, and she would be all right. This was probably why baby Carolyn cried so hard until Mrs. Stoody rocked her on Stockton Island.

Mom used to be able to call on Dr. Moody from the Sanitarium just south of town when Carolyn had a spell. She would cry very hard and wouldn't stop and her breath would smell so bad. By the time the doctor got to the house, she'd be over it. Or, Mom would take her to the office and the symptoms would be gone by the time she arrived.

Dr. Moody thought it was ulcer-like, and empathized with Mom, saying, "By the time you get her in here, whatever it is broke and all of the symptoms are gone. So, we didn't think there was anything wrong with her." But Dr. Moody finally saw the symptoms, and sent the new parents to Dr. Tucker in Ashland. He then sent them to Duluth to deal what turned out to be a kidney problem. She'd already lost 20 percent of one kidney.

They told Mom and Dad that Carolyn would need a certain medication for the rest of her life. Unfortunately, the medication wasn't getting where it should go and they still had a crying baby. Exasperated, they went back to our family doctor, Dr. Guzzo. After reading her file, he knew what it was but couldn't put his finger on the syndrome's name. This was the early '50s, before the ability to input symptoms in Google and hit "search." Dr. Guzzo spent an entire evening looking through medical books in his office until he found the name and treatment. The medication was an herb, and IT was black and thick and horrible.

Mom said, "Try to get IT down a three-year-old. But we did." IT turned out to be an herbal remedy made by Morgan Meyers in his pharmacy downtown. Carolyn described IT as "stuff" that looked like coal tar and was thick as molasses. It worked its way through to the bladder or wherever the infection was and relieved her symptoms. She was in the fifth grade before her body was able to fight off this problem. She had to swallow this glop until then.

As a toddler, Billy had a tendency for his temperature to spike up to 104 degrees, and for no observable reason. Mom would take him to the hospital where they would sponge him down to drop the temperature and send him home. Not as serious as Carolyn's problem, but just as exasperating.

Mom suffered a case of influenza when Karen was two or three. She got up from her misery to find Karen climbing around on the kitchen counters. Instead of going after the imp, she shuffled to the phone, dialed the school and told them to send Jan or Carolyn home ASAP. At this point she had such a high fever that she couldn't stand upright any longer. Karen was left to rummage in the kitchen while Mom staggered to the bedroom and collapsed. She woke later to hear Jan in the kitchen corralling her little sister.

When Dad got home he packed up his wife and admitted her to the hospital. The staff did the basics to cool her down and stabilize her. Later that night, the nurse came in and took her temperature. She smiled the sadistic smile of one who has worked a long time in

health care. She informed her patient, "Lucky you. Your temperature went down one degree. If it had stayed up we were going to
put you in a full ice bath!" She smiled again. Mom was in the hospital four or five days before she recovered. She now gets a flu shot
every year.

Karen, the little shyster on the counter, was born with a urethra
that was pencil thin. At three years of age her kidneys had shrunk
to the size of a 50-cent piece. Everything was backing up from the
bladder to the kidney. She would be in pain and feel sick. She
couldn't 'hold it' because the bladder and kidneys weren't large
enough to store anything. When she said she had to go, she had to
go now. (And she was in pain.)

Mom watched the little girl bring down wet bedding in the
mornings and see the look of misery and unhappiness in her face.

Karen went go through a number of surgeries in Duluth and
Ashland hospitals to stretch the urethra. They even gave her a test
for tuberculosis but it was negative. By the time she was 9 she had
recovered from all the problems. The doctor told Mom if she'd waited six months more before seeking treatment, Karen would have
died.

So much for illnesses. There were also a couple of accidents
along the way.

Billy once stepped out of the tub, slipped and fell through the
bathroom window, slicing his wrist on the broken glass. Jimmy had
had first aid training, having been a ski patroller at Mt. Ashwabay.
He applied a tourniquet to the spewing wrist. He and Dad got a pair
of pants on Bill, wrapped him in Dad's security blanket, and loaded
him in the middle of the front seat of the car (we still had bench
seats in the front at that time). Before Dad drove away, Jimmy
quickly gave Mom instructions on how to release the pressure off
the tourniquet every 15 seconds or so to get some blood flow into
Billy's hand.

It was 13 miles to the hospital in Washburn, down that two-lane
winding road. Dad went 70 miles an hour, and probably held his
breath the whole way. The cops spotted him, but the officer knew
Dad and later said, "If Jim Frostman was going 70 miles an hour,

there was a reason and I wasn't going to stop him."

There was another time when going to the hospital was not an option. Karen was eight months old and toddling as a little one will toddle. There was a huge snow storm outside. She fell and hit her head bad enough that Mom called the doctor. From her description, the doctor said she possibly had a concussion. There was no way to bring her in for an office visit because the blizzard would make the trip more dangerous than just staying home with the injury. So Mom spent the next couple hours keeping Karen awake per the doctor's orders.

During better weather, Karen got a trip all the way to Duluth to get urgent medical attention. It was one of those incidents we loved to remind her about for years to come. She stuck a dime up her nose and got it lost up there.

She said she was in the bathroom washing up for bed. She soaped up her face, saw a dime somewhere, picked it up and was just sliding the dime around the soapy skin on her cheek when it accidentally slipped up her nose. She came walked into the living room where Mom was knitting and dropped the news. Mom looked up the nostril and in the depths saw the corrugated edge of the dime. She got a tweezers and tried but could not get it out.

So they loaded up the car and took her down to Washburn to the hospital. The doctor couldn't get it either. So he said, "You've got to take her to Duluth."

Mom figured it could wait until morning, so they went home and went to bed. During the night Karen came down and said her throat hurt. Nothing was visible so Mom sent her back to bed.

The next morning they headed for Duluth. The doctor there looked in her nose and couldn't see anything. Mom told him, "You know, during the night she came down and said her throat hurt. He said, "Down to X-Ray!" They found the dime to be well on its way through the digestive system. It would pass the natural way. The doctor's parting comment was, "She's darn lucky it didn't go sideways and get stuck."

Let's see, what else. Eric once came home with his head stuck on his shoulder. A couple of days in the hospital with muscle relaxers took care of that. Billy broke his neck in high school but nobody knew it. It was discovered when he had an X-ray as an adult. So Mom and Dad lucked out with that one. I guess Billy did also.

Legal Issues

Dad fished the *Ruby* for 24 years. Being on the lake was his passion but as time went by there were factors that made the thought of retirement more enticing. Through the years fish prices could literally drop as he entered the harbor. Lifts measured in tons were becoming a thing of the past. The price of fuel was climbing. Then there was his health, two incidents that took him into the court of law and finally increased government regulation.

As Eric had mentioned, Dad's first heart attack came around 1980. He was 50 and the world of roasts, gravy, ice cream, high cholesterol and a family history of heart disease had caught up with him. His heart problems did not control him. He accepted the fact and dutifully carried his nitroglycerin everywhere with him. He even swallowed his pride and control, if just for one day, and turned the wheel of the *Ruby* over to his youngest son. There was a limit to how much control he was going to give up.

He'd had to fight a court battle with the State of Michigan, where they accused him of setting nets in Michigan waters. On July 4 and 5, 1975, the Michigan Department of Natural Resources confiscated four gangs of nets and all their contents. Dad was furious and called on friends across the region for help. He got written statements from a pilot in the Air National Guard and a Master Mariner, both stating the data used to place his nets in Michigan waters were flawed. He hired lawyers to defend him in court. He first lost the case in the Michigan court system. He then took it to Wisconsin and had the verdict overturned. It was a hard fought legal, mental, emotional and financial battle. On January 24, 1980, Jim finally received notice that he could travel to Michigan to recover his nets.

He also got caught up in Operation Gill Net in 1982, a sting operation where a dummy company was set up to lure commercial fishermen into illegal activities. Dad received a letter received from "Tri-State Food Co." out of Wilmette, Illinois. They were looking for suppliers to provide fresh fish. They said they would pick up the fish and pay for the order immediately upon pick up. What they were fishing for were fishermen willing to supply lake trout without the tags required by law. It was a sting operation during a time some fishermen were going through financial hardships. And the fantastic prices proved to be too enticing.

Dad and others in Bayfield took the bait. In the end, Dad got off light. It cost him $5,000 in fines and immeasurable humiliation. He was lucky to evade jail time. Other fishermen had equipment confiscated, much greater fines imposed, and for some, the loss of their freedom, all imposed by the State of Wisconsin.

To Dad, the state had always seemed to support the sport fishery to an extent exponentially greater than the support they gave to the commercial fishing industry. In 1973 a quota of 100,000 pounds of trout per year was imposed. Twenty percent went to assessment programs, 40 percent went to Indian fishermen and 40 percent were split between the 21 non-Indian commercial fishermen on Lake Superior. In 1991 the Wisconsin Department of Natural Resources reduced the number of lake trout that could be caught, and required the fishermen to attach those hated tags on each and every trout they caught. Then a footage limit of 100,000 feet for trout was imposed. This equated to 10 boxes a day and the fishermen would be done fishing in 9-10 days.

The restrictions were touted as an effort to protect the environment, but came at the cost of a viable commercial fishery. Dad estimated that with these regulations, his income that year would drop from $50,000 to $5,000. Dad and a few close fishermen friends finally petitioned the state for a buyout. They drafted a convincing argument.

In 1996, the State of Wisconsin offered a cooperative retirement agreement to the 21 licensed commercial fishermen in the

Wisconsin waters of Lake Superior. The offer came with financial incentives, much to the ire of some across the state. With this agreement the state hoped to "enhance lake trout restoration efforts and the quality of the sport fishery while preserving the economic viability and stability of the remaining commercial fishery."

The agreement required the fishermen to surrender their commercial fishing license, quota tags, and not use their boat or their gear in any commercial fishing operations within the state. Once the license was surrendered, it would not be reissued.

After 66 years on the lake, Dad signed the agreement.

Mom

After all the years Dad spent as the major breadwinner, he now easily transitioned into a position as Mom's hired help. She had worked for a sail repair shop in town and eventually bought the business. Together she and Dad repaired sails, made and repaired dodgers, biminies, sail and boat covers and branched out to make canvas bags.

It wasn't that she had to convince him to help, he just couldn't stay away. In short order he could be found shoving canvas through a sewing machine, crawling on the floor to trace the outline of a sail, or, together with Mom, clambering around sailboats to measure for orders. He continued to be on the city council and the United States Coast Guard Auxiliary, but was happy to join his wife in the new challenges that came with the shop.

They set up in a building by the marina, across from the old Allwoods. The business enlarged their circle of friends and acquaintances to include those folks floating around the islands on fiberglass and powered by canvas.

The UPS man made frequent deliveries to the store and to the house and didn't even knock, he knew he was welcome to open the door and drop off the packages. Not only the UPS man, but all sorts of customers started coming to the store and the house, and knocking was always optional. Usually you'd hear them call hello from the inside porch.

For Mom it was a culmination of a long and colorful series of occupations. Maid on Madeline Island, stocking shelves at Johnson's grocery store, working the line at the beanery, picking herring at the docks, tying eyes on fishing poles, selling real estate,sewing T-shirts for Munsingwear, bartending and waitressing at Juniors, cleaning quail on Madeline, salesperson at the Easter Seals store downtown, counting votes on Election Day, and through all the years she continuously knit and took in sewing.

She did all this while raising seven kids. Parent-teacher conferences, mother-daughter banquets, school concerts, volleyball games, basketball games, softball games, wrestling matches, weddings, parenting her parents, and all the other duties accepted in the course of a lifetime filled the time available.

Soap operas were never even on the agenda.

RV-ing

After 40 years of marriage, raising children, and working hard to earn a living, my parents decided it was time to treat themselves. They bought a 1984, 28-foot *Southwind* mini motor home. I was shocked. I never expected my parents to do the camping thing. They were supposed to stay at home so I could come visit. Mom and Dad ended up using that RV to come visit me.

My first son was a year old when the RV phase began. At this time my husband and I were also working and living in Rocky Mountain National Park, just uphill from Estes Park, Colorado. One summer day I glanced out my kitchen window expecting to view Ponderosa pines, Deer Mountain, a pristine meadow and maybe see a coyote or mule deer wandering by. Instead, the Frostman 28-foot mini motor home was planted right in the middle of my vista. And it was filled with my family.

I picked my jaw up off the floor, picked up Parker off the same floor and staggered outside. We planted ourselves in the driveway, happily shocked as all get-out, and watched as my parents, my oldest sister and her daughter and son piled out of the RV, cheering and shouting greetings. Parker stared at the gang for a while, then nuzzled his head into my shoulder and bit me.

Mom and Dad used the RV locally on summer weekends, joining a group of their friends to camp around northern Wisconsin. They also took solo trips such as trekking to Laughlin, Nevada. My parents had discovered casinos. It was such a contrast to winters in Bayfield. Eat cheap, play Keno and stuff nickels into the slots, what a life!

Laughlin was where they lost a belt as they descended down the highway from Kingman, Arizona. They didn't know they'd lost it until they attempted to leave that Sunday morning. What a day to look for an engine belt for a *Southwind* motor home. After four trips to Bullhead City, Dad actually found the right one.

The second *Southwind* was gas powered but at 32 feet in length, they had room to breathe. After this upgrade, they abandoned winter ice fishing and joined the annual snowbird migration. Along with traveling partners Red and Ruth Ann Compton, each winter they would go tandem on a route that took them to Florida, Arizona, Nevada and finally home to Wisconsin. These trips were full of visiting with friends and family, touring landmarks, dealing with mechanical ailments, being stressed and blessed by the kindness of strangers and their own opportunities to reciprocate.

On the foursome's first major trip, this second RV developed a mind of its own. It began a habit of stopping itself. Then it wouldn't start. Let it sit for a while and it would start. Red finally got fed up with its antics and put his foot down. He said, "We're going to put this thing in a garage and I'm going to go from the license plate to the trailer hitch! We'll find out what's wrong with this thing!"

True to his word, Red found a garage that allowed Dad to park on the grass in the back so Red could operate. Red searched and searched and finally found the culprit. It was the gas filter, tucked almost inaccessibly up against the firewall. The booger was chuck full of dirt. When the engine was shut off, all the goop would drain out. Once it drained long enough, the engine would happily start. Then, as the engine did its thing, the goop would start cycling through the filter and plug it up all over again.

`This RV had other personality traits as well. It didn't like going up mountains. It would c-r-a-w-l. Red used to say, "Well, you girls got to get out and push!" It also liked to overheat. They took it to a garage but the mechanics were never successful in solving the mystery. Only after trading it in did they learn that the timing was off. Ah, the joys of owning and getting rid of RVs.

The third and final RV was a 1989 model, 36 feet long and a diesel. It was comfortable, it started when it was asked, and it went up the mountains without complaining. The route now included a couple of weeks in my Georgia driveway. Gramma and Grampa would back the RV into my 40-foot driveway and have little room to spare. My son Dillon could have crawled out his bedroom window and landed on the roof of the RV. He and his brother were enthralled with this portable house.

The diesel gave them a few problems such as the day it seemed to be void of any power. That evening, as they lamented the lack of energy over brandy and seven, their neighbor in the campsite next door just couldn't help but provide some advice. He also had a diesel and some experiences maintaining it. After examining under the shell, he discovered that one of the big intake pipes had been ripped off. A part had also been bent inward so there wasn't a tight seal or some mechanical something. The man loved solving the problem, Mom and Dad were happy to be rid of the headache and together they all had a good visit.

Later that evening, Dad noticed a young couple at a campsite having trouble with their car. Dad and another camper walked over to be nosy (nosiness was an obligatory camping behavior). Dad found out that they were heading for New Orleans. They had pulled a boat down, and they didn't have any money to fix the car.

Dad came back to the campsite and said to Mom, "D'ya have any money on yuh?"

She responded, "Yeah."

He said, "They don't have anything."

Mom said, "I have $40 bucks in cash."

So she rolled up the cash and walked over to the couple. She handed the wad of cash to the young woman and said, "Here you can use this." Then she smiled and quickly walked away. The surprised young woman called back a confused, "Thanks!" She then began to unroll the wad of cash with curiosity. When she realized what she had, she yelped and ran over to her boyfriend. And she started to cry.

Dad had been hovering nearby to enjoy watching the gift giving. He came back to the RV and said to Mom, "Why didn't you stay there, she wanted to give you a hug!"

The next morning, as Marcie and Jim broke camp and headed

for the highway, they had to drive right past the young couple. The man waved at Dad to stop and brought over a broken auto part. He wanted to show Dad what the money had allowed the young couple to fix.

Down the road, on Highway 10, Mom and Dad blew a tire. It was an inside tire so they could keep going, just not as fast. Dad said, "Where's the next town?" Mom fumbled with the map and found a nearby town that might have tires. They pulled off the highway, and immediately found a garage. Unfortunately the mechanic was off that day. But the manager knew of another garage, so he gave them directions and sent them across the bridge.

Mom and Dad were hopeful, until they took a turn and came upon the sign, "Road Closed - Construction." Now they had no idea where to go and started feeling lost and a bit vulnerable. Then down the road came this beat-up truck with three black men. The men stopped and asked where the Frostmans were headed.

Mom and Dad suddenly felt very much out of their element. Their world had revolved around very pale Scandinavians, Chippewa Indians and low humidity. The south was so different. They had to rely on their gut feelings. A trait of Northern Wisconsin people growing up in the 30s and 40s were very trusting, so Dad told the driver where they were going. The man started to give him lengthy directions. He watched Dad's face and finally said, "You're a little confused, aren't yah? Just follow me, I'll take yah."

So Dad followed this guy for quite a ways through secondary roads. Mom looked at him and queried, "You know where you're going?"

Dad said quietly, "No."

But they continued to follow the truck. Much to their relief, a garage appeared in the distance. The three men had done a good deed and Marcie and Jim were thankful, except that the guy didn't have the size tire they needed. Ugh. This guy directed them back onto I-10.

Back on the interstate, they became that annoying slow-moving RV that backed up traffic. This was not how Dad usually drove. But with a blown tire, he couldn't travel very fast. A big semi called on the CB and complained, "Can yah speed it up a little bit?"

Dad replied, "I can't, I got an inside dual blown."

"Oh," he responded. Then the trucker did them and everyone else on the road a favor. He gave them specific and exact directions on where to go. Twenty minutes later the tire was replaced and the RV was up to speed and heading down the highway once again.

As the years and miles rolled by, the Tampa, Florida region kept calling them back. Red had brothers and sisters who settled into Zephyrhills. After a few winters in St. Petersburg, the foursome began spending time in Florida in a quiet and pleasant trailer park on the outskirts of Zephyrhills. There was a farm across the road. It was calm. It was peaceful. There were Bayfield people all over the place. It felt right.

One day, just for the fun of it, Jim, Marcie, Red and Ruth Ann decided to go look at a "senior citizens" mobile home park. They were all in this one trailer looking around when Jim disappeared. He returned shortly and nudged Marcie.

He said, "C'mon, I want you to look at this."

By the end of the day Red and Ruth Ann had purchased the first trailer, and Jim and Marcie purchased the trailer next door. And neither couple knew what the other couple was up to.

They were now residents of Florida, for winters anyway.

Finding Joy in the Empty Nest

In 1999 Mom and Dad celebrated their 50th wedding anniversary. The basement of Bethesda Lutheran Church filled with many guests who had attended the wedding back in 1949. More friends from across the years and across the miles poured in to the little church to celebrate with our parents. And then there were all of us kids, our spouses, in-laws, the grandchildren, and, if I count my fingers correctly, even one great-grand child in attendance. It was a wonderful day with wonderful company, wonderful food and in the forefront, a couple still deeply in love.

Marcie and Jim had spent their entire married lives setting the example for us kids; by the way they lived their lives together, how they showed us love, taught us the golden rule, set boundaries for us, provided for us, and did everything as best they knew how. Of course, outwardly we didn't always follow their example, but inwardly we kept their principles close to our hearts.

We would leave the nest and follow our own paths in life, spreading across two continents and floating on the ocean. It seemed that wherever we went it was a great place for our parents to follow.

****

Carolyn was the first to move out and obtain a vacation destination for the folks. A wedding conveniently came before she and her new husband moved to Kansas. This was doubly good for Mom. She wanted new carpeting, so she ensured that the wild post-wedding party was held at the house. The plan worked perfectly.

1999 - *Marcie and Jim celebrated their 50th wedding anniversary.*

After the ceremony at Bethesda, there was a reception at the "hotel." Then half the town met in our yard, kitchen, dining room, living room and other places we probably don't know (nor want to know) about. It was wall-to-wall people, champagne and activity. Dennis Beatle, a young member of the crew at Coast Guard Station Bayfield whom we had basically adopted, had his VW Beetle parked in the yard, too convenient to the kitchen door and one sick partier. Suffice it to say, the car was mistaken for a trash can.

The next day the house carpet was in the same condition as

Beatle's car. Trashed. Mom was *sooo* happy! (For the house, she was sorry about the car.)

Carolyn settled in Wichita, and after the lake iced up, Mom and Dad would drive down to visit. One year the ice left so early that Dad couldn't make the trip. It didn't stop Mom. She, her sisters and their husbands loaded up in a pickup truck with a camper on the back and headed south. Not a lot of preplanning went into this trip. A big part of not planning was not telling Carolyn that they were coming.

When they got down to Wichita, Uncle John called my sister and started a causal conversation, just as if he were still home in Brookfield, Wisconsin. Using interviewing techniques, he found out what her evening plans were, where she was going for dinner, what time she would be at the restaurant, etc and etc. Little did she know, she was helping to set herself up for a surprise.

The five arrived at the restaurant, which had a large plant just inside the door, blocking the view between patrons and the front door. They hid behind the plant until they had devised their plan. Once set, Snookie, John, Dolly and Gene all casually walked together past Carolyn's table and were seated. Carolyn was oblivious to their presence. Then Mom walked by, purposely strolling at a snail's pace. This time Carolyn looked up, saw Mom and slowly registered in her brain that her mother was not in Wisconsin but standing right next to her. She let out a scream.

****

Jan got married in Bayfield at the Catholic Church. After the wedding, in true Janis fashion, she and her new husband did the unordinary. They toured the town from the trunk of a 1931 Model A coupe. No, not inside the trunk. They had taken the trunk lid off and fashioned a back seat where they could sit together, laugh and wave to everyone as they were chauffeured through town.

****

Jimmy would tour Colorado and Germany, courtesy of Uncle Sam. Mom and Dad never got to visit him in Germany, though Mom would discuss the lack of phone calls and letters from the boy with his commanding officer.

Later Jimmy would take a position as first mate engineer on a private yacht named the *"Dreamboat"*. It was an 84 foot Trumpy, built in 1961. Jimmy described it as "old classic meets modern design." The varnished woodwork was "gleamy and glossy" according to my brother. His engine room had black tile floor so shiny that you could see the reflection of your smile in it. Jimmy also took pride in rubbing a shine on every piece of brass, bronze, chrome, and stainless steel under his care.

One winter Mom and Dad visited Jimmy during his layover in Palm Beach. He was able to arrange for them to spend the night on board and go for a cruise. They were tickled with the idea living for a day on such an elegant boat, seeing the sights and being wined and dined. They were also blessed with the company of the wife of their best man, Doris Shovick, who lived nearby and was more than elated to join them for the outing.

Jimmy, his crew member and high school buddy John Spencer, took them for a ride up the inter-coastal waterway and served them cocktails and hors d'oeuvres on the deck. He remembered that seeing the smiles on their faces made every minute of the trip so worthwhile.

This was the time where cell phones were in their infancy, and Jimmy had access one on the boat. He asked Doris what her oldest daughter's phone number was and she rambled it off. What she didn't know was that he was dialing each number as she said it. As they motored up the waterway, Jimmy handed the phone to Doris. He, John, Mom and Dad all watched with glee as Doris related her escapades with one of her children so far away.

****

I chose to get married in an open air cathedral. Actually it was a rock ledge at Acadia National Park. I left home in 1982 to pursue a low paying career as a seasonal Park Ranger on the west side of Mt. Desert Island on the Maine coast. I ended up meeting the man of my dreams, another seasonal who would be that summer's Seawall Campground manager. It was a great choice in that it gave my folks an excuse for an out of town vacation the next summer (and a great choice in a husband, by the way).

Randy met his future in-laws the next August, a couple of days before the ceremony, when we drove to the Ellsworth airport to pick them up. We watched as they disembarked from the small plane onto the tarmac. I gulped a little as I watched Mom slowly made her way down the stairs. I had last seen her in May when I had stopped home on my way from Lake Mead National Recreation Area to Southeast Harbor, Maine. (It was just a little out of my way.) It was shortly after that visit that she quit smoking due to my niece's asthma. There was an obvious weight gain, but she looked great and we continued to celebrate her new lung power with local Maine cuisine.

Dad had so much fun with this celebration that he lost his lobster. It escaped while we were having dinner at a quaint little restaurant in Bass Harbor. Dad had his plastic bib on, and was following all the instructions on how to approach his dinner. He grasped the lobster by the tail in one hand and the body in the other. He broke the tail off like you're supposed to, except that the tail flipped out of his hand and flew across the room. Not fazed one bit, he calmly got up, walked passed a few tables, said hello to a young couple, picked up his tail and returned to his seat to finish his dinner.

The day before the wedding we traveled to Schoodic Peninsula to attend the annual Lobster Festival. Good food, lobster boat races and engine exhibits, what more could a commercial-fisherman/father-of-the-bride ask for? The day was topped off by one of the boats blowing its engine during the race. Dad had lots to talk about when he returned home to the boys.

The wedding was held at Wonderland, a rocky ledge on the edge of the ocean, half a mile down a gravel fire lane. We enjoyed the walk, Mom in a dress, Dad in a suit and I, strolling between them, wearing the wedding dress Mom had made for me, and my curly once white-blond hair covered by my sister's veil. Around my neck I wore a necklace. That morning, as I dressed at Mom and Dad's motel room, Mom brought out this necklace and asked if I wanted to "borrow" it for the wedding. It was a pink cameo, aged with time, encased in a gold frame. I looked at it and then looked at her, curious about its history. She said the cameo came from a tie clip of Grampa Cousineau's. He also had cuff links that matched. During the depression the family needed money, so he sold the cuff links and the gold from the tie clip, but kept this cameo. When we lived in Belgium, he had Gramma ask Mom if she wanted it. He was too afraid to ask himself, afraid of rejection. I smiled as she secured it around my neck.

The only controversy of the day was when I confided to Mom that the pastor officiating was a Congregationalist. She looked at me and quipped, "Don't tell your father!"

****

Karen took us west again for her wedding. She and her new husband hosted the family at a bed and breakfast in Dillon, Colorado. It was a long weekend of visiting, eating and having fun. The altitude was a little tough on the old man, but with Lake Dillon right there, he and I did some driving around to check out the water. He had actually come to this area a few years before to go elk hunting, so he knew a little bit of the lay of the land. And then there were plenty of shops, so he and Mom had to get out also.

****

Eric got married at Bethesda. The service went well, however the tux fitting apparently did not. The night before the service, Eric took the suit out of its bag and tried it on. Mom looked at the sleeves dangling near his knees. Maybe not that far, but his hands were well up the arms of the jacket. And then the pants needed suspenders or they would fall to his knees.

Mom was so angry with the rental company that she took matters into her own hands. With needle, thread, sewing machine and measuring tape, she began to alter the tuxedo. The whole time she muttered that she wasn't going to pay any damage fees for the alterations she was making. Just let them try. Oh gosh was she mad!

****

Billy topped us all when it came to weddings. It took him until 2001 to find a bride and schedule a wedding, but he did and it was memorable indeed. His fiancé was a British spitfire and the wedding was in an English castle. So my rocky ledge and Karen's bed and breakfast were upstaged, if only just slightly. He flew Mom and Dad over and Karen tagged along for the event. And wouldn't you know, the folk's luggage got lost.

Luckily both mother-in-laws to be wore the same size. Mom ended up wearing an outfit borrowed from the bride's mother. And, according to local custom, all the women wore hats to the ceremony. (It was in stark contrast to my wedding, where it looked like the Mafia had gathered on the coast. Everyone was wearing dark sunglasses.)

****

After the wedding, Billy gave Mom and Dad a gift. He put them on a plane and sent them off on a tour of Norway. The two unlikely world travelers landed in Oslo, took the Bergen Railway to Myrdal, the Flam Railway to Flam, a ferry through the Nærøyfjord to Gudvangen, a bus to Voss, and another train to Bergen. They spent a couple of leisurely days touring Bergen, and then boarded another ferry for a trip up the Sognefjord. They stayed in Balestrand in the largest wooden hotel in Europe before taking more ferries and trains back to Oslo for the return trip home.

The dates of this trip are forever marked in history. Bill's wedding was September 8, 2001. Karen flew back to Colorado on September 10. Mom and Dad left Great Britain and flew to Norway. As the events unfolded against the World Trade Center, the

Pentagon and the field in Pennsylvania, we kids were frantic about the whereabouts of our parents.

I knew the folks would be staying at the Opera Hotel in Oslo, so, with the extent of my Norwegian language to include counting to 10 and praying for dinner, I dialed the number. The desk clerk answered in perfect casual English. I was shocked. (I need to get out more.) He quickly connected me to my parents' room and I found Marcie and Jim happy as clams, safe and sound.

Mom took the unfolding world events in stride. She said everything was fine, there was no reason not to finish their trip and if they could not get home on schedule, so be it. Norway was normal, beautiful and after living lives as children of immigrants, they were enjoying the opportunity to touch the site of their Scandinavian roots. They went sightseeing, shopped for Norwegian sweaters, and checked out bi-hull ferries.

After years of struggling to make a living and raise seven children (Mom figured it took 29 years to get us all through high school), Mr. and Mrs. James Frostman were empty nesters on their second honeymoon, having the time of their lives. It was just the two of them, and they embraced the opportunity to spend time alone with each other as they explored the world.

It was something they had dreamed about, over the course of 51 memorable, wonderful years.

1996 - *The Thundering Herd (as we affectionately call ourselves):*
Back: Eric, Karen, Carolyn. Middle: Janis, Mom, Dad, Bill. Front: Jim
and Connie

Photo by Dillon Marcy

About the Author

Connie Marcy is the fourth of
seven children born to Jim and
Marcie Frostman, and readily
admits to being the cause of a
number of her mother's gray hairs
over the years. Raised in Bayfield,
Wis., Marcy graduated from UW-
Stevens Point, spent 15 years as a
naturalist, law enforcement ranger
and fiscal clerk, working in nine
national parks across the country.
She is currently Deputy Budget
Officer at the Federal Law
Enforcement Training Center,
Glynco, Ga.

Great books for great readers at www.booktraveler.com!